To Tom

Make Your Difference!

Will Marré

SAVE THE
WORLD
AND STILL BE HOME FOR
DINNER

ALSO BY WILL MARRÉ

Your Dreams on Fire
Reclaiming Your American Dream PBS Documentary
Good Fortune: Grow Your Business and Save the World at the Same Time DVD
Lifeology: Coaching Lessons for a Well-Lived Life DVD

OTHER TITLES IN THE CAPITAL CURRENTS SERIES:

The Ambassador: Inside the Life of a Working Diplomat by John Shaw

Baby at Risk: The Uncertain Legacies of Medical Miracles for Babies, Families, and Society by Ruth Levy Guyer

David, Goliath and the Beach Cleaning Machine: How a Small Polluted Beach Town Fought an Oil Giant—And Won! by Barbara Wolcott

March to a Promised Land: The Civil Rights Files of a White Reporter, 1952-1968 by Al Kuettner

The $100,000 Teacher: A Teacher's Solution to America's Declining Public School System by Brian Crosby

The Other Side of Welfare: A Former Single Welfare Mother Speaks Out by Pamela L. Cave

Torn Between Two Cultures: An Afghan-American Woman Speaks Out by Maryam Qudrat Aseel

Serving Our Children: Charter Schools and the Reform of American Public Education by Kevin Chavous

Suffer the Child: How the Health Care System Is Failing Our Future by Lidia Wasowicz Pringle

Save 25% when you order any of these and other fine Capital titles from our website: www.capital-books.com.

SAVE THE
WORLD
AND STILL BE HOME FOR
DINNER

How to Create a Future of
Sustainable Abundance for All

WILL MARRÉ

Capital Currents

CAPITAL
BOOKS, INC.
Sterling, Virginia

Capital Books, Inc.
Sterling, Virginia

Inquiries should be addressed to:
Capital Books, Inc.
P.O. Box 605
Herndon, Virginia 20172-0605

Library of Congress Cataloging-in-Publication Data
Marré, Will.
  Save the world and still be home for dinner : how to create a future of sustainable abundance for all / Will Marré. -- 1st ed.
    p. cm. -- (Capital currents)
  ISBN 978-1-933102-78-8 (alk. paper)
  1. Self-realization. 2. Values. 3. Social values. 4. Change (Psychology)
  5. Satisfaction. I. Title. II. Series.
  BJ1470.M37 2009
  170'.44--dc22

                                                            2009015001

Printed in the United States of America on acid-free paper that meets the American National Standards Institute Z39-48 Standard.

First Edition

10 9 8 7 6 5 4 3 2 1

**Dedicated to My Grandchildren
and Your Grandchildren**

Sources and Evidence

Rather than footnoting the text, I've included extensive endnotes citing sources and evidence for my case for the future and our role in creating it. The inspiration for these ideas is not limited to references cited on a page. I have benefited from so many mentors, clients and conversations throughout my life that I want to acknowledge everyone who has touched my life with either challenge or encouragement. All were necessary. So, for those unnamed but influential, thank you.

CONTENTS

Part Five: Design

Part Six: Desire

Part Seven: Sustainable Abundance

Part Eight: Relationships

Part Nine: Lifestyle

Part Ten: Career

Part Eleven: Just Start

THE TRAIN

I grew up on a ranch. When I was in high school in the mid-sixties, our family would sit down to raucous Sunday dinners, where strong opinions would fly back and forth faster than the gravy boat and the homemade biscuits. My dad was big on self-reliance and responsibility. During these noisy dinners, he would constantly challenge us to think for ourselves instead of trying to fit in with friends and family members. He'd often say, "You have three choices: to stand for something that matters, to be a selfish bully, or to be invisible—someone who just fits in."

Then he'd put his elbows on the table, look me in the eye, and say, "So what are you going to stand for?" Conversation would lull, and I'd just sit there staring at my mashed potatoes, thinking, "He doesn't even know who Mick Jagger is."

I didn't get it. Now I do.

Most of us don't live the life of our Promise. Instead we manage trade-offs. We cope. We get used to things that should drive us crazy, whether it's a long commute, an abusive boss, empty relationships, irrational debt, or a world consuming its own future.

It's as though we are on a sweltering train, sitting on sticky vinyl seats, chugging to nowhere. Occasionally, we look out the window and see beautiful views of mountain streams, vineyards, and wildflowers. But the train is moving too fast for us to do anything but look and wonder. When it does stop, it stops in rundown sections of aging cities. Scary places where graffiti covers the concrete walls and the scent of trouble fills the air.

So we stay on the train of our current habits, comforted by the fact that the train is crowded with people just like us. This must be real life, we tell ourselves, because almost everyone we know is on the same train. So we adjust to the constant sweat of our own anxiety and tell ourselves it's normal. We accept the state the world is in, thinking there's nothing we can do about it. We get used to riding a train being driven by other, more powerful people. We accept the absurd rules spelled out by the conductor because that's what everyone else is doing.

Well, nearly everyone.

The irony of it all is that the people we admire most are those who get off the train. The people whose lives reflect our own dreams are usually those who behave differently from the rest of us. They are people who make extraordinary choices. Usually at some risk. They jump off the train in order to live how and where their hearts desire and to make their signature difference. They create careers that uniquely express their purpose and engage their talents. They love in bold and unexpected ways. It is those who are different from the rest of us, not our fellow train-riders, that we secretly wish to emulate. We marvel at their originality and guts.

What we don't realize is that they are just as scared as we are. The only difference is, they get off the train in spite of their fear.

Of course, some of the people on the train don't seem worried at all. These are the riders sitting in the air-conditioned comfort of "first class," snuggled in butter-soft leather while they eat, drink, and devour entertainment. These passengers seem neither desperate nor confused. They know, from observing the lives of the "economy class" riders, that they are living the "good life." A life full of fine stuff and stimulating experiences. Their biggest fear is boredom.

Yes, boredom and meaninglessness are the quiet background music in first class. So it's the job of those who serve them to keep them constantly distracted by providing finer wine and more mouth-watering desserts. More, ever more. And when the train stops for first class riders, it must stop at ever more dazzling resorts. Filled with extravagant rooms, original art, and world-class floorshows—each stop more opulent than the last.

The first class passengers also have moments of private doubt. Not often, but sometimes, the externals of their lives are so rich, they usually drown out the inner voice. But in those rare moments of reflection, these passengers, too, admire those who are different. Those who make extraordinary choices. Those who find meaning and joy in life without having to constantly buy it. Those who are not forever chasing hyperstimulation and seem to be content with enough. Those who don't just donate to good causes, but are performing good causes.

I spent years helping people get a better seat on the train, the seat they really, really wanted. Many ended up very successful but not in a bone-deep way. Not in a way that made them deeply fulfilled. Finally, I started asking people if they'd like to get off the train. Surprise—almost everyone wants to. All I have to do is ask.

Getting off the train doesn't have to mean quitting our jobs, our marriages, or even our neighborhoods. What it means is changing the way we live the lives we're living. How we do our jobs, our marriages, our personal lives. Getting off the train most often means changing our life right where we are.

Yes, I know. Sitting here, reading this book, it's easy to agree that to live an extraordinary life, extraordinary choices are necessary. It's easy to understand that each of us has a Promise that is unique to us. It's easy to believe that each of us is perfectly designed to fulfill that Promise, that our traits, talents and interests are signposts to our greatest possible life. All of that is easy enough to understand.

But, I've found it takes more than understanding and inspiration to actually get off the train. Many of us rise from our seats and head for the door. Far fewer actually open that door and leap off the train to follow their own path. The major reason for the hesitation is that it is scary to trade the certainty of the life we know for a life we might gain. We do a masterful job of convincing ourselves not to take the risk.

Be assured: The risk is not real. It's a mirage. But you'll only know that after you jump.

The real risk is in riding the train to the end of your life and wondering what might have been. Wondering if you really did what you came to do. Wondering if you made the greatest impact you could. Wondering if you stood for something that really matters.

It's time to stop wondering and start doing.

HOW TO ENJOY THIS BOOK

After years of helping people jump from moving trains, I fully realize that everyone is in a different place of readiness to make changes. For some of you just reading these pages to see if there are some ideas you haven't considered may be satisfying. Often meaningful concepts are filed away and are retrieved later when the need arises. Great. Go for that.

But for others, your need or desire for change is powerful and present. If that's you, please wrestle with these challenging ideas and the people whose real stories I tell. Read with the energy of a mixed martial arts fighter locked in a cage with a life you want to change. To do that, when invited to in the text, go to the SavetheWorldBook.com website and complete the assessments and exercises, answer the *Change How You Think About Change* questions, and get the insight you're seeking so you'll know when to jump from the train. We need you. All of us.

PART ONE

WHAT'S MY PROMISE?

CHAPTER 1

THE PROMISE

"Save the world and still be home for dinner." The voice rang triumphantly from my cell phone. "That's what I want!"

Ah, the moment I'd been waiting for. I had been doing leadership consulting with Melissa for months now and she was finally answering The Big Question. The question I ask when I first sit down with a client. The question I *keep* asking, over and over. The one that earns me many an irritated stare and protracted silence.

Four simple words: "What is your Promise?" Four simple, terrifying words.

Oh, I get plenty of great sounding answers from the senior executives I counsel. Answers they think I want to hear like, "I promise to grow the company at 20 percent annual compound growth," or, "My promise is to create a great place to work, to be an employer of choice," or, "I promise to be there for my kids . . ."

Really? My experience is that most of the time our promises are overused phrases we've heard somewhere else, recycled to fit our present circumstance.

So I keep pushing. I keep hammering. What is your true Promise? What do you really want? What do you deeply long for? What are you willing to commit to? And eventually what I get, four times out of five, is a blank look and a confession: "I'm not really sure." Okay, now we're getting somewhere.

What do I mean by a Promise? It is the most powerful commitment we can make. People who wish to lead fulfilling lives make their Promise on two levels. On one level is a public Promise, a leadership Promise, a commitment to help make a better future for the people around us. When we make a genuine public commitment to help create a world of more opportunity and less pain and stress, people sit up and pay attention. Whether we're making a Promise to our company, our co-workers, or our friends, other people are energized when they know that we can be counted on to make tomorrow better. If we are unwilling to make a Promise we gradually become irrelevant. No one will follow. No one will care.

The second level of Promise is one we make to ourselves: a personal Promise. It is the commitment to live our lives in a meaningful, fulfilling way. It's the Promise to have enduring relationships and follow our healthy passions. It's the Promise to *be who we are* and *do what we came to do*. To fulfill our nature and do our noble work. Without a Promise we will only cope. Exist. We will live in a constant state of reacting, hanging on, hoping for things to change.

A Promise is a sacred commitment. It is far more than wishes, hopes, or even dreams. A Promise with a capital "P" is a clear-eyed vision of a future we can count on.

TO SAVE THE WORLD AND STILL BE HOME FOR DINNER
This comes back to the question I'd been pounding Melissa with.

"How can you make a difference in the world if you don't even know what you want, what you stand for?"

Finally, her answer came. Maybe it was sparked by the hour and 20 minutes she'd spent in rush-hour traffic, the three marathon meetings, and 14 panicked business calls she'd had to return, only to arrive at daycare—late again—to find her four-year-old in anxious tears. Or maybe it was just the voice of her soul spontaneously bubbling up through a crack in her everyday, habitual thinking. Whatever the source, her answer was unambiguous: "Save the world and still be home for dinner. That's what I want!" Melissa hung up the phone with a decisive click.

Her words stuck in my head. Save the world and still be home by dinner. A modest little Promise. Isn't that what we all really want, though? *To save the world and still be home for dinner.*

Ten Years to Save the World?
Save the world and still be home for dinner. After all, the world certainly seems to need saving. Global surveys of both citizens and CEOs reveal

that all of us feel we must do things differently to create a future we want our children to grow up in. It seems that the horsepower of industrial capitalism and the magic of modern technology are accelerating our consumption of natural resources so quickly that we are running out of everything we need to sustain ourselves. Today it's oil; tomorrow it's water.

Add to that the horror potential of modern weaponry, ranging from new biological plagues to nukes in the hands of emotional tyrants. Then factor in the problems of economic instability, health care, poverty, education, violence and environmental destruction, all slowly simmering over a fire of a rapidly growing human population set to exceed to 9 billion in 40 years and what do you see? It's called the problem of "simultaneous complexity." That's a technical way of saying that there are so many big challenges happening at the same time that they seem to be growing too overwhelming for humans to solve. In simple terms, we're living in a ticking time bomb with an accelerating clock.

In fact, many experts say that we have only ten years to save the world. It's not that in ten years we can solve all of our problems. Rather, it's that we must change the direction we are all headed in and start heading toward a sustainable future. This must be done within ten years. It will require a sweeping change in our leadership and business paradigms.

Perhaps sounding such an alarm seems overly dramatic. After all, great strides are being made around the world to reduce suffering and increase opportunity. But is it fast enough? We live in a time of paradox. Today we have the most people in history who are billionaires and the most who live in extreme poverty. The most obese people and the most starving. The most well-educated and the most illiterate. The greatest personal wealth and highest personal debt. We live in an age with the highest volume of communication and rapidly growing social isolation.

We live at a time when the richest country in the world has the highest rates of depression, takes more mood-elevating medicine and has the highest rates of suicide and divorce than any other. We live in a world in which the largest armies with the latest technologies cannot pacify people with crude bombs and an iron will. We live in an increasingly connected world. Where the poisons used in China may kill our pets and sicken our children. Where the gasoline we buy today may fund the terrorist's attack of tomorrow. Where airplanes bring us foreign flu.

And unemployment and fear and despair in Africa, Southeast Asia and the Middle East may make the world of our children's future less free and more limited than our own. And, of course, none of us know how climatic change will disrupt our lives or cause sudden suffering.

But this we do know. More than ever, everyone matters. What we believe, what we choose, how we act, all of it matters. The vulnerability of our interdependence and the leverage of technology make the risks of unforeseen events greater than ever. We don't like to think about this. Because we hate thinking about what we cannot control.

Most of us are too busy living our lives to think about how we might want to lead them. But personal leadership is what our world seeks right now. We might have had confidence that people in charge of things knew what they were doing, but recently man-made catastrophes of our banking system, our energy crisis, our educational failures point to a steady stream of blunders that impair all of us. We can't escape the personal suffering caused by impersonal decisions made by small groups of people who simply believe that what they know is all they need to know. But it isn't. Our old institutions are failing because they were designed for fewer people with smaller problems. They are simply overwhelmed by the velocity of modern change. Our model of how the world works is outdated. We need bigger goals, better methods, and higher motives. What's at stake is nothing less than the future of humanity.

If there is an answer, it's that saving the world is up to us. Each one of us, individually and collectively. It is fruitless to deny that we all share in the consequences of these problems. Or to waste our energy blaming the powerful, the greedy and stupid for bringing us to the brink. Or to delude ourselves into thinking that some charismatic leader or magic technology will save us.

Personal Leaders

The fact is the big institutions of government and business need *us* to push *them*. Big organizations and most of their leaders are trapped in the gravity of their own size. All bureaucracies tend to do is jealously guard the status quo, avoid risk taking, offer compromise solutions, cross their fingers and hope for the best. I know. I've spent most of my professional life trying to help large organizations become psychologically healthy places to work. Most of the time it's like painting the Golden Gate Bridge. Staying ahead of the rust and corrosion of toxic self-interest is a never-ending task.

But today is also a day of astonishing new opportunity. Our individual and collective voices are being amplified by the Internet, social networks, citizen blogs, and other exponentially empowered technologies in a way that gives each of us a greater voice than ever before. Creative choices and new ideas can now spread quickly across the globe like benevolent, healing medicine. Change can happen at a breathtaking pace.

I am convinced that if the future will be saved, it will be because you and I exercise our greatest individual gifts as personal leaders. I don't mean we all have to start fast-growing social enterprises; rather, I mean that we must stand for something that matters. And to do that, we must commit to consciously creating value in our lives, in a way that makes highest use of our individual talents and desires. That's what this book is about.

So, I'm not writing here about 101 ways to save energy, eat fiber, or wear underwear made from soybeans. This book is not a scare-fest. Nor is it about taking on more guilt for participating in the world's addiction to consumption. I am not asking you, necessarily, to make do with less or raise your fist to "the man." There are plenty of others doing that. That sort of thing may, in fact, be helpful. But I just don't believe that any kind of negative, oppositional focus will be enough to solve the problems that confront us. It's time to move our focus beyond the things we must *stop* doing and onto the things we must *start* doing. It's time to stop fighting *against* bad ideas and fighting *for* good ones.

And that comes down to each of us fulfilling our unique Promise, our positive vision for the world and our own lives. The great thing is, we don't have to be world-famous heroes to make a difference. Sometimes listening to Oprah or watching a documentary on Mother Teresa or Nelson Mandela can be more overwhelming than inspiring. Right? I mean, how can we ever measure up to lives like those? We feel like giving up before we even try.

But the challenge, for each of us, isn't to be famous or even "great" in the world's eyes. The challenge is to stand for something that is unique to us and our circumstances. And to do it with joyful, positive energy. We will not keep our Promise through self-denial and life-draining sacrifice. Our Promise is not so much a burden as an *opportunity* to do what we are uniquely designed to do. And to do it well everyday. In the real world of our personal lives and careers.

Sustainable Abundance

Our quest is nothing less than *sustainable abundance*. By sustainable abundance, I mean an abundance of everything that really matters in life, both material and spiritual. This is humanity's essential challenge. Every human being wants a chance to live a decent life. The poor everywhere aspire to the middleclass blessings of electric light, clean water, transportation, education, even heat and air conditioning. It will not work for those of us in developing nations to say "oops" we got ours but used up all the natural resources and hit the power switch to climate change so you can't have what we have. At the same time it would be catastrophic to temporarily profit by turning the whole world into an out of control consumption machine. What we must do is choose a new future. A future striving for universal abundance that is wholly sustainable. This is the abundance that comes from creation rather than exploitation.

For too long most of us have *exploited* ourselves, our talent, our energy for something smaller than our greatest value. A paycheck. True abundance is not found just by turning our work into money. It is the genius of turning our ideas into value and our time into purposeful energy.

To create a world of sustainable abundance means we must first find the heartbeat of *our own* personal sustainability. We must find the pulse of life we can maintain that doesn't burn us out or exhaust us, but enables us to be fully present in each moment filled with both gratitude and new solutions. Citizens of the 21st century need to be able to lead their lives, their communities, and their enterprises in a way that improves their real standard of life while nurturing environmental vitality and bringing dignity and opportunity to every human being. This is not overly idealistic. It is not a resource problem. It's a challenge of will.

Our leadership Promise and our personal Promise, it turns out, are flip sides of the same coin. Both are fulfilled in exactly the same way. If we can imagine ourselves being a better person, then we must become that person. By pursuing the life we authentically desire, the life we *yearn* for at our core, we achieve life's deepest purpose…genuine integrity. After years of helping people off the train, I am convinced that what we all truly desire at our core is to maximize our unique Design, Drives, and Desires. We all want to *be who we are* and *do what we came to do*. And when we do that, we simultaneously make our maximum contribution to ourselves, our families, and the world.

What a wonderful piece of symmetry. Saving the world does not come from beating our heads against the wall or giving up our personal dreams, but from living the life we were uniquely designed to live.

YOUR CALL

So I am pulling the emergency stop cord on the train and calling you to uncover your greatest gifts of talent, energy, and passion and to start using them so the rest of us can benefit. This is your authentic mission. This is how you were designed to "save the world."

I am also asking you to "be home for dinner." That is, to have a life. I am encouraging you to nurture and enjoy your most rewarding personal relationships. I am asking you to take time to play. I'm asking you to hike, golf, surf, paint, travel, garden as if you had six months to live. I am asking nothing less than for all of us to live with a new level of purpose and a new level of joy.

Above all I am reminding you that when you change *your* world, *the* world changes!

The life we all really want is the one we were perfectly designed to live. In the end, that's the only life that is both abundant and sustainable. And when we each live a sustainable life, *we create a sustainable future for all of us.*

In helping people discover their dreams for nearly 30 years, I have come to believe that, like Melissa, all of us have a noble intent. But fulfilling that intent does not come from criticizing ourselves and flailing away at unreachable goals; rather, it comes from listening to the theme music of our lives. At different stages of our lives, those lyrics call us to serve our families, focus on our neighborhoods, contribute at our work, commit to our local communities or to faraway places. We hear this theme music more with our hearts than our heads. And when we follow the tune, our lives take on a gentle, sane, and nurturing rhythm. Sustainable abundance.

We all want lives of genuine meaning. We all want lives that create value and leave the world a better place for our having walked here. But we also want to enjoy the process. To feel love, connection, belonging. Excitement and stimulation. We want quiet time to think, to *not* think, to watch the geese fly. To enjoy a little beauty and romance, to sleep an extra hour now and then and to have those rare days in which we don't have to solve anyone's problems. To live a life we both value and enjoy.

That's the good life. Is that too much to ask?

No, it isn't, I have come to realize. It's the *only* thing to ask.

"Save the world and still be home for dinner" sums it up. To *save the world* means to stand for something that matters, make our unique contribution to a sustainable future, and to add value to the lives of others. To *still be home for dinner* means to do it our way. A way that fulfills our heart and satisfies our soul. A way that is not frantic or controlled, obsessive or fear-driven.

When we are fulfilling our true Promise, we don't have to take time out to smell the roses because we are constantly in the garden. Our lifestyle, relationship, and career choices are woven together in a single tapestry that reveals a picture of profound and constant life satisfaction. That is our dream life. Save the World (making our maximum contribution), and Still be Home for Dinner (enjoying life to its fullest)—the two themes that create sustainable abundance.

OUR BIG CHOICE

The only way to achieve sustainable abundance is to invent it. If we view our planet with all of its people as one big adaptive system, we have two choices. The first is mal-adaptation. This choice will create a future fundamentally driven by increasing scarcity and competition characterized by economic and military wars and immense suffering. The second choice is positive adaptation driven by entrepreneurial invention of sustainable agriculture, lean manufacturing, no waste consumption and increasing human health, human rights and human opportunity. The second choice is not automatic, but making the right choice during the next ten years is maybe the most important choice in human history.

CHANGE HOW YOU THINK ABOUT CHANGE

What kind of person do you aspire to be?

What is keeping you from living your sustainable life?

CHAPTER 2

CHANGE YOUR WORLD
AND THE WORLD CHANGES

The whole idea of making your signature impact on the world and at the same time living a life you thoroughly enjoy nearly every-day may seem unrealistic. I thought so too. But then, a few years ago, I began meeting scores of people who are living exactly this way. It all started when I was recruited to speak about the purpose of leadership by The Graduates Club, a nationwide organization that provided educational events to business schools and universities. This led to the founding of The American Dream Project, a campaign dedicated to examining and redefining the American Dream in terms of sustainable abundance. The Project took me to community events and town hall meetings across America—from Silicon Valley to Atlanta, Phoenix to Chicago, Boston to Philadelphia and Los Angeles.

The subject of leadership prompted both me and the audiences to ask some really fundamental questions such as: "What kind of society do we want?" and "What kind of future do we want?" These questions led us back to our nation's founding and the ideals of Life, Liberty, and the Pursuit of Happiness. These town hall meetings became a basis of an award-winning documentary, *Reclaiming Your Dream*, which aired on PBS stations across the country.

As the American Dream Project grew, my colleagues and I built a website and developed an in-depth questionnaire-assessment that more than 20,000 Americans answered encompassing a wide cross section of ages from high school students to 80-year-olds and increasingly people from all over the world. What we learned was nothing less than inspiring. The world is changing. Right now. And that change is being led by citizens rather than leaders. The demands of employees and consumers, from moms and dads, single adults and students, are for a sustainable future. Not a future with less for some, but a future with more for all. This is a future built on the initiative and creativity of people you've never heard of doing things that all add up to a revolution of how we live, love, and work.

What really opened my eyes were the people I met at our events. Our organizers recruited local people living extraordinary lives. Purposely, we chose people who weren't famous. The point was to show what the pursuit of happiness means when ordinary people focus their gifts on serving others while maintaining a personal life of vital relationships and a sustaining lifestyle. What was remarkable to me was that in every community I visited I met people who are saving the world and are still home for dinner.

That journey is the inspiration for this book. All of the stories I share are about real people most of whom I personally know. (I've changed some of their names for their privacy). The people I've written about are just like you and me. And that's the point. We all have the opportunity to make our difference right here, right now. All of us. These people are living proof of that.

One of the most remarkable individuals I ran into was Abraham Keech. He was introduced to me by an equally remarkable individual, Chris. I had known Chris for many years, having recruited him over 20 years ago to work with Stephen Covey and me to teach organizations *The 7 Habits of Highly Effective People* around the world. Chris is now the president of the Human Performance Institute of Johnson & Johnson in Orlando, Florida. I contacted him about our town hall meeting soon to be held at Public Broadcast in Atlanta. He told me an astounding story.

LOST AND FOUND

It seems that about a year earlier, a college professor he knew showed him a videotape of the Lost Boys of Sudan. This now famous story recounts the terrible tragedy that had begun in the 1980s in Southern Sudan. Thirty thousand boys aged three to 12 were orphaned by Civil War. Mothers were raped and enslaved, fathers killed or herded into labor camps. Thousands of young boys were driven into the desert in a matter of days.

Without adult leadership, these children survived by eating leaves and, at times, drinking their own urine. Thousands died of illness and exposure. Finally they began a thousand-mile march to Ethiopia. They marched for months. At night they slept in circles, each taking turns to sleep in the outer ring where many died being dragged away by lions. It was a journey of horror and unimaginable difficulty.

When they arrived in Ethiopia, they were settled at a refugee camp. In time, the Lost Boys became a political problem. One night they were awakened by bullets ripping through their camp. Militants drove them into the raging Gila River where thousands drowned and others were killed by hippos and crocodiles. In all, only about 16,000 of the Lost Boys survived the journey to new refugee camps in Kenya. They had seen their brothers and friends die of starvation, disease, and violence, yet they created a society of support. If one boy happened to get a candy bar or a sweet, he followed the "one bite rule" and passed it on. Instead of *Lord of the Flies*, they became *Lord of the Rings*.

A few years ago the U.S. government agreed to resettle 4,000 of the Lost Boys in the U.S. A political science professor introduced the story of the Lost Boys to my friend Chris, who at the time was a hardworking independent consultant with five children of his own, aged two to 22. Like most of us, when Chris heard the story he was moved to outrage and compassion but didn't know what to do.

A few weeks later he found himself at the airport returning from a long trip. At a Cinnabon stand he noticed a tall, thin young man whom he guessed must be one of the Lost Boys. They have a distinctive look––many are over 6'3" and rail thin. Without hesitation, Chris introduced himself to this 19-year-old Sudanese, whose name was Abraham. They exchanged phone numbers.

A month later, Abraham and three friends had dinner at Chris's house for Thanksgiving. Abraham asked Chris if it would be okay if he brought all of his "brothers" back for Christmas. He informed Chris there would be 12 in all. You see, the camps had made these boys brothers in a way that was deeper than sharing the same DNA. These boys were living in U.S. apartments with each other, no adults. The oldest ones were trying to help the youngest ones get high school diplomas and somehow find a way to college.

After Christmas dinner, Chris became emotionally overwhelmed by the boys' plight. What could he, Chris, do to help? At his greatest moment of anxiety he said he remembered the inspirational energy of Helen Keller's admonition that he had recently read: "I am only one, but still I am one. I cannot do everything, but still I can do something; and because I cannot do everything, I will not refuse to do something that I can do."

At that moment Chris said he felt as if his "heart was being ripped out of his body." He must do something.

That night he resolved to "adopt" Abraham. Not in a legal sense, but to treat him as a son—to coach him, to support him, to put him through college. His own son, Ryan, was a sophomore at a local university. Chris decided he would treat Abraham exactly as he treated Ryan, offering him a place to stay on holidays, money for tuition, coaching, whatever Abraham needed to get launched and become self-sufficient.

By the time Abraham was a senior in college he was studying international relations and had already founded the River Nile Institute, a village school in Southern Sudan aimed at educating boys and girls from his village to become leaders of the future. Abraham used his story to raise money first for books and supplies, then for concrete building materials. He told the village leaders that he would only get the school built if education was mandatory for both boys and girls—something new to the southern Sudanese culture.

The Courage to Matter

Today Abraham lives in his own village, is married to a local girl, and helps to expand his school to raise up a new generation of African leaders. And of course Chris and his family still stay in touch with their Sudanese son.

All of this is real. Imagine Abraham's possible excuses for doing nothing. His childhood traumas were unimaginable. No one would have blamed him for wanting to live life as far away as possible from the problems of Southern Sudan where poverty is still the rule. But Abraham has a gift for speaking, a gift for leadership, and a vision to make a difference.

As for Chris, he's an ordinary man with an extraordinary heart and a gift for courage. When Chris voluntarily took on the obligation to help Abraham, he had his own family to support, five children to educate, and no savings. But when we have the courage to act on love, we simply see things differently. When we act on that motive, the world changes.

Life is a choice.

Chris matters. Abraham matters. Because they have the courage to matter.

You matter too. All it takes is the courage to get up from your seat on the train. The courage to be the leader you would most respect.

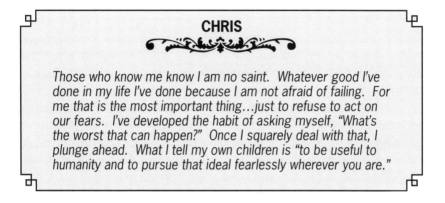

CHRIS

Those who know me know I am no saint. Whatever good I've done in my life I've done because I am not afraid of failing. For me that is the most important thing...just to refuse to act on our fears. I've developed the habit of asking myself, "What's the worst that can happen?" Once I squarely deal with that, I plunge ahead. What I tell my own children is "to be useful to humanity and to pursue that ideal fearlessly wherever you are."

RADICAL CHANGE

Each of us really can change the world. This is the message I am teaching both my business clients and university students. They are skeptical at first. They've been filled with false stories of why they can't make a difference, or worse that they don't need to. But once they open their eyes to the power of their personal leadership, they become positively jacked with ideas to save the world, right now in their current workplace, their community, their own home, or best yet, in all of these places. They light up from the heat of their Promise. Then they act. It's amazing. And it's real and it's now.

So is this possible? Yes.

Change—world-shaking, paradigm-exploding change—is here now. Our research confirms this. And our historical presidential election, the struggles of business-as-usual and the financial collapse of old institutions are all in-our-face evidence that our old assumptions are collapsing.

And what an opportunity this presents for us all.

The radical change we're undergoing right now is going to affect the way human beings will interact with each other and the environment from here on out. And when you start to see unexpected people do unexpected things, or unexpected organizations behave in new ways, or new institutions begin to blossom out of thin air, you can be sure that change is accelerating even faster. Let's look at six areas in which we can see this happening right before our eyes.

We see it in our **popular culture**. We are not surprised when Oprah calls out for greater social justice and personal integrity. We are amazed, though, when rock star Bono does it not only with passion but also with intelligent action. Or when playboy actor George Clooney travels to Darfur or bad boy Brad Pitt and over-the-edge Angelina Jolie adopt orphans and choose to live part-time in Africa. Whether you believe these are sincere expressions or publicity stunts is beside the point. Popular culture is shifting.

We see it in **philanthropy**. When Bill Gates resigns from business and convinces Warren Buffet to give his fortune away to solve society's problems or when Bill Clinton and George Bush work together for world relief, or when large-scale giving is built into the core business models of corporations such as Google and eBay, something is up.

We see it in **business**. When eco-conscious Patagonia clothing company pioneers the use of organic cotton in tee-shirts, it's cool. But when they teach Wal-Mart how to do it, it's jaw dropping. When the largest for-profit company in the world transforms itself into the largest seller of organic food, fair trade coffee and organic clothing in the globe, when it converts part of its truck fleet to alternative fuel and mandates recycling, we must sit up and take note.

When eco-friendly countries like Denmark get much of their power from the wind, we are not too impressed. When new companies like SunEdison create a brand new business by installing the solar panels for free in exchange for a 10-year contract to buy the generated electricity, we appreciate the eco-innovation. And when big box outfits like Staples start putting solar panels on their stores and warehouses to cut their energy costs, we take notice. But when old Maytag plants in Iowa are converted to make giant wind turbine blades, we know we are witnessing a transformation.

Yes, when mainstream entrepreneurs and venture capital firms start scaling up large businesses using new solutions that are better for everyone, something is happening.

We even see it in **globalism**. Fifteen years ago, when offshore manufacturing was still young, standards of manufacturing quality and working conditions were left to local factory managers. Abuses were common and few people spoke up. What started 10 years ago as protests against Gap and Nike for using sweatshops is now going mainstream. New standards are being set for fair labor practices, overtime and child labor. Large manufacturers and retailers are now demanding parts and products built in factories that are certified. Of course, there will always be cheaters and outlaws; that's not the point. The point is that there is a rising tide of change that we can all help to accelerate.

What's been happening is nothing short of a revolution. Our expectations about the things we buy—how they work, how they are made, how long they should last and how they can be recycled—have been dramatically raised because citizens worldwide are demanding it.

We see it in our **workforce**. Recent global surveys confirm that a growing majority of us have an appetite to change the world. In fact, corporate recruiters report one of the most common questions asked by highly sought-after job candidates is what the prospective employer is doing to contribute to humanity and the environment. 80 percent of us want to work for companies that contribute to society and heal the planet. A similar percentage of us want to do something vital in our communities right now.

Most of all we see it in our **personal lives**. When our high school and college-age kids start volunteering more than Americans have in a century, it's inspiring. When millions of Boomers begin seeking redemption from self-focused lives, it's downright revolutionary. When ordinary people like you and me take the future into our hands by striving to create happy and sustainable lives we can look in the mirror and see leaders.

We can lead from wherever we stand right now. We can make our signature impact on the world and at the same time live a life we thoroughly enjoy everyday, or at least almost everyday. The root of leadership is not power or position. It is a willingness to make a public and personal Promise. A Promise to stand *for* something that matters. A Promise to create a life that matters to us. When we are clear on what we stand for and we stand for it wisely in meetings, at work, in conversations with friends, in our choice of product purchases, in what we demand from elected leaders, and how we speak up in our communities, we are, as Gandhi said, "becoming the change we seek."

EMOTIONAL LIBERATION

Whenever I do leadership workshops on creating sustainable abundance there comes an "aha" moment. People start to shake off feelings of helplessness and open their eyes wider. They begin to sit up in their chairs and stretch their necks higher. They reach a point of "I am going to make my difference" and are ready to do something. It's called *emotional liberation*. It is necessary for all big change.

We are emotionally liberated when we can "feel" a new future. The "old future" is the future we are headed for if nothing changes. That's what makes us feel helpless and angry. When we can envision a new future, a different, better future, we are liberated. Emotional liberation gives us the energy to think new thoughts, make new decisions, and take charge of our own destinies. Emotional liberation moved Chris to "adopt" Abraham. And Abraham liberated himself from his horrific childhood to build a future-changing school in Southern Sudan. Emotional liberation is hot energy. It's the only fuel that will power us past the leaders of the status quo, who use fear to make *their* priorities seem like the only priorities.

When the purpose and practice of leadership changes, the world will change.

We have a world in need and a newly emerging resource of committed leaders. We only need to give ourselves *permission* to lead.

We have the tools to create a better future, but we have to use them now. It's time for a generation of new leaders to step up. These leaders must be aware of the great challenges of our day and have the know-how to yoke the power of the marketplace, the inventiveness of entrepreneurialism, and the promise of technology to a powerful will to benefit humanity.

Who are these leaders? They are you and me.

CHANGE HOW YOU THINK ABOUT CHANGE

If I was to make one small choice that could be world saving, it would be...

CHAPTER 3

REALEADERSHIP FOR A NEW FUTURE

It is inspiring that we can be the change the world needs by liberating our own leadership. It's also a major challenge. For forty years business schools and management books have promoted leadership practices that sought to turn everything into money. And just like King Midas who turned his loved ones into cold and lifeless gold, we are succeeding, sucking the life right out of our children's future.

So what if all of our problems were caused by one thing? Just one thing. And what if that one thing was that we didn't have the right goal? As long as our goal is to make as much money as we individually can, we are doomed by the inherent limits of competition. When we change our goal to create sustainable abundance, we open a new universe of opportunity based on collaboration. It's not that competition doesn't have its place. It's just that instead of competing *with* each other, we can compete *for* each other. We can realize that we're on the same team. The team called humanity.

We will never achieve our new goal of sustainable abundance with the leadership models of the past. They are simply too small, too restrictive. The kind of leadership that is needed today is what I like to call REALeadership.

The four cornerstones of REALeadership are:

1. Be Responsible.

We are responsible. That's the simple truth. We are responsible for the consequences of our choices not only on our customers and employees, but also on our families, the environment, the community and the generations of the unborn. That's not all. We are also responsible to make a Promise, a personal commitment to create a sustainable future. Denying our responsibility makes us irrelevant as leaders.

2. Be Ethical.

To be ethical in the new future is to be actively moral. That means going beyond the Golden Rule of doing unto others as you would have them do unto you. The new moral standard is *do as much good as you can*. Create the *Greatest Total Value* you can. For everyone, all the time. Why else lead? Why else live?

3. Create Abundance.

Abundance only begins with conservation. It also requires creation. It demands invention. It requires creating something with unique value and then constantly recreating *more* unique value. Unique value that benefits humanity, heals the environment, and enables you to also enjoy an abundant life.

4. Create a Legacy.

Our legacy is our impact on the future. Our legacy is built one act at a time. It is not something begun in our old age. It starts as soon as we do. The world needs saving. We need new solutions we can implement as fast as possible. If you aren't going to save the world then get out of the way. Make room for someone who is.

The REALeadership model isn't just for leaders of big corporations. It's a way of framing our challenges into opportunities for any size enterprise, even for individuals. In fact, according to the U.S. Census Bureau, of the 24 million businesses in the U.S., 18 million (75 percent) are one-person enterprises. So REALeadership applies to how anyone might lead their business or their life. It is simply a way of thinking and behaving so that decisions are made with the whole world in mind.

The great news I tell everyone is that real change will not wait for enlightened leadership at the top. We cannot wait for institutions to re-invent themselves. We must re-invent them. REAL change happens when we lead from the bottom and the middle. Yep, that means us.

BE A REALEADER

I was introduced to Mike by the CEO of a giant global manufacturer of active apparel. He was proud of Mike because he had created something new out of the sheer force of his own Desire. Mike is an unlikely leader. In fact he describes himself as an eco-bum. He grew up in southern Maine where he spent every spare moment hiking, fishing and, by age 11, surfing. Yes you can actually surf in Maine. It gets downright gnarly in winter. Nature was Mike's escape "from all the voices in my head," he says. Like so many of us, nature's silent energy connected to his soul. After a frustrating two-year stint at Boston University, Mike transferred to the University of New Hampshire where he worked for the Environmental Network and lived in a farmhouse. He spent the next ten years hugging trees, snowboarding, surfing, and hiking all over North and Central America, Africa, and Australia. He paid for it all by waiting tables. Hardly a star MBA in the making.

At 30 he woke up one morning in his mother's basement and it dawned on him that if he didn't do something different he would be waking up in this same basement at age 40. He felt a growing urge to do something bigger than his self-focused adventure life. He had no idea what it was. So one day, armed with an irrelevant resume, he got a temp job at Timberland, the environmentally conscious footwear company. He was a new-product fit-and-wear tester, which meant he lent out new shoes to hikers and construction workers to see how they worked. Sound like leadership yet?

Well, as it turns out, it was. By stepping up to the call of his inner voice, Mike decided to take his Timberland job seriously. He became responsible for his Promise and became an expert at eco-friendly manufacturing.

His temp job turned into a permanent one and within a few years he found himself in southern California being interviewed for a job for Reef, a surfer sandal company. Reef had been started by two Brazilian brothers and had grown into a global footwear phenomenon. In terms of surfing, working for Reef was a dream come true for Mike. Sure, the thought of trading New England for the congestion of paved-over southern California repulsed him, but his desire was to do the most good he could. He considered his new position as a product line manager was an opportunity to make a much bigger impact. He left the eco-monastery of Timberland and became a missionary for sustainable abundance.

MIKE

I think what's important is that I didn't make big changes until I had enough experience and self-awareness to passionately commit to what is most important to me. Life always demands compromise. What guides me is knowing when to back off and when to take a stand. Real change is driven by relentless patience as well as relentless passion. I'm like a dog chomping on a rag being yanked by the status quo. I may not bite, but I won't let go.

It wasn't easy at first because everything he wanted to do with sustainable or recyclable materials cost more, and his bosses wanted better products, not more expensive ones. However his commitment to succeed was cemented by his visits to Chinese and Indonesian factories as he looked for manufacturing partners. He saw factories filled with people huddled into dirty workstations surrounded by swarms of mosquitoes. Mike said his mind went wild with the negative impacts of globalism and vowed that Reef would never exploit the desperation of others to make a buck.

It was while listening to Bob Marley that the idea of Redemption sprung to mind. It was a moment of emotional liberation. Mike developed an idea for a new line of shoes, sandals, shorts, and shirts made almost entirely of organic or recycled materials made in humane conditions. At first he was nearly alone with this vision, but his passion attracted a small, talented group of colleagues at Reef. Reef Redemption was born, featuring very cool products with a very cool story. He collaborated with Rob, a famous surfer, who symbolized the "leave no footprints" philosophy of the sustainable adventure trend. With some inspired help they made a minute-long video that told the Reef Redemption story and posted it on the web. Mike's project became the fastest growing part of the company. That's the power of thinking abundantly. Mike never set out to be a leader. Leadership called him. He just wanted to stand for something. He does.

So can we.

Being a REALeader calls upon each of us to take responsibility for our talents, our visions and our dreams and to create sustainable economic value in our lives, right where we stand, right now. It means we no longer look to "the Man" to provide us with lifelong career paths. It means we blaze our own trails. It means we each become "the Man" in our own careers and forge a unique career path where we can excel like no one else. It means that if we are going to work for a company, we do it on our own terms and we do it for a company that holds values we believe in and that honors what we bring to the table. We insist upon it.

ALL OF US CAN BE REALEADERS

Leadership has been hijacked by business schools over the past forty years. They, along with most of the leadership development industry, have defined leadership as a series of skills and attributes such as decisiveness, discipline, vision, inspiration and the like, but by these definitions Hitler and Stalin were as much leaders as Churchill and Roosevelt. By developing our current business and political leaders using this "skill" mindset, we are witnessing a massive epidemic of leadership failure. REALeadership deals with the first principle of real leadership—the leader's intent. The first question of leadership is, "What am I trying to accomplish?" If we have noble intent, purpose beyond self-interest, and we seek sustainable abundance for all, then we are building on the foundation of real leadership.

CHANGE HOW YOU THINK ABOUT CHANGE

What do you envision your future to be in 1 year? 3 years? 5 years?

PART TWO

NO FEAR, NO EXCUSES

CHAPTER 4

BEING BOLD

E levating ourselves high above our circumstances, as Abraham has done, or courageously creating opportunity for others, as Chris has done, or changing the policies or products of your employer as Mike did, is not as impossible or farfetched as it seems. In fact, it is right within our grasps. And it is how we *save the world*.

What's hard is seeing the opportunity. What's hard is giving ourselves permission to start. To act. It's hard to allow our most noble intentions to take wing. It's hard because our current society is preoccupied with superficial goals and because our fearful emotions are not wired to take bold steps no matter how obvious and practical they might be. The result is that many of us are living in ways that are neither sustainable nor abundant.

But every one of us can make our difference as Chris did. All we have to do is keep our Promise to act on our noble intentions. When we do, the ripple effects spread outward, multiplying themselves in incalculable ways.

Unfortunately, many of us never make our greatest impact. We allow too many crippling fears and limiting assumptions to get in our way. But when we have the courage to act *despite* those fears and assumptions, boldly fulfilling our Promise, great things start to happen.

NO FEAR

One of the most powerful examples of the magic of commitment to your Promise is an educator named Sarita. I honored Sarita at a San Diego town hall meeting for the American Dream Project. For years Sarita's inner voice told her she was stuck. She denied herself opportunities, blamed her teenage misjudgments for her problems, and rationalized that change was totally unrealistic.

And she had a point. At the age of 16 Sarita had dropped out of school. At 26 she found herself with a GED, two children, and a low-paying job at a school. She was lucky enough to have a school principal who believed in her and said, "You are so much better than what you're doing; you should be running this place. Make something of your life, the world needs you." So at 30, Sarita went back to school. It took six years for her to get a bachelor's and a master's degree, all the while supporting and raising her children. She wanted to get through school so badly that she actually enrolled in two junior colleges at the same time so she could take 28 units simultaneously. Pretty amazing.

After graduating, Sarita worked her way up in a school district from teacher to dean to assistant principal to principal. She then became director of instructional support in a different district. It was everything she thought she wanted, everything she had worked so hard to achieve. She was working in a powerhouse district and held a prestigious title. But she was also commuting three hours, which kept her from being home for dinner. She was frustrated because she didn't feel that she was really able to give 150 percent to her job or make the biggest difference she could.

So she did the unthinkable—she quit her job. People were shocked. They thought she had been fired! Then they thought she must be dying from a terrible disease. Why else would someone do something so crazy? But Sarita's response was simply, "Why do we wait until we're told that we're dying to change our lives? I didn't want to do that . . . I just knew that somehow I would find a place where I could do more. Where I could get home at the end of the day and feel good about what I was doing."

So Sarita traveled to Brazil, the land of her family, to gain some perspective. She wanted time to reflect, to think, to listen. One day she found herself in an Internet café and decided to check on job possibilities back at home. Up popped a new posting for principal of Monarch School. Monarch is a school for homeless and at-risk students. These are not kids that are left behind; these are kids that have disappeared. Imagine not knowing if, when school gets out, you are going to return to where you slept the night before. Imagine not knowing if your parent will still be there, or where you can find them. Those are the students of Monarch.

Sarita experienced a moment of clarity. Of blinding commitment. Her Promise stepped from the shadows. When she came back to the states and interviewed for the job she told the panel of interviewers, "It doesn't matter if you hire me because if you don't, I'll still volunteer." That's a Promise. A big, fat bold one.

They made her principal. Today her school is open from 7 a.m. to 5 p.m. every week day, and every Saturday she runs programs that give these kids opportunities to go to San Diego Chargers games, the symphony, the opera, to play tennis, to go to the beach. Sarita also makes it possible for many of these kids to graduate and go to a university. Sarita is energized by her life. She says, "I'm living my dream right now. I know that I am privileged to be in an environment working with incredible educators and support staff that believe in students who are at risk of failing and slipping through the cracks, and I believe that if we can have an environment where each of us sees a potential in each and every student, we can change lives and we can make a difference."

Sarita had plenty to fear—going back to school later in life with children to support, leaving a prestigious and secure job, the disapproving looks of others, entering an environment of "rough" kids—and she could have made plenty of excuses. But instead she took up the torch of her Promise, lit it with the brightest flame, and marched right into the darkness of a school for the forgotten. And she fulfills her Promise every day. She tells me she can't wait to get up in the morning.

Imagine if more of us were like Sarita. Just imagine.

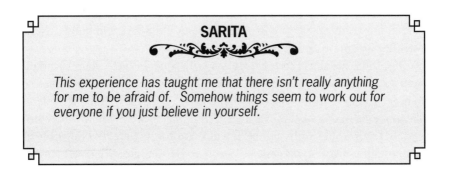

SARITA

This experience has taught me that there isn't really anything for me to be afraid of. Somehow things seem to work out for everyone if you just believe in yourself.

OUR UNIVERSAL EXCUSE

Very often the enemy of our Promise is the universal excuse, "I don't have time." We're simply too busy to think about our Promise. Too busy to choose as Sarita chose.

Most business clients I counsel leave the house between 5:30 and 6:00 in the morning and return home between 7:00 and 9:30 in the evening. Then they work at home. And on weekends. In the car. On the boat. On the *toilet*. If they're not working, they're *thinking* about working. It's what they believe is required. Today, social research reveals that nearly everyone feels time-bankrupt and constantly stressed with activity overload.

Why? With modern technology helping us accomplish tasks faster, communicate more easily and manage our lives more efficiently, we should have more leisure time than ever. But what's causing us to feel this stress is that our free time is filled with other people's urgencies, our own made-up deadlines, a barrage of trivial communications, and an ever-present media stream of anxiety-ridden news, entertainment, and advertising. Most of it is the equivalent of "empty calories," just empty mental junk food pulling our attention 24/7.

THE ILLUSION OF URGENCY

The answer to our stress is supposed to be something called work-life balance. This is achieved, we are told, through time management. But it's an illusion. We try to balance work, family, and play on a preset schedule. The problem is, nothing important ever happens on schedule. Great opportunities and painful crises usually show up inconveniently. Living by time management ensures that nothing ever gets our full attention. When we're at work, we're thinking about our child's soccer game that we're missing; when we're at our child's soccer game, we're working on our "Crackberry."

For three decades I fought this war with time. In fact, when I worked with Stephen Covey teaching the world *The 7 Habits of Highly Effective People*, I helped to develop a Seven Habits time management system. The big idea of the system was to differentiate between what's truly important from what's only urgent. It was great for its time, but the tools of technology constantly assault its premise. By the late '90s most people had given up on time management because *everything* had become urgent. We had traded in our day planners for Blackberries and iPhones to keep us fully connected to our work lives via a digital leash.

This is supposed to improve productivity. And so more and more of us Information Age workers have surrendered to round-the-clock work availability. Like Denny's, we're always open. And as the abnormal has become normal, many of us have begun to tell ourselves that we actually *like* being tethered to our jobs. We tell ourselves it is simply necessary in the twenty-first century. After all, the competition is always working, so we'd better be.

This is a very goofy story that most of us now believe. It's called mal-adapting—adapting to something that we should not tolerate. This new story of normal life is missing something vital. Being busy, connected, and always "on" may make it seem like what we are doing is vital, important, and meaningful to us. But is it? Or is it the stress energy simply creating an illusion of importance?

DOES IT MATTER?

Important sounding job titles seduce us into thinking that what we're doing really matters. But it's not the job itself that's important; it's the quality of our Promise. Nearly two decades ago when I was conducting a retreat for a group of senior General Motors executives, I asked them, "Would the world truly suffer if G.M. ceased to exist? If it simply vanished from the planet? Wouldn't everyone just buy Toyotas, Fords, or Nissans?" The executives, of course, got very agitated. I continued, "Who was the biggest chariot maker in ancient Rome, and who cares? Why does your work matter? If you're not creating transportation that is sustainable, easy to build, easy to fix, with enduring quality and recyclable materials, why make it? The world doesn't need more of what it already has too much of." The room thundered with silence.

The question was supposed to be outrageous. Unthinkable to stimulate new levels of thinking. Who knew it would actually become a valid question? The tragedy of General Motors is that it is full of bright, hardworking people who have spent their work lives creating less than what is possible. Less than what is needed. The problem is not in work ethic of the workforce or the brilliance of the engineers or designers. The problem is the goals of G.M.'s leaders.

The point is that most of us spend most of our time thrusting our creative energy into extremely demanding work whose value we never question. Others of us work frantically to support a lifestyle we don't intrinsically enjoy. We're just used to it and think it's what we're supposed to want.

Most of us have been programmed to pursue someone else's dreams. When we're pursuing such a false dream we often become "possessed" by a feeling of self-importance and indispensability. Or we become intoxicated by the high of using our minds to achieve other people's goals. Healthy motivation becomes so twisted that we work ceaselessly, ignore our higher aspirations, and lose our friends, our families, and finally our health.

And for what? Much of the time we are working at an unsustainable pace to live an unsustainable lifestyle. And we don't question it.

If we are working purely for someone else's agenda, we will never make our work "our own." We won't infuse our work with our unique Promise as Sarita did. We won't make our difference. We'll become like a 15-watt bulb lighting an emotional jail-cell we wish we could escape.

Somewhere deep inside, though, we all sense that our life has a purpose. In our rare moments of stillness we hear an inner voice asking us if we are doing *what we came to do.*

WHY WE CAN'T HEAR OUR OWN HEART
In today's world it is increasingly difficult to quiet down and listen to our inner voice. We are constantly bombarded by the Grid, the media-industrial matrix that permeates our lives. The Grid is our cell phones, our pagers, our laptops, our Blackberries. It's the fax machine, the television, the radio, the 24-hour news channel with the live updates crawling across the bottom of the screen, the OnStar system in the car, and the email that's piling up even as you read this. The Grid urgently beeps and buzzes and pings as it constantly insists that our attention is urgently needed. And once our attention is captured, we are simply too distracted to *have* a Promise, let alone act on it.

The Grid never sleeps. It hums away, seven days a week, demanding not just attention but allegiance. After all, if we miss that email at 9:30 on a Sunday evening, our world just might collapse. Someone else might *win.*

The Grid makes it easy for us to abdicate true leadership of our own lives because it tells us what to do. What to want. It gives us prefab priorities. It sets the goals for us —wealth, accomplishment, position, *winning.* Winning at *what,* we're never quite told, just winning. The Grid makes life easy, in a sense, because we don't have to think or feel for ourselves. We don't have *time* to. At least that's what we're programmed to think.

What's going on is nothing less than a battle for our independent thoughts. The Grid distracts us from our authentic desires and substitutes them with trivial or damaging ones. New brain research confirms that what we repeatedly think actually creates new brain circuits called neural pathways. They are like logic highways our thoughts travel on. Increasingly these highways are paved with the Grid's opinions and assumptions.

We all have the capacity to build our own logic roads to take us to our unique best life. Or we can travel the logic highways pre-paved by the bulldozers of the Grid. Every day the Grid sends thousands of dump trucks down our mental highways, filled with ideas of how we should live. These honking, smoking trucks are jamming every on-ramp to our brain's attention and taking over our choice-making powers.

To the Grid, only the superficial life counts. The Grid bombards us with images of the rich and famous and successful. It shows us what happens to losers. It catalogues our flaws and tells us what products we can buy to fix them. It shames us into accepting its standards. If we don't follow its urgings, we're bad parents, lousy lovers, weak employees, or failing leaders. Losers. The Grid unites us all in one big, generic, all-purpose dream. We don't *need* to come up with our own.

The Grid treats nothing more contemptuously than yesterday's stars, yesterday's successes. Yet it relentlessly sells us the idea that power, fame, and fortune are what really count. It insists that if we solve this problem or achieve that goal, it really *matters.* So we let the Grid drive us, motivate us and tell us what to care about. It fills our minds with discontent and keeps us obsessed with trivia. We hook up to it like an IV unit, mainlining mass-produced ideas about what's important.

The Grid doesn't care about your Promise. It doesn't care about sustainable abundance in your life. It doesn't care about your children. It only cares about "more now." That's what sells products; that's what fills our garage with stuff we don't use. When we're marching to the drumbeat of the Grid, we get up in the dark, come home in the dark, solve meaningless problems all day, and eat dinner at a drive-through.

And don't get what our souls want.

Maybe it's time to stop managing our time and start fulfilling our Promise.

WORK-LIFE HARMONY

So what's the answer? Well, for most of us, the solution isn't dropping out and moving to Costa Rica to play with the monkeys. Trying to "live simply" is not the real answer to our anxiety either. Going back to *Little House on the Prairie*, wearing Birkenstocks®, and having granola for dinner will not solve our problems any more than a raincoat will save us from a hurricane. No, the solution is something much deeper, richer and more interesting.

We need to change the model we use to look at our lives. Most of us unconsciously view life as teetering on a scale, with consumption on one end and work on the other. We attempt to achieve balance by placing some food, shopping, booze, or TV on one end of the scale to counterbalance each chunk of stressful work we put on the other side. An empty chunk of pleasure balancing an empty chunk of labor. Using this model we are able to push ourselves through another day, another week, another year. But this type of balancing act never leads to fulfill-ment and never eliminates anxiety. That can only occur when we are pursuing our Promise.

Our Promise is found in life-work harmony, not in a constant bal-ancing act. The model is a tapestry, rather than a scale. Life, relation-ships, and work are woven together in a seamless fabric that creates sustainable abundance for us as well as others. In this model, our work serves our life and our relationships because it is in harmony with *who we are* and *what we came to do*.

Living this new model in the twenty-first century requires a con-scious choice to become the "cause" of our lives instead of the "effect" of someone else's. It requires that we stop striving to fulfill someone else's agenda and start seeking to fulfill our own Promise.

CHANGE HOW YOU THINK ABOUT CHANGE

If you could work anywhere, for anyone, or do anything you wanted and money wasn't an object, what/where would it be?

CHAPTER 5

NO EXCUSES

As I teach university classes and workshops in Leading for Sustainable Abundance, many adult students tell me they are inspired but frightened. They share a powerful belief that if I commit to my Promise I won't be able to pay the mortgage, credit card bill, or even the lunch tab. "Besides," they say, "my boss is not interested in saving the world. He tells me he is just trying to save my *job* so I'd better work harder doing what I am doing."

They continue, "How? How? How? Can I do it? In *my* situation?" Indeed that is always the core question. But the question is just the form of an excuse. The reason most of us don't seize our Promise and throw our whole selves (and souls) into it is that we're mentally constipated. We won't act unless we're positively certain of our actions. Unless we're 100 percent sure that how we are acting is the "one best way." But the one best way is an illusion. An impossibility. When we substitute certainty for courage and wait for the right time and circumstances so we can be certain of success, we sabotage our own leadership.

It's hard. Certainty, after all, is certainly attractive. Others seem to be very certain. We hear certain people all the time. Business meetings, politics, talk radio, religion are all filled with voices that sound certain. Sometimes friends or spouses also sound dead certain about our life. But they are pretending. They pretend to have all the facts or at least all the facts that matter. But they don't. No one can. It's just fear talking.

The future is always beyond our certainty because the truth about everything is simply far more than we know. In fact, it is more than we are designed to know. The wisest people are open to raw, ragged reality. The fact that the future is always uncertain does not scare them. They

see life as a project "under construction." They are not afraid to look reality in the eye and embrace experiences that run contrary to yesterday's
plans and assumptions. It's in the details of reality that our opportunities
lie waiting.

Nevertheless, we wait because our need for certainty convinces us
that we must be the primary cause of positive change, so we cease to
change at all. What's holding us back is the Single Cause Fallacy. We
tend to assume that a particular problem has a particular solution. We
tend to assume that saving the world happens one big change at a time.
So if we can't bring about that change, why bother? That's the Single
Cause Fallacy. It's one of the dark tricks of certainty.

When our minds are enslaved by certainty we are locked into an
Either-Or picture of reality. We think *either* my life is a platform to fulfill my Promise, *or* it isn't. Either-Or thinking shuts down our insight
toward hidden possibilities because it insists that if one statement is true,
the other must logically be false. For instance, if I don't have enough
money to quit my job I can't really do much to save the world. But life
is not a true/false test. It is an essay question. And the essay our life is
writing is a story of interconnectedness. If we just act today on what
we already know, it may unleash a chain of virtue whose impact is far
beyond our imagination.

IT'S ALL CONNECTED

We live in a world of immense unseen opportunity. It's a world that's
vastly more complex than our minds can grasp. For a simple illustration,
think of a recording artist preparing to go on stage to receive an award
for his new CD, *Cynthia Smashed My Heart into Tiny Pieces.* He wants
to thank all those who helped him create the CD. He soon realizes that
he must consider *everyone* who inspired all of the songs. Virtually every
person the artist ever met inspired the CD's contents in some way or
another. So now he must look into *their* lives too. Who influenced *them*?
And, then, who influenced those people? And them?

And what if that snowstorm had never happened in 1979? His ex-
lover's parents would never have met and Cynthia wouldn't have been
born and he would never have written the title song. So the entire history
of global weather becomes a factor. Gutenberg's printing press contrib-
uted to the CD cover. But what if the Chinese hadn't invented ink in the
first place? China must be thanked. And what were the influences that

caused Thomas Edison to invent the phonograph? What if his second grade teacher had never struck his head on a tree branch and gotten a crucial idea that inspired his legendary student? The entire evolutionary history of trees, then, becomes a vital factor. Then there is the influence of our entire culture, technology, and the economy that comes into play.

If you ask enough questions you will see that you cannot think about the CD without taking quite literally *everything that has ever happened in the history of the universe* into account. Everything influences everything else, is part of everything else.

Nothing exists as a separate event. There are no single causes for *anything*. No matter what the scientists, pollsters or talking heads on TV would have you believe. What this all means is that we can all be part of the bigger "cause" of the effect we seek. We all have a role to play in the drama of humanity.

BOTH + AND

What does all this connectedness mean on a practical level? It means a new kind of thinking is required. Both + And thinking. Both + And thinking as opposed to Either-Or thinking will lead us to insights that are impossible to see any other way. Both + And thinking is the creative power that seeks higher level solutions to every problem that plagues us, individually or globally.

Both + And is a powerful tool to resolve tough ethical dilemmas. For instance, in ethics classes I lay down a tough standard. I propose that the core mandate of ethics is to never cause avoidable suffering. I get a lot of nodding heads. Then I suggest the suffering caused by layoffs of people working for profitable companies qualifies as unethical leadership. Gulp. Now people aren't so sure they like my definition of "avoidable." *Either* we meet our obligation to shareholders *or* we make less profit than we could by tossing people overboard is the typical objection. I remind them that consumers view the first social responsibility of business is to its employees. It turns out consumers don't care if you recycle if you treat your own people like trash. So, how can we *both* help creative, loyal people stay employed and prosper the shareholders?

Kim started with her company as a receptionist at age 20. A single mom, she eventually earned her MBA at night and worked her way up to vice president of marketing. Then when the company was floundering, she was named president in hopes she could turn things around. Instead of following textbook turnarounds and laying off hundreds, she rallied her employees in a national series of town hall meetings in which she challenged them to come up with practical cost savings or revenue growing initiatives. Hundreds of good Both + And ideas were generated. Scores were implemented. The bleeding stopped almost immediately and hurricane-like growth whipped up within months. The person she put in charge of running this resurrection project was a leader of their maintenance department. It turns out he had both brains and tattoos!

Both + And thinking is at the core of sustainable abundance. Old disconnected Either-Or thinking drives a fear-based mindset that asks us to choose between abundance and sustainability. This low-level thinking tells us we must choose one desire or another. One value or its opposite. We can *either* live a meaningful and poor life *or* a rich and empty one. We either work for a non-profit or sell-out to the Grid. It's not true. We can stay in our current job *and* make a difference. We can serve in our communities *and* have plenty of personal time. The point is we can make our difference right where we are.

NOTHING IS IMPOSSIBLE

Peg, the director of Grameen Foundation's Human Capital Center, recently told me the story of the greatest and most unlikely Both + And solution of our time. Bangladesh is a country the size of Wisconsin with 143 million people. In 1972 everyone, well almost everyone, was grindingly poor. Dr. Muhammad Yunus, an economics professor teaching in the United States, decided to return to his native country to try to make a difference. He had no idea.

Poverty really triggered Dr. Yunus. He hated it with a ferocious passion. It robs humans of everything: their health, education, future, and most of all, it daily assaults their dignity. He went to a poor village to try to understand why poverty has such a tenacious grip on so many. To his dismay he discovered that although most of the poor worked hard every day, they made no economic progress. The most direct reason was they had no access to affordable capital to grow their tiny craft enterprises. Instead they borrowed money at punishingly high interest rates from a village moneylender who also demanded to be the sole middleman for their crafts. He paid them so little for their work and charged interest so high they never made enough to get ahead.

Dr. Yunus decided to become their new banker. He loaned several women a total of $27 and encouraged them to sell their crafts directly in the marketplace. Suddenly they were no economically liberated. They were entrepreneurs. Their profits enabled them to increase production, hire others and send their children to school. But wait. These borrowers had no education, no business experience and no collateral. Dr. Yunus' actions made no sense. *Either* you loan money to people who are good credit risks with proper collateral *OR* you lose your shirt. Right? Not exactly. Not at all in fact.

What if instead you could *both* loan money to poor, asset-less, uneducated women, charge reasonable interest *AND* have almost no risk? What if, in fact you could create a banking model that enabled the poorest of the poor to become self-reliant within months, have 80 percent of their children attend school and enjoy a repayment rate of over 98 percent for 30 years? And what if that Both + And model is now used by hundreds of microfinance institutions around the world with 133 million of today's poor raising themselves from the death grip of poverty because of innovations made by an obscure economics professor that no one took seriously? Well, if all that really happened, you'd give the man the Nobel Peace Prize for bringing more of the human race out of poverty than any individual in history.

And that's what happened. Dr. Yunus was awarded the Nobel Peace Prize in 2006 all because he stared down the impossible gloom of Either-or thinking and embraced the innovation of Both + And. How? The primary innovation was "social" collateral in which a small group of women from the same village promised to co-guarantee each other's loans. These groups also become peer business consultants helping each other execute new ideas to accelerate growth. Turns out the power of a social contract can be far more potent than a purely legal one.

The critical lesson Dr. Yunus teaches us here is that when we refuse to accept the unacceptable, which are nearly always the alternatives of an either/or challenge, we ignite a blowtorch of inventive ideas and weld together unthought-of Both + And solutions. If Grameen Bank can thrive, truly anything is possible. No, every good thing is.

EITHER-OR MAKES US WEAK

Our Either-or thinking enables us to invent causes, motives, and reasons why we can't pursue our Promise. These false stories become our elaborate excuses for why we cannot act on our desires.

Excuse stories allow us to DENY, BLAME, or RATIONALIZE. These are the three main mental-emotional tools we use to prevent ourselves to living our potential. They blind us from our Promise.

MENTAL EMOTIONAL TOOLS

DENY

"There isn't a problem." "This problem is normal."
"Everybody's doing it."

To deny means to pretend a negative situation doesn't exist or to pretend a problem isn't really a problem. "I have no problem. My life is fine as it is. This problem is normal. I shouldn't expect more. Sometimes you have to be patient and wait for things to change." To deny means to selectively filter out, or minimize, any evidence that might suggest that our current choice is not a healthy or productive one.

BLAME

"It's not my fault." "He won't let me."
"It's someone else's job to fix the problem."

To blame is to say, "I don't like my situation, but it's not my fault and I can't fix it. My spouse needs to change her attitude. My supervisor needs to recognize my talent." Or, "I can't do anything to create a sustainable future because my boss would never go for it. The company culture doesn't support it."

We often blame our obligations, responsibilities, and the stubbornness of others for the "stuckness" in our lives. We don't change because we are waiting for people or situations to change for us. "After the organization changes, then I can change. For now, I think I'll have another beer."

Sometimes blame has a foundation in reality. Those in powerful positions often don't care about our Promise. Their roadblocks are both wide and tall. But it turns out, blame, even legitimate blame, is no excuse for not pursuing our Promise.

RATIONALIZE
"What's happening doesn't matter and change is
impossible anyway." "It is what it is."

To rationalize we literally tell ourselves "rational lies." Lies that
make superficial sense. Most of the time these lies are constructed
around two false ideas: (1) even though this aspect of my life or my
job is less than I want it to be, it doesn't matter, or (2) change is
impossible. To rationalize also means to tell ourselves that change
would probably create a situation that is even worse. This becomes
our excuse not to change.

In business it is easy to rationalize that we can't afford to be
environmentally responsible because our foreign competitors are not.
In non-profits it is easy to make excuses for lack of progress because
of tight budgets, reduced giving, or inadequate staff.

In our own lives we have our list of well-worn reasons why we
must cope with things as they are or lower our expectations for
personal fulfillment.

Rationalizations are excuses that make sense. But they are arti-
ficial limitations. The truth is that whatever your perceived limitations
are, there are others in similar situations who are succeeding and
living a life they find deeply satisfying.

THE COURAGE TO LEAD INSTEAD OF BLAME

Remember Kim. After she'd transformed her company's direction from
straight down to straight up, her board of directors began considering
taking the company public. Kim was worried that this would enrich the
company's bottom line but bankrupt its soul. So she wanted out.

You see Kim had always been willing to do things differently. Her
company's business is training students who have been "left behind" by
traditional schools and putting them on a career track to earn $50,000 to
$120,000 a year by teaching them skills for a skill-starved world. A huge
part of Kim's success, and the company's success, was her Promise to
educate the whole person. She enlisted the help of education experts to
teach sophisticated science, technology, engineering and math skills to

students who previously struggled near the bottom of their high school class. Kim is the real deal. But her "excuse story" was also very real to her.

First she denied she had an opportunity to lead. "The Wall Street analysts and the Board will never go along with my vision," she told me. "All that will happen is that we'll race to the bottom churning students through a system instead of changing lives." Then she told me she was thinking of accepting a position as a regional director of a large national charity.

"So," I countered, "you're ready to blame some board members for what they might do. Then you're rationalizing that it doesn't matter if you quit because you can work for a name-brand charity. What if instead you lay yourself on the line? What if you both declared your Promise and gave them a chance to support your vision? What if you convinced the shareholders that they will prosper best by always doing what's best for your students?"

I told Kim to think about it over the weekend. She called me on Monday saying, "I know what I want to do. I am going to change the world or get fired for trying." Six weeks later she held a meeting with hundreds of company leaders. Several board members were present. She painted a vision for the company that connected the challenges of the past to the opportunities of the present with the brush strokes of her Promise for the future. At the conclusion, the audience erupted in a standing ovation. Even the crusty "suits" were softened by the power of her clear conviction.

Kim's commitment to a Promise that mattered to her (and to the over 100,000 graduates of her schools) created a new future for her students. What made it possible was that at her moment of truth she stood up and declared her truth. She refused to make excuses for not pursuing her Promise.

CHANGE *IS* DOABLE
Denial, blame, rationalization, and the trap of Either-Or thinking—all are well-honed mental games we play to keep us in a state of inaction in which we believe that change is impossible or unnecessary.

But here's the thing. Change is only hard as long as you resist it. What I often tell people is that most of the time small changes create big

NO EXCUSES AT WORK

Many of the management students I teach want to fulfill their Promise by making Corporate Social Responsibility (CSR) an authentic part of their work. They envision "green" business practices that eliminate waste and reuse and recycle resources. Or they want to volunteer their skills or encourage their employer to partner with an aligned non-profit. But most of these young managers are sure their ideals will either fall on deaf ears or face strong opposition. After all, times are tough. But I counter, what if you made the case that Corporate Social Responsibility is Corporate Social Opportunity? (For a great example of how someone made change at work by making a case for Corporate Social Opportunity, visit SavetheWorldBook.com and read "It's Not My Bag.")

QUESTION: *How do we overcome denial of Corporate Social Responsibility in the workplace?*

"We're not a charity; it's not our business."

"We don't have social and environmental responsibilities beyond what we're already doing."

ANSWER: Ask, for example, "What if we had social and environmental opportunities to create more profitable value?" Then provide relevant examples of companies saving money through sustainability efforts to eliminate waste (e.g. Wal-Mart) or creating new value with products and services that benefit humanity (e.g. micro-loans to the world's poor, which creates self-reliance and new customers). Show that "doing the right thing" can be a viable, positive business choice, not a burden.

QUESTION: *How do we overcome blame that we can't do more to create sustainability in the workplace?*

"We can't because Mr. X won't let us."

"Our customers don't value green stuff."

ANSWER: Do it anyway. Create a small pilot project with like-minded people that's off the radar. Keep it small at first, with little risk. Get a quick success and document it. Repeat it to ensure it's a trend and not a fluke. Then present the results and request more opportunity.

QUESTION: *How do we overcome the rationalization that we don't have the resources to create positive change?*

"Business is tough right now, so I guess my ideas should wait."

ANSWER: Build a positive coalition with:
- A leadership sponsor—Convince someone with a budget and authority to support your idea.
- Passionate vision—Make your vision vivid and visual; use pictures, film, charts, statistics, etc.
- Practical experimentation—Make the first step a low-risk one with measurable rewards.
- Phased implementation—Break a big idea into three manageable phases: Phase one is your practical experiment that offers low risk and measurable results. Phase two expands the experiment to a wider range of trials. Phase three is full-scale implementation.

results. If you change 5 percent of your life, you can often change the way you feel about the other 95 percent.

In business, small, successful changes will often ignite a storm of enthusiasm that gives leaders courage to support more positive change. In our personal lives small positive changes create momentum that eventually change everything.

On the other hand, sometimes a whopping change is needed. You need Sarita and Kim-sized courage. But if you're crystal clear on your Promise, you can find the courage to do extraordinary things, even in the face of fear. If you're content to leave your Promise on the back burner though, that courage will never come to boil.

Our Promises change us. They make us more creative, more productive, and more loving. But we'll never know what our genuine Promise is unless we come face-to-face with *who we are*.

For that we must ask ourselves bold questions.

Are you ready?

CHANGE HOW YOU THINK ABOUT CHANGE

The reason I am unable to be the person I aspire to be in my relationships, career, and lifestyle is...

What are you currently doing to balance your life? Is your balancing act leading to a fulfilling life?

SAVE THE WORLD RIGHT NOW

Over my decades of searching for ways that our work, our careers and businesses might serve humanity better, I have discovered many inspiring people and enterprises. But, for me, nothing comes close to the world changing impact of microcredit. Dr. Yunus' discovery that nearly all of us have a self-reliance gene is the best lever for changing the world. His work in providing tiny loans to the poor so they can develop profitable businesses has probably done more good for more poor people than any other single economic initiative in world history. I know. That sounds extreme. But he actually won the Nobel Peace Prize because of the positive social, health, education and human rights impacts that follow economic self-reliance. His vision is nothing less than to end poverty. Period. The Grameen Foundation, which was established with Professor Yunus as founding board member to spread the impact of microfinance globally, is working to make his dream of ending poverty a reality. The clock is ticking on the international community's goal of cutting poverty among the world's poorest families in half by 2015 (that's about 700 million people). Yes in five years. It's possible. It's actually happening.

So to put my commitment on the line, I decided to pledge $1 of my royalties from each book to the Grameen Foundation to help make this happen. You can help too.

Go to StopPovertyNow.org

Make a contribution to sustainable abundance by helping local organizations that enable striving mothers in hopeless situations become entrepreneurs. Give all you can. Be bold. After all, we'll all be home for dinner, so why not do something to save the world right now.

PART THREE

WHO AM I, AND
WHY DOES IT MATTER?

CHAPTER 6

WHO AM I?

If I had to trim down to one sentence everything I have learned in nearly three decades of coaching people to fulfill their Promise, it would be this:

**We cannot know what our true Promise is
until we know *Who We Are*.**

WHO AM I?
This might sound like an odd assertion, but most of us don't really know who we are, what we truly want, or what deeply motivates us. We were never taught to ask these big questions.

- Who am I?
- What do I deeply desire?
- Why does it matter?

In fact, we were taught to avoid such soul-stretching queries. Instead, the small questions, like: "What time should I get up for work?" or "When are my taxes due?" have dominated our lives. I know. It's crazy.

Most of us are on "automatic pilot" most of the time. The American Psychological Association says that 95 percent of our daily thoughts are habitual. Since most of us think as many as 50,000 thoughts a day, that's a lot of repetitive thinking. It means for the most part we live our lives unconsciously. Too rarely stopping and thinking. Too rarely pondering our choices, our responsibilities, and our opportunities to *be who we are* and *do what we came to do*.

KATE DISCOVERING KATE

If we are "lucky," something happens to pull us out of our small questions into something much bigger. One warm spring night I walked onto the set at Georgia Public Broadcasting for an American Dream Project town hall meeting. As I shook hands with 27-year-old Kate, I noticed wisdom in her eyes. We were honoring her for starting Kate's Club, an organization dedicated to helping children who had experienced the death of a parent deal with their grief and loneliness.

As Kate told us that night, her mom died when she was twelve. Her dad retreated into his own sorrow and her older brother who was in high school, chose to spend most of his time away from home. Kate vowed to be normal, happy, and popular, just as if her mother were on a short vacation. So she lived with a deep sadness hidden by her big personality.

At the end of her junior year at the University of Virginia, she volunteered to be a counselor at a summer camp for kids who had lost parents. The first night the head counselor asked Kate to make the kids feel comfortable by telling her story. Kate said she was seized with fear. She had never told her "story" to anyone. She never talked about her ache, her feelings of anger, and the damn unfairness of it all. She never talked about the fear of her own mortality that was so amplified by her mother's death.

And then she did. That night at camp she discovered a worthy purpose for the pain she had carried for years. She learned that by sharing her story she not only healed herself but opened doors for others to heal by telling their stories.

After graduation Kate became a marketing manager and was building a good life for herself. But at 25 she felt vaguely empty. At dinner one night with her father, he asked her what her true dream was. She surprised herself by telling him she'd most like to build a place in Atlanta where local children who have lost a parent or a sibling to death could come on weekends or after school to talk and help each other.

Her father calmly looked at her and said, "Well then, that's what you should do."

Her jaw dropped. "I have no idea what to do. I don't know how to start a non-profit. I'm a not a psychologist or even a trained counselor."

Her dad's eyes locked on her, and he said, "None of that matters, just start."

So that's what she did. Today Kate's Club is a thriving Atlanta Charity serving hundreds of children who would otherwise suffer in silence.

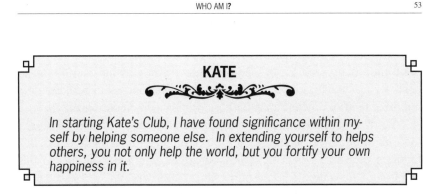

KATE

In starting Kate's Club, I have found significance within myself by helping someone else. In extending yourself to helps others, you not only help the world, but you fortify your own happiness in it.

Kate had no power or permission to do what she did; she just did it. There wasn't any career plan. There was no job to apply for. But there was something much stronger. It was the voice of her own soul, telling her to stand for what mattered to her.

Kate told me something I'll never forget. She said the suffering from the loss of a parent when you're a young child is terrifying. Not only do you feel abandoned, you also feel guilty for the inevitable fading of your memory of that parent. You feel guilty for laughing again. But the real, deeper fear this brings up is that if you can "move on" from your mother's death that must mean everyone will move on after yours. In other words, she said, "We are confronted with the terror of our own seeming insignificance." I told you she was wise.

This fear of not mattering is the deepest human fear of all.

Strangely, inexplicably, the way most of us deal with it is to fritter away our one chance to matter in the way we are uniquely designed to. Our greatest fear is that life is meaningless. Then we spend our life proving it by living that way. It's the saddest kind of self-fulfilling prophecy.

But if we wish to live a life in which we DO matter, it stands to reason that we must first have a true understanding of *who we are.*

ROCK STARS, MOVIE STARS, AND ATHLETES

When asked who we'd like to be, a great many otherwise reasonable adults reply that they would choose to be famous actors, rock stars, sports heroes, or retired hedonists. Basically rich, famous, and lazy. This is the Grid's programming. But there are probably fewer than 5,000 actors who really make a living in film and television, and fewer than 5,000 athletes who get paid anything for what they do. How many rock musicians rise to the level of "star?"

So what does that mean to the rest of the 300 million Americans and 6.8 billion people on Earth? Do our unique souls really want us all to become movie stars or American Idols? To eat Godiva chocolates in a hot tub day after day and play endless rounds of mediocre golf?

No. It's just that from the time we were infants, we've been taught to think of ourselves as our bodies, our thoughts, our achievements, our families, our stories, our ethnicities, our tribes, our "inner narrators," our emotions. Our haircuts. Our sports shoes. Our cars. We've been taught to look for our identity in just about every conceivable place but the right one.

JUST WHO DO YOU THINK YOU ARE?

To save the world and still be home for dinner we have to know *who we are* and *what we came to do*. We have to take the time to ask and to answer the big questions. Otherwise we'll waste precious time on trivia, make excuses, and settle for whatever table scraps we can get out of life.

But to meaningfully answer the question of Who We Are, we first have to look into some scary territory. We have to ask what is *humanity itself* and what is our place in the cosmos? What does it mean to be a human here on our little blue planet in the early twenty-first century?

For unless we have at least a reasonable answer about what it means to be human, we can't possibly know what it means to be *this* human called me.

WHAT DO YOU BELIEVE?

I need to plunge in and take a big chance. I am talking about belief in the Divine. I know, I know. Why do I have to bring it up at all? Nothing is more controversial. But it matters so much. This is not about religion. It is about our source of meaning. It is about the "why" we live our lives. It is about "what we are," which actually comes before "who we are." So here's what I propose. I'll tell you how I think about belief and non-belief and you tell me what you think. (Go to SavetheWorldBook.com and join the discussion).

First, all of us should be humble about our own ignorance. The smartest minds have peered into the tiniest building blocks of nature and what have we found? "Holy crap!" seems to be the most appropriate response. All we really know is that reality is staggeringly different from what we commonly think it is. Turns out, there are no "real" objects. None. There is no such thing as solid substance! It's invented by our brains. The universe is 99.9999 percent nothingness, punctuated by little fluctuations of *whatever* that blip in and out of existence millions of times per second. What is this mysterious whatever? We don't know. What causes the blipping? We don't know. Where do the blips go when they blip out of existence? We don't know. Why do they come back? We don't know.

We don't know. We don't know. We don't know.

We have no idea what anything in the material world really is. Nor do we have a clue as to *why* anything exists. Anything. Think about that for a moment. Our ignorance is grand, magnificent, overwhelming, stupefying. All we have really learned in centuries of science is how much we profoundly *don't* know.

That being said, we all have a choice to make. As I see it, there are two general possibilities, two scenarios. Both scenarios have their supporters. Both sides use science to back them up.

Scenario #1 is that we are "accidental humans;" the result of a cosmic chemical spill. A random mass of colliding electrons guided by unseen forces that proceed without any cause or meaning.

Scenario #1

Under Scenario #1, consciousness is just a by-product of biochemistry––an epiphenomenon, as the scientists say. If we accept this possibility, then all meaning is self-invented, a comforting illusion to save us from despair. With Scenario #1 values are simply the preferences we invent to help us get along. This view of accidental humanity is quite popular among the highly educated. In fact, it has become *de facto* religion in most of our colleges and universities. I have personal friends who are "positive atheists" who work tirelessly to better humanity just "because." Yes, they amaze me. It's a vivid demonstration of our core human need to give, love, and serve that's beyond all reason. I see my selfless atheist friends as secular saints acting like human weather vanes directed by the unseen winds of a loving force. To me, their passionate purpose serves as silent indication of a divine imperative rather that its negation.

I am not naïve enough to think that non-belief will motivate most people to pursue their noble Promise or create a future of sustainable abundance. Where can we find evidence that *human* virtue can be sustained by large numbers of humanity based simply on "self" control? History is clear that when humans decide that we are the pinnacle of all intelligent life, it opens the door to genocide and child abuse being just as legitimate as charity work because if there are no universal values, life descends to survival of the fittest. If you think this is far out, consider the long list of early 20th century leaders that believed in selectively breeding out what "science" said were low IQ races: Woodrow Wilson, Theodore Roosevelt, George Bernard Shaw, John Maynard Keynes, William Keith Kellogg, Margaret Sanger, and Winston Churchill to name a few. Eugenics was a very popular fake science. It was the scientific excuse for Nazism.

In fact, several bloodthirsty twentieth century tyrants used their own version of Scenario #1 to justify their actions. We all know what happened. It led to the slaughter of over 150 million of us. If Darwinism is the soulless mechanism of creation, what we end up with is a life based on competing for power instead of one of meaning. That's because once you blow through the thin wall of humanism, ferocious self-interest is the only thing that makes sense.

I know there are people who claim religion has done more to harm humanity than non-belief ever has. But all the wars, intolerance, and torture didn't happen because of a belief in a divine unseen world. It happened because humans are corrupt. The fact that religion doesn't tame man's evil doesn't mean that life is meaningless. To the contrary, it makes life's intrinsic meaning even more important.

All attempts of the "accidental humans" camp to create secular meaning are in the end meaningless. After all, if meaning is made-up, then it really isn't meaningful. And living without real meaning is not fulfilling—never has been. It also makes science, art, spirituality, our work, our families and even love itself meaningless. Just diversions on the road to nowhere.

Scenario #1 isn't personally satisfying either. It never deeply addresses the "Who am I" question. Even science itself admits this when its guard is down. Science can tell us a small bit about how a thought is transmitted in the brain, but it can't tell us a thing about *who* thinks and originates the thought. It can tell us a small bit about how perception works, but not a thing about *who* is doing the perceiving. It can tell us a small bit about how the brain communicates with the leg and the foot, but not a thing about who has the idea, "I think I'll go to Krispy Kreme this morning."

Scenario #2

Scenario #2 says that there is something more to us. It says that we are significant humans. We are part of something that goes deeper than the electrical wiring of our brain. We are connected to a greater intelligence, a transcendent spiritual energy that is at the core of everything.

Scenario #2 isn't made-up woo-woo. It, too, has science behind it. Its reality begins with understanding $E=mc^2$—Einstein's discovery that matter and energy are one and the same and that energy cannot be destroyed, only transformed. Every physical thing, according to Einstein, is really just energy in a particular form that our particular senses interpret as matter. And energy cannot be destroyed, only changed in form. We don't actually live in a material world. Matter is just energy. It is technically non-material. And the name we commonly use for things non-material is spiritual. Spiritual energy, imagine that.

What's intriguing is that the laws that govern *how* energy changes form seem to depend on intelligent consciousness. Decades of repeated experiments performed by scores of mainstream renowned physicists have categorically shown that human intention powerfully affects the behavior of matter/energy. Period. It's no longer up for debate. In fact it's this property of physics that makes electrons behave in ways that make electronic circuit boards possible. It's ironic that every computer chip is a reminder of an invisible unexplainable reality. A spiritual world.

There's more. Our awareness is not a result of our brain's biological ability to think; rather our brain's abilities seem to come from our deeper non-biological consciousness. Thanks to new super-sophisticated brain surgery we now have clinical evidence the individual human consciousness does not depend on our brain being alive. That's right. We now know that we can have zero brain wave activity for prolonged periods and still have conscious awareness of what is happening while our brain is switched off. Now that's amazing. (If you want to read about a clinical account of independent human consciousness, read *The Scalpel and the Soul* by Allen S. Hamilton M.D.)

WHO CARES?

We are intellectually arrogant when we think what we do know is more important than what needs to be known. But what we don't know appears to be far more significant than what we do know. For instance, in Scenario #1, the central question of life—*Who* is doing the believing or doubting or thinking, experiencing, deciding, loving?—is completely ignored because it is inconvenient and can't be answered by experimentation. The "who" question is beyond science, so traditional science pretends it's not important. If we are all "accidents" of nature, there is no who.

So if all you and I are is the minute-to-minute result of our brain chemistry, our personal identity is a mad illusion. And survival is the only thing to pursue. But if "selfish genes" are what drive us, why does a person run into a burning building to save a stranger? Or even a stranger's *pet*? Did we simply evolve to cooperate? In Scenario #1 we logically shouldn't care about anyone else. Not even our children. Because when we're dead, we don't exist.

So the future doesn't matter. Nothing does. But we do care. We can't help it.

In Scenario #2, we are not, at our essence, physical, biological hunks of matter that have learned to think. Rather our biological bodies are only the temporary manifestation of some essential, eternal energy––what spiritual teachers have for millennia called our souls. In that case, the source of our true desires and noblest intentions is much deeper than our individual story, our personality, or our brain chemistry. We are part of an abiding, universal consciousness temporarily housing itself in our body.

What's the importance of all this? Well, if Scenario #2 is true, then most everything the Grid tells us is important isn't. At least not in the way we think it is. With Scenario #2, our soul belongs to a deeper spiritual reality. And in that reality love does matter. In fact, it matters most of all. And if love matters, then so do my grandchildren and so do yours. And so does the future we are creating for them. I don't know about you, but I'm putting my chips on Scenario #2.

WHY THE BIG QUESTIONS?

The Grid doesn't like us to ask questions about the significance of human life. For if we really believed in our own spiritual essence, if we really believed that the source of joy in life lay *within* rather than without, we would stop buying products to make us feel complete. We would stop marching to the Grid's tune and start dancing to our own.

I, on the other hand, love to ask such questions. Because what I have found as I ask people, "What's your Promise?" and watch them dig for an answer is that they come face to face with their own significance. When we take the time to wipe clean the lens of our hearts and minds, the face of God stares at us from every direction.

The truth is, if we don't believe that we are part of something purposeful, something bigger and more lasting than ourselves, we'll find it difficult to sustain the motivation to live a truly valuable life. If everything is ultimately pointless and all meaning is made-up, then what we do in this life doesn't really matter. With this attitude, we will be constantly drawn into the endless stress of seeking pleasure and avoiding pain. Accumulating *stuff* instead of meaning.

But what if we believed that human beings *are* deeply connected to one another and to a vaster intelligence—I mean *really* believed it, not just mumbled the words on Sunday morning? And if energy cannot be destroyed, doesn't that open the possibility that each of us will survive death in some way? What if we understood that the person we were becoming on the inside was the only thing that mattered because who we are becoming is the point? The point of everything.

Then everything changes. Cutthroat, competitive motives just won't do anymore. Nor will small-minded, fearful, self-protective ones. We are forced to come to the conclusion that we are all engaged, together, in creating one legacy.

And that legacy is this: a healthy, sustainable planet filled with healthy, sustainable human lives.

CHANGE HOW YOU THINK ABOUT CHANGE

What's your Promise?

CHAPTER 7

IS MY INNER VOICE MY TRUE SELF?

O nce we've summoned the courage to answer the big questions about *who we are* as humans and whether we humans matter at all, we can move on to the question of "How do *I* matter? Who, in fact, am I?"

"Where does my sense of identity—my sense of I-ness—come from?" It's a critical question. For our Promise is squarely rooted in whatever we perceive as our individual identity.

Figure 7.1: The Identity Cycle

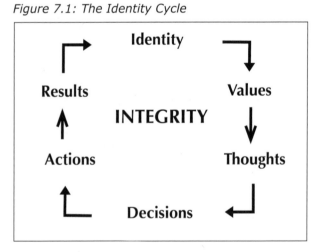

IDENTITY DRIVES EVERYTHING

The quality of our lives, from top to bottom, is determined by our identity. Identity—who we think we are—drives every choice we make, whether consciously or unconsciously. It generates our values, thoughts, decisions, actions and real-world circumstances. It determines if and how we might lead.

Identity is the role we play in life's drama. The trouble is, most of us get off to the wrong start. Instead of looking inward for identity, we choose an external role, a character of sorts, and that outer character becomes the protagonist of our made-up story. All of our lines and actions flow from the character we've chosen. If I'm playing the part of Gang Member, for instance, I fight my enemies, sell drugs, and intimidate my teachers. If Doctor is my identity, I fight to save the life of the gang member wounded in a street fight.

Our identities dictate our values. Our values give rise to our concerns, our obsessions, our habitual thoughts. These thoughts drive our decisions, which, in turn, lead us to action.

Our actions produce real-world consequences—a trip to prison, a Chief of Surgery appointment—that further confirm our sense of identity, making that identity increasingly more real to ourselves and to others.

> **I choose gang member as my role.**
> **I ice a rival.**
> **My gang brothers cheer and high-five me.**
> **I am Gangster.**

> **I choose stockbroker as my role.**
> **I have a successful year.**
> **I buy a $100,000 Mercedes.**
> **My colleagues cheer and high-five me.**
> **I am Stockbroker.**

> **I choose father as my role.**
> **My son is on a traveling soccer team.**
> **I spend my holidays going to soccer tournaments.**
> **Other soccer dads cheer and high-five me.**
> **I am Soccer Dad.**

You get the idea. Over time, I *become* the character I am playing. Pretty soon I can't pry myself off the stage with a crowbar.

Identity sets the boundaries of our lives. It cements our sense of place in the world. It makes us feel more secure. Less fearful. Less alone. At least for a little while.

We look to our fellow character types to figure out what kind of life choices we should be making. What kind of car are the other stockbrokers driving? Which suburb do the other doctors or lawyers live in? What type of eyeglasses are the other college professors wearing?

Instead of making authentic choices, we make choices based on the part we're playing. Our lives are dictated, to a large degree, by what we think we must do to remain members in good standing of whatever club we have decided to join.

The Grid plays right into this. It feeds us a steady stream of images, products, and pre-made desires to help us play our chosen part with a higher approval rating. We maintain an illusion of freedom by making individualistic choices on trivial matters, such as which color Porsche convertible to buy or whether to plant trees or flowers on our front lawn in Sunnydale. But we allow the big choices, the meaningful choices, to be dictated by what we see as our external identities.

This isn't good enough if we want to live our Promise. If we want to make the courageous choice to *be who we are* and *do what we came to do*, then we must reconnect with the raw and unadorned "I" that was there before we started reading our lines from an actor's script.

We must ask, "Who am *I*?" Really. Underneath our *Self-Concept.*

OUR TROUBLESOME SELF-CONCEPT

Early in life, no later than age five or six, we make the unpleasant discovery that some people don't like us. As babies and toddlers, we had been eager, innocent learners. We didn't try to protect our Self because we didn't really *have* one yet. We simply tried stuff —walked, talked, threw toys around. If we didn't get the results we wanted, we tried something new or changed our goals. There was no real sense of self-involvement; there was just doing and being.

This was the stage of psychological innocence. But now things change. We go to school and suddenly realize that we are not all the same. Billy is stronger. Josie is prettier. Kenny has cooler stuff. We begin to be judged, compared, graded. We develop what Robert Kinsel-Smith calls a Comparative Self. A mental idea of how we stack up. We become ashamed of our shortcomings. The idea, "Uh-oh, I may not be good enough," creeps in. It scares the hell out of us.

Meanwhile, we're busily authoring our Self-Concept, that story we tell ourselves about ourselves that begins to define our sense of identity. We become extremely protective of this Self-Concept. We look for ways to make it stronger and more durable in our minds. We pad it with personal folklore selected from memories and defensive strategies. The more we pad it, the more real it seems to become.

We begin to mistake our Self-Concept for *who we are*. The more primal part of ourselves is plastered over by persistent thoughts and stories—likes, dislikes, opinions, accomplishments. We begin to believe the ideas we've constructed *about* ourselves to *be* our actual self. The real me.

Our Self-Concept filters the world so as to validate itself. It denies, distorts and rationalizes reality to preserve its own myth. That myth can even be an extremely limiting and negative one—"I'm no good," "I'm learning disabled," "I have terrible luck," "I'm just not a leader"— as long as it's something predictable to hang onto. Whether the Self-Concept is positive or negative doesn't really matter all that much. What does matter is its preservation. Why?

Because our Self-Concept cares about one thing above all: Certainty. It craves stability. Security. The Known. Anything unknown is terrifying. Even though a negative self-image may not win us great rewards, the emotional payoff of certainty trumps the risk of change.

Underneath it all, our Self-Concept is driven by fear. Fear of annihilation. It knows it is a flash in the cosmic pan. It knows it soon will die. This terrifies it. And so it gets busy trying to fake its own permanence.

And here's where the Fundamental Error of human life occurs: Rather than identify with the part of ourselves that actually *is* eternal, we throw our support to our Self-Concept. It's what we're taught to do. It's what our parents did, and their parents and their parents. It's what the Grid tells us to do—to identify with our Self-Concept and to spend our lives trying to make our un-real Self-Concept our real self.

Most human lives are not driven by growth and creativity but by constant validation of their Self-Concept. Denying, distorting, rationalizing. It's exhausting.

IT'S JUST BANANAS

When I ask clients, "What do you really want?" I usually get some pretty fast answers. "Success." "Peace and quiet." "A million bucks."

MY INNER MONKEY

When I went to first grade my ears stuck out. I had pillow lips and big round eyes. As fate would have it, my favorite toy was a stuffed chimpanzee named Zip. Zip often made the trek to school with me, dressed in his red overalls and yellow shirt. It wasn't long before teachers and students began to notice an uncanny resemblance between my chimp sidekick and his human companion. I became known as "Monkey Boy." I actually *liked* this. It gave me an identity distinct from the other kids. (Even at that age I had trouble distinguishing the value of being infamous from the value of being famous.)

I bolstered my "Monkey Boy" identity by dominating the monkey bars during recess. I swung with great enthusiasm and became the Robin Williams of chimp noises. When not besting the bars, I loped through the sand, knuckles dragging on the ground. I actually began to consume several bananas a day. This was 50 years ago, before therapy was a common option.

As long as my identity was tied up with Monkey Boy, my drives and desires revolved around consuming bananas and mastering the monkey bars. Fortunately, my mother performed an "intervention" and got me back on track before a veterinarian had to be called in. The point is, having my identity centered on being Monkey Boy was having no identity at all, because Monkey Boy was not who I really was. I had just seen too many Tarzan movies. My desires were being fed by a Self-Concept based on a story I was telling myself about how absolutely cool it was to be a monkey.

As grown ups, we often get sidetracked by all kinds of sophisticated "monkey boy" stories about ourselves.

"An extra round of golf." Or something gloriously vague, like "to make a difference." Or "to retire and teach;" there's a common one.

The problem with these answers is that most of the time they are just plain bananas. Monkey Boy food. They don't arise from our real identity; they come from the fretful inner dialog of our Self-Concept.

You see, our Comparative Self, the part of us that's preoccupied with how we stack up against others, is always sizing up our Self-Concept and comparing it to others. The dialogue between the Comparative Self and the Self-Concept becomes the non-stop soundtrack of the typical unexamined life:

> "Ferguson has a new SUV. You're his boss. Shouldn't you be driving a better car than he does?"

> *"Yes, but I'm not materialistic, I'm pro-environment. I told everyone that at the last meeting."*

> "Still, it doesn't look good. People will talk."

> *"But I have Deep Values."*

> "Ferguson has Deep Values, too, but he still drives a nice car."

> *"Okay, okay, I'll look into a new SUV—as long as it's a hybrid!"*

That noisy inner dialogue constantly overlays our experience, continually evaluating us as acceptable and lovable or unacceptable and inadequate. And we constantly jump to its demands.

For many of us, this inner voice becomes the identity we think of as "me." But we are more than the voices in our heads.

Much more.

CHANGE HOW YOU THINK ABOUT CHANGE

What stories about yourself are keeping you
from living the life you most desire?

CHAPTER 8

FACE TO FACE WITH YOUR OWN SOUL

B ut can this inner voice really be ME? Well, it *calls* itself "me," it thinks of itself as "me," it defends itself as "me." It's always there, ever evaluating, ever managing, ever worrying. Ever running the show. Constantly assessing not only my actions and motives, but also those of everyone around me.

This inner voice *must* be me. Right?

Nope.

This self-critical or self-congratulatory voice in your head is simply the running dialogue between your Self-Concept and your Comparative Self. It is the drama your mind is desperately trying to compose about you. It is not you.

Our inner chatter is kind of like the banter between Al Michaels and John Madden now on *Sunday Night Football*. One is calling the play-by-play, the other is doing the color commentary. We start to think this running chatter is the game itself. But the real game is being played down on the field.

To believe you are your inner chatter is seriously nutty (even though we've all done it). Think about it—who is your voice talking *to*? That becomes the really interesting question.

As long as we believe our Self-Concept and its running dialog constitute our identity, we are trapped. For nearly a century, traditional psychotherapy focused on lying on a couch describing, not *ourselves*, but our Self-Concepts. If we dragged up enough stories about our traumatic childhood, the theory went, we would be free. But Freudian psychotherapy doesn't really work because neither the id, ego, nor the superego is *who we are*.

Trying to make our Self-Concept healthy is like trying to have healthy cancer. Can't do it. It's just replacing one story with another. Switching from an internal horror movie to an internal romantic comedy might feel better in the short run, but it is not a long-term answer.

"Okay, then, if I'm not my inner voice, then who am I?"

We're getting there. I'll give you a hint. The answer is found less in the part of you that makes all the inner noise and more in the silent part that hears it.

WHO AM I? LAURA'S STORY

Most of us coast along, believing that we *are* our Self-Concept, dancing to the tireless voice in our head, until life's tires blow out. Crisis happens—death, loss, betrayal, suffering. The ground shifts. The rules suddenly change. We wake up one morning, look in the mirror and say, "Who am I?"

A couple of years ago I was advising Laura, a chief marketing officer of a high-tech firm in Silicon Valley. Laura was married with two daughters, 11 and 13. As her photos attested, she had been a pretty young woman. Now 44, she was aging nicely, but aging no less. Her husband of 17 years was a struggling software salesman. One fine Christmas season he announced to Laura, out of the blue, that she was "too good for him" and that he wanted a divorce. Furthermore, he had never really loved her.

Oh, and by the way, he was in love with her "best friend."

Laura's friend was a hard-bodied gym bunny. And it turned out that Laura's daughters actually *liked* her betraying friend. So Laura had no allies.

Laura's self-worth deflated like an old beach toy. She faced the classic crisis: beliefs and expectations shattered by reality. Her theory of life had let her down. She had tried to do everything right. She'd been a good, supportive, attentive mate. A great financial partner. An emotional anchor. She had done everything she could to make life turn out just right. And it had fallen apart regardless. Everything she had hung on to as meaningful had suddenly slipped away. What she'd thought was her Promise had disappeared.

Laura had plenty of time to reflect. Half of every week the girls went to Dad's new condo and Laura sat alone with a glass of wine, philosophizing. And sobbing. Laura didn't know anything anymore. Who she was. Why she was here on Earth. What she wanted to do with her life. She called me and asked for help. She didn't want to resort to denial, blame, or rationalization; and she didn't want to just suck it up. She wanted to embrace new expectations for her life, but she didn't know where to start.

I told her that she needed to get to a deeper place. She needed to answer the big "Who am I?" question. I told her that if she was up to the challenge, there was a way to start. It might go against the grain of her traditional thinking and business training, but it might provide a breakthrough.

Laura was desperate, so she said, "Okay."

THE "WHO AM I?" REFLECTION
I told Laura that what she needed to do was a simple three-step process:

(1) Unplug from the Grid,
(2) Ask deep questions, and
(3) Listen.

I taught her a very simple form of reflection that I've found helps individuals come to a place of insight into who they are.

I told her that this simple, but powerful technique does not demand special ability, arduous self-discipline, or any kind of religious belief. It only requires a sincere desire to know who you really are—apart from the circumstances of your life story.

Though variations of this method have been taught for centuries, I stumbled across this one in a little gem of a book by Paul Brunton called *The Secret Path*, first published in 1934. Brunton tackled the question of identity by eliminating what we are NOT. Brunton says that we are not what we believe, what we perceive, what we think, what we feel, or what we do. Nor are we any of the following things:

• Our achievements
• Our memories
• Our tribes
• Our jobs
• Our opinions

- Our past
- Our stuff
- Our behavior
- Our IQ
- Our tastes
- Our interests

How do we know this? Because we can think *about* all of these things. We can stand apart from each of these elements and consider it objectively. In the same way, we can stand back from the chatter of our inner voice and observe it playing in our heads like a CD—a CD we can choose to play, pause or eject.

Who, then, is the ME that stands behind all of these functions of perceiving, thinking, feeling, and doing? That is what Brunton urges us to focus on.

If I am not any of my mental, physical, and emotional operations, then who, indeed, am I?

As I explained all of this to Laura, she gave me a dull nod of intellectual understanding but her eyes betrayed an attitude of, "What in the hell are you talking about?"

I said, "You can either continue in your pain until it slowly scabs over, then spend the rest of your life being super-sensitive to betrayal, or you can become stronger, wiser, and clearer on what your unique path is. The choice is yours, Laura, but you have to choose." I asked her to think about it and said I would get back to her in a week.

A week later I did not find her any more alive or optimistic. She said that her work was going fine but that she was performing like a robot. As soon as she was alone all she wanted to do was either drink wine or jump off the nearest bridge. She said she felt dead inside. Then she sat up in her chair and said, "But I am willing to try what you're talking about. So what exactly is it?"

I explained to her that it was very simple. All it required her to do was to ask certain key questions, be still, and listen. I explained, "I can't describe for you what to listen *for*; but I will tell you one thing, it's not your inner chatter, it's not the punishing voice telling you how you failed or what you could have done differently to save your marriage. It's something way beyond that."

I told her to ask these questions in "rounds" and to write down her insights after each round. I suggested she devote an hour to this exercise at first and that later she could string questions together and listen more and more deeply without taking notes.

She tried to put a sparkle in her eye, but her inner flame was down to small embers, which I thought was probably perfect for this exercise. The lower the defenses, the easier it is for the truth to slip through.

Round #1

I told her to find a place where she could deeply relax and feel undisturbed. I said she should begin the exercise by releasing as much tension as she could from her body and detaching from her emotions. Above all, I told her to stop trying to fix her current problems with her mind. Her current thinking wouldn't allow her to fix her problems at the root level, or even understand them.

I told her the first question to ask herself is, "I am not my body, who am I?" Then I told her to listen to her body.

I told her to let her awareness run down to her feet, up her legs to her torso, shoulders, head, and arms. To notice any pains or areas of tension and discomfort.

"Describe your sensations to yourself in a completely detached way," I said. "If you feel an itch, try to just notice it objectively it without scratching it. If you feel tight, resist the need to stretch."

And then I said, "Imagine leaving your body. Move across the room and imagine looking at yourself sitting in the chair. What do you see? Gently keep asking the question, 'I am not my body, who am I?'"

Deep down we all know we are not our bodies. When my mother, for example, was in her 80s, she partied with eleven life-long friends whom she met in high school. All were widows. When she talked to these friends on the phone, she became that girl who took them tooling around in a 1940 Ford convertible. At 85, my mother still felt as if she was 18. She was not the body that she saw in the mirror. She repeatedly told me that it seemed like that flesh and blood costume she was wearing belonged to her mother, her grandmother, or some alien being. It was not her. No, we are not our bodies, and this is what I wanted Laura to understand.

I told Laura that there are other questions she could ask. Who would you be if your body was in a wheelchair? Who would you be if you were 80 years old? Who would you be if you were disfigured or robbed of speech?

Understanding that we are *not* our bodies is critical to understanding who we really *are*. The Grid feeds us the notion that we *are* our bodies and gives us a daily list of health and beauty problems so that it can sell us products to solve them. If I believe I *am* my body, my motives will revolve around whatever pleases me physically, things like food and sex. Or I may become a gym junkie or a plastic surgeon's best friend, ceaselessly striving to perfect my outer form.

Our bodies are simply vehicles of our self-expression. We are not our bodies.

I told Laura to wait 24 hours to do Round 2.

Round #2

The question for Round 2 is, "I am not my *thoughts*, who am I?" I told Laura to treat this question the same way she treated the question in Round 1. "Sit in the same place, try to be as relaxed as you can and just sit back and observe your thoughts as if they were written on a blackboard. See if you can identify with being the writer rather than the idea. Observe your thoughts, worries, and obsessions as they pass, without trying to change them. Just be the audience.

"Notice what thoughts grab you and control your decisions. What thoughts chronically dictate your opinions? Do your opinions bring you happiness or do they just make you feel like you are "right" and others are wrong? What are the threats or worries you can't stop thinking about? Can you begin to see these thoughts as separate from you, the thinker?

"You are not your ideas. You are not your opinions or your prejudices. You are not your thoughts. Who are you?"

I asked Laura to try to imagine where her thoughts were before they popped into her head and where they go after they disappear.

All psychologically healthy people change their minds when they get new information. New ideas replace old ones if we ease our firm grip on our comforting beliefs before a crisis forces us to. For instance, Global Warming first came to popular awareness in the 1980s. At first the convincing data was incomplete and changes we would all need to make too uncomfortable for us to "believe" it. As the scientific data mounted and visible evidence of things like disappearing ice caps mounted, many of us changed our ideas about what humans needed to do to create a sustainable future. I saw this first hand with many executives who vigorously opposed the "inconvenient truth" simply because it assaulted their plans and beliefs. But some of them began to thaw their frozen view of reality and started seeing opportunity in a "green" economy. Some actually made complete 180s and became champions of eco-responsibility. All of us can change our minds.

The point is we are more than our present beliefs. What we don't know is far greater than what we do. Life is filled with possibilities we can't yet see. Our problems are loaded with opportunities. The greatest gift we can give ourselves is a strong open mind.

Our thoughts are merely blips of energy and information that pass through our brains. We can watch them go by. We can actually change them. So they cannot be who we are.

Whatever Laura believed about her past or thought about her future could change if she wanted it to.

I could tell by Laura's eyes that I had given her more than enough for now. I said, "Try that for the next few days, then give me a call. I have two more questions for you."

When Laura did call, I was hoping she might have had some kind of breakthrough. But I could tell from her tired voice that not much had happened. "Yeah, so I did your 'Who Am I?' questions and I'm still wondering who I am. What else have you got?"

I explained, "Laura, this isn't a microwave solution. This is like eating raw food that you grow from your own garden. You're in the stage where you're just planting the seeds. You need to be willing to do this for as long as it takes. Are you ready for the next two questions?"

"Fire away," she said.

Round #3

The third question is, "I am not my *emotions*. Who am I?" This time I told Laura to begin as she had before, but now to notice any anxiety, impatience, anger, fear, or other emotion that she might feel. I told her to imagine her life as a movie and herself as the main character.

"What feelings are driving your performance?" I said. "Can you see how you're creating those feelings? That you're playing a part? Your feelings are not creating you. An actor can walk away from a grueling emotional scene and have a completely enjoyable evening. So can you. Who would you be if you weren't angry, sad, lost, or lonely?" I challenged Laura.

There was a long silence on the phone. "Okay. I wrote that down. What else?"

"Listen, before I go on, I just want to make it clear. These are not just metaphors. You really aren't your emotions, Laura." Then I told her about how I learned that something deep inside me was turning my emotions on and off like a light switch.

One day I was reading the riot act to my son "Fun Boy." He was 15 and living like a feral creature in my home. His room was a rat's den. Junk everywhere. Clothes, books, papers, candy wrappers. "How many times do I have to tell you to clean your room?" I roared. "You're a health hazard, a disgrace . . ." Blah, blah, blah, I continued my parental rant until the phone rang. It was a colleague from work.

"Yes, Ron," I said, instantly snapping into soothing professional consultant mode. "I have the presentation down and we'll knock it out of the park," I assured him, smiling with confidence. I hung up and immediately resumed my red-faced tirade. "How can you be so disrespectful? Is this the thanks I get for all I do for you? . . ."

"So, who was it that went from crazed parent yelling at his 15-year-old to super-smooth consultant, and back again within moments?" I asked her. "Who was turning my emotions on and off in an instant? Look Laura, if you *identify* with your emotions, you are little more than a drama victim. Life will be a constant soap opera driven by ever-changing feelings of jealousy, anger, fear, lust, or rapture. When we assume that our emotions are *central* to who we are, we become swept up in them. But our emotions can change like the wind, based on external triggers. So they *can't* be the essence of who we are. There is an inner chooser. You *can* choose your emotions. Even now," I counseled.

There was a long silence as if she was saying, "You have no idea how bad I feel and how I don't deserve to feel this way." I stayed with her silence, saying nothing.

"Okay, so do you have a fourth question?" she finally ventured.

"Oh there are as many questions as you have pain for, but I think four is what you need, at least to get started."

Round #4

The final question I urged Laura to ask was, "I am not the roles I play in my life. Who am I?" I explained, "This is the question that asks you to 'dis-identify' with all the stuff you've been taught your whole life that you are. With this question I want you to really step outside your life as you currently know it. I want you to begin to really see the you that is beyond your accomplishments and your career. I want you to see who you are if you weren't a mother, an angry ex-wife, or a member of your church. Really imagine yourself in a different culture or time period. Who would you be if you were raised in China or born in Renaissance Italy? Who would you be if you were either born in a ghetto or the child of millionaires in Manhattan? Who would you be in your essence?

I have found it's especially hard for high achievers to "dis-iden-tify" with career achievements. Many people I counsel literally cannot imagine who they would be without their jobs. But the truth is, often our careers merely happen to us. They are not who we are. They merely define one aspect of our temporary life con-dition. We are more than any of our social roles. Mother. Demo-crat. Catholic...anything.

"If a car accident claimed the lives of your whole family," I asked Laura, "would you still exist? If you found out that the religion you be-longed to was a scam, who would you be?

"You are not the part you are playing," I reminded her. "You are the actor. You can step off the stage and remove your costume any time you

want to.You can be star in a different movie. A hero story, for instance. What kind of movie do you want to star in?"
    I further reminded Laura, "You are not . . .

- Your achievements
- Your memories
- Your tribes
- Your opinions
- Your past
- Your stuff
- Your beliefs
- Your behavior
- Your IQ
- Your tastes
- Your interests
- The "voice-over" narration in your head

"You are not any of these things because there is always a deeper part of you that is aware of them—that is *listening* to your story, that is *having* the perception, that is making the choice, that is *holding* the opinion."
    I challenged Laura to go through the entire soul reflection every day for 40 minutes, hitting all four steps . . .

- I am not my body
- I am not my thoughts
- I am not my emotions
- I am not my roles

    . . . plus any others that she felt defined by, she would discover something amazing. "There is more to you than you know," I said. "If you persist with this meditation, you *will* discover it. Your job is to be alert to the answers, wherever and *however* they pop up in your life––insights, coincidences, new mentors, new opportunities, new relationships. Ask and listen and you will discover who you are beyond your current sadness."
    Of course, I am telling you Laura's story because it worked. Not all people stay with the deep questions long enough to gain insight, but

Laura did. Suffering can be a tremendous motivator. Laura was diligent. She asked the big questions over and over. Some days the pain was so great, she just openly wept about the condition of her life. But she kept asking.

Then it happened. She came face to face with her own soul. I asked her to write down her experience and for her permission to share it with others. This is what she wrote:

I was sitting on my couch going through the "Who Am I?" meditation for the umpteenth time. I only had one light on in the corner of the room. I was tired and depressed. As I began my reflection, something new washed over me. It was a flood of love. Love more intense and more complete than anything I thought possible. It was pure joy. In the next instant I was filled with profound understanding that love is everything. That love is the substance of the universe. I was overwhelmed with peace and the understanding that everything was all right and everything would always be all right. In that moment I experienced my own immortality. I knew I would never cease to be. The real me would never die. This experience has changed everything for me. Most of all, I have learned that I have nothing to prove and there is nothing to be afraid of. Ever.

Laura had the single most important experience a human being can have. She *got* it. Call it Enlightenment, Satori, Epiphany. She knew in a single flash of insight that her inner life was eternal, that love was the only thing real, that fear, death and separateness were illusions.

This kind of realization is a very big deal. A show-stopping, earth-shaking, life-altering deal. It changes everything: how we live, how we lead, how we love. Everything.

"But what if I don't have a sudden awakening?" you might ask. Don't worry. Most of us do not have a single, direct experience that lights up our soul. Rather, our inner landscape must be illuminated one lamp at a time. But Laura's mega-insight gives us a tantalizing glimpse of what lies in store for us if we stay on track.

As long as we keep doing this kind of reflection and asking the big questions, those inner lamps *will* turn on. And that mother of all insights–

–that our inner essence is eternal and that Love is all that matters—will ignite our lives. If not all at once, then in a slowly mounting blaze.

So what happened to Laura after her illumination? Well, she decided that she was going to quit doing the safe thing. Being the chief marketing officer of a software company, she realized, did not really express the way she felt designed to save the world. She joined a local university to teach, among other things, social entrepreneurship. Now she loves the fact that her business background allows her to speak from experience about how businesses can create a more sustainable world.

Nobody gave Laura permission to pursue her new passion for teaching. Nobody needed to. She discovered her own soul. Oh yes, she also eventually found the love of her life and got remarried.

Laura's Self-Concept would never have found her present life. It took Laura's soul to create it.

CHANGE HOW YOU THINK ABOUT CHANGE

Answer the question: "Who am I?"

CHAPTER 9

OUR SOUL

What we discover when we persistently ask the deep questions about "Who am I?" is nothing less than our soul.

Yes, our soul. I know that's a big and weighty word. But that's okay, because it's a big and weighty subject.

Soul, as I mean the word, is not some poetic spiritual abstraction or article of religious dogma, but the core essence of who we are as living, breathing, feeling, thinking human beings. Our soul is the deepest dimension of our awareness, a silent intelligence that underlies all of our mental and emotional functions. Our soul is not the object of our thinking. It is the thinker. The "me" before my thoughts. It is the sacred essence of our individual identity.

Our soul is whole. In fact, it is our wholeness itself. It is the source of inner integrity. It is where subject and object merge into one; the thinker and the thought are one and the same. It can't be talked or thought "about," it is known only by direct experience. First-hand. Once we experience it directly, we simply *know* it as the most real aspect of who we are. It is knowledge beyond "belief." "Belief," in fact, becomes irrelevant. Doubt becomes irrelevant. Our soul-based existence comes before doubt is possible.

Our soul, rather than being a subject of debate, is the *one experience in life we cannot deny.* Our soul is not our thoughts; it is what makes our thoughts possible. Ironically, it is our soul that enables us to doubt our soul's existence! Otherwise we'd simply be a pit bull or a toad. An animal. But we're not. To put Descartes dictum in the right framework, it's "I am, therefore I think," rather than the reverse.

The soul is connected to the source of intelligence that makes the whole universe tick. The same vast and silent intelligence that orchestrated the Big Bang and manages the galaxies and formed our bones and brain and toenails from a few organic ingredients is still at work. And that intelligence is available to us, at any moment, to help us live the life we were designed to live.

The soul is much, much, much, much, much, much, much, much, much, much, much, much smarter than our thoughts. Did I mention "much"?

The soul, in a sense, is the junction point where we as separate individuals connect with the universe as a whole. Our soul has two-way vision, inner and outer. It wants to express its identity in our very unique human form, but it also wants to serve a bigger purpose. Our soul has nothing to prove. In fact, our soul doesn't need anything. It is complete in and of itself.

What it *wants*, now that is a different matter. My decades of experience working with others to find their Promise have convinced me that our soul's desire is to express itself in its highest form. Our quest is to fulfill our own integrity. To fulfill our most noble intentions.

That's our real Promise.

THE "WHAT" AND THE "WHO" OF IDENTITY

Identity has both a WHAT component and a WHO component. When Laura had her transformative experience, she saw her true essence and the true essence of all human beings. She saw the WHAT. WHAT we are, at our deepest level, is an eternal Being "putting on" a temporary form called human. This is the deep core of our identity. We have no hope of knowing WHO we are as individuals unless we first understand that WHAT.

But there is more to the whole identity matter. You and I share the same eternal nature, true, yet we are different. I am not you. You are not me. Human beings are amazingly diverse and unique. Why? How can this be? If we are all essentially the same at our core, then why are we all so different too? Why do I need an individualized ME? What does being ME mean?

Well, the way I have come to see it is this. Here in this fragmented material world, the wholeness and perfection of God (Universal Mind, Source, the Implicate Order—whatever word you want to use for it) can't be contained by any one being. It must be divvied up. We embody perfection *collectively*, by each being the most perfect me that we can be. We are like facets of the same gem, all part of the whole, but expressing that whole through unique shapes and colors. Only when we all shine does the gem reveal itself in its full glory.

WHO you are, then, has monumental significance. No one else in all of space and time will reveal the facet of the Eternal that you can. If you believe that you are only nature's accident or if you're too busy "making a living" to *be who you are* and *do what you came to do*, you'll pull the plug on the creative adventure that is your life.

And dodge your Promise for the rest of your life.

The "Who Am I" question is the all-important central question of life because it frames all the other big questions. It is the "What is the point of all this?" question. It provides the paradigm of our lives. Answering that question leads to an understanding of the three big D's that reveal our Promise:

- Drive–What motivates us?
- Design–What are our unique gifts?
- Desire–What do we really want?

Knowing who we really are opens us up to look at what *Drives* us day to day, minute to minute. If our Drive is rooted in the animal selfishness of the "accidental human" model, we won't be interested in proclaiming a genuine Promise. We'll follow our nose like a bloodhound on the trail of self-indulgence, external success, or obedience to someone else's ideology.

If, on the other hand, we see ourselves as having a higher purpose, we will adopt the kind of Drive that will unleash our Design (most unique gift) toward the true Desires of our soul.

Drive, Design, and Desire. When the three are aligned, our power to make and keep our Promise expands as we fulfill our part of the Big Bang.

PART FOUR

DRIVE

CHAPTER 10

MY MATTERHORN

"The Matterhorn. We've got to climb it, Will," my friend George decreed. George was 70 and had recently tackled the Grand Tetons without any problems. He assured me I could easily handle the Matterhorn. I believed him. Big mistake.

Too soon, the date of destiny arrived and I found myself standing in downtown Geneva with George, my friend Chris, my son Adam ("Fun Boy"), and several other friends all hyped up on superficial "high fives." *How did I get involved in this?* I thought. No matter. The Matterhorn was going to be a great father-son adventure. One for the books.

My enthusiasm continued unabated until I stepped off the little tram in Zermatt, our destination. And then I saw IT. Jutting up against the Swiss sky like a monument to madness carved by an insane God. An incomprehensibly vertical pyramid of solid rock nearly three miles high. The Matterhorn. It literally snatched my breath away. My knees buckled and I plopped myself on a bench.

Only two words came to mind: No way.

Climbing to the top of that hell-tower was not even within the realm of possibility. At least my decision was a simple one. I was not going up. Period. The only decision remaining was how I would break the news to Adam.

As if on cue, Fun Boy marched up beside me. "This is going to be the greatest thing we've ever done, Dad. I can't believe you brought me here." He looked out upon the Matterhorn and his face transformed into the shining reflection of fearless vigor.

I couldn't find the words to tell him my decision just yet. Not when he was looking so damned *inspired.* So I painted an encouraging smile over my inner grimace. I spent the next few days faking it. I studied Matterhorn climbing books and even spent a scary afternoon with a very mean retired Swiss guide doing practice climbs. He kept yelling at me to "dance the rocks" while I clung to a 1,000 foot limestone wall dangling from his homemade ropes. No way. No way in hell. Every second of preparation convinced me I would never make it. I just kept smiling.

To climb the Matterhorn, you spend the first afternoon getting to the Hornli Hut. The Hut is a base camp for the final 5,000 feet. Getting to the Hornli Hut is not a big deal. You take cable cars up a good part of the way, then hike the rest. The Hornli Hut is located at 10,000 feet, two-thirds of the way up the Matterhorn. It's the last 5,000 feet that kill. Sometimes literally.

I devised a plan. I would hike to the Hornli Hut with Adam and Chris, *then* announce my decision not to climb to the summit. I'd send them off in the wee hours of the morning and greet them with cheers when they returned. It was still going to be great I kept lying to myself.

I felt like a fraud and a failure as I went to the mountain shop to rent the climbing gear I knew I wouldn't be needing. This included crampons for my boots. Crampons are spikes you put on when you get within the top 13,000 feet and hit the glacier ice. Right.

We began our hike. I kept to myself so as to avoid Adam's relentless enthusiasm. Three cable car rides took us to a place called Schwartzee. So far, so good.

The hike to the Hornli Hut quickly squashed any last grain of optimism.

I'd been told by the guide that it should take about an hour. Two and a half hours later I staggered up to the door, tired and sore. Adam had made it in 45 minutes. He was waiting for me in shorts, a tee-shirt and a huge smile.

The Hornli Hut sits directly below the summit. From this viewpoint, the peak shoots straight up into the sky. An entire, demented, vertical mile. It was even scarier than I had envisioned. My mind couldn't even wrap around it. In the deepening afternoon shadows, it grew more ominous by the minute.

We checked into the Hut and sat down to a meal. Climbers from all around the world circled the table. Most were tan, with skin like leather and zero body fat. I kept looking for someone older, less fit, or less experienced than I was. I couldn't find anyone. Now and then Adam would catch my eye with a twinkle and I would look away.

After eating, I found a place outdoors to be alone with my pack. I juggled items around, trying to keep it light. I was still going through the motions of preparing to climb. This was crazy. I needed to tell Adam I was chickening out, but my Self-Concept wouldn't let me do it. I wanted to be Hero Dad, not Wimp Dad.

At around 10:00 p.m. I crawled into bed. My plan to talk to Adam had evaporated. I lay there with saucer eyes. Of all places to put a window, they had stuck one directly in front of my mattress. A full moon lit the stark ridges of the peak. The only thought that kept playing in my head was, "This is insane. Call it off."

My stomach burned. Pressure was mounting inside me like the old furnace in *The Shining*. I felt boxed in and bereft of acceptable options. I was about to attempt the scariest thing I had ever done and was completely unprepared. Yet I couldn't bring myself to tell Adam I was out. My Self-Concept wouldn't allow it. For days now, its inner conversation had been creating a din in my head, reminding me what a fool I was, what a failure I might become.

As my panic reached an unbearable pitch, I asked myself over and over, "What can I do? What can I do?"

Then suddenly something shifted deep, deep inside. A voice answered. Quiet. Steady. Still. Not in words, but in a rush of clarity. It was the voice of my soul. I immediately knew the answer. It was so obvious, it seemed almost silly.

Until that moment I had been so focused on my drive to climb the summit of the Matterhorn and avoid total embarrassment, I had lost sight of what my real drive should have been: sharing this experience with my son. But now my intention had suddenly shifted. I realized that I loved my son and I just wanted to have this experience with him no matter what the end result was. If *I* didn't make the summit, it didn't matter. This was about *Adam*, not about me. What a liberation!

Suddenly, for the first time in days, I was able to experience the present moment. I looked around the dark Hut with fresh eyes. I walked outside on the deck and gazed up at the mountain. I looked down at the flickering lights of Zermatt. It was one of the most beautiful sights of my life.

All that mattered was that I be with Adam, in support of him, as well as my seemingly fearless friend, Chris. I would simply climb the mountain until I couldn't climb any farther. And then I would stop. No biggie. All I could do was do what I could. As I released my goal of summiting the Matterhorn, I felt warm blood rush back into my body. I could breathe again. I went back to my mattress and promptly dozed off.

Around 3:30 a.m. I was awakened by motion. Tomy, my guide, appeared and said, "Let's go." I asked him about climbing with my son and Chris. He said, "We'll wait for them later, we must go now."

I gave Adam a big hug. I was now able to *share* his excitement instead of being frightened by it. This wasn't about my Self-Concept anymore. I just wanted *him* to have an incredible experience. That was my only motive. With a laugh, I told him I'd see him *somewhere* on the mountain.

I could not believe how vertical the ascent was. It was so much harder than I thought it would be. It was like climbing a stone ladder in the dark. With only the flashlight on my helmet, it was hard to see beyond my hands and feet. This turned out to be a good thing. The dark kept me from seeing the edges. I climbed onward, using both feet and hands.

Tomy kept pushing me and we kept moving at a relentless pace that made my heart pound like a two-stroke engine.

The message I kept telling myself was, "I'll go as far as I can and then I'll stop." At dawn, we reached the midway point. There was a crude hut perched on a cliff where climbers could shelter in bad weather. Perhaps this would be a logical place for me to turn around and head back. I asked myself, "Can I go on?"

I knew I could. So I did. The climb got steeper after the hut. Finally, we arrived at a narrow ridge that angled up to the last steep face of the summit. We still had over 1,000 feet to go. From here on, all the rocks were ice and snow-crusted. We put on our crampons.

I looked up at the ragged summit, but it didn't have a hold on me anymore. I stayed focused on just doing what I could. I was so involved in putting one foot after the other that I didn't seem to have any psychological space for fear.

The hardest challenge still lay ahead. Shortly after putting on the crampons, we reached the first ice wall. No one had told me about the ice walls. Four vertical walls, 15 to 20 feet high each, had to be climbed by jamming our crampons into ice and pulling ourselves up by ropes. By this time, my legs were rubber so I had to rely on arm strength. After each wall, I asked myself, "Can I do one more?"

When I finally reached the top of the fourth wall, I was 600 feet from the summit. I was also spent. The combination of fatigue and altitude had sapped the last of my reserves. I felt no great need to continue but now wanted to. I called upon my emergency fuel tank and found there was a tiny bit of gas still in it. I started moving again.

Finally, about 50 feet from the summit, I heard a voice, "Hey, Sir Edmund Hilary!"

I turned. "No way we're going to the top of that mountain without you," Chris said. Then he shouted, "It is not about the mountain; it's who you climb with that matters." I was so, so tired. So grateful. I couldn't help it. Tears escaped my squinting eyes of disbelief.

We hugged and then we hiked the last few steps to the summit together. Once at the top, I collapsed. I was exhausted at a level I had not imagined possible. But I had made it. Amazing.

The climb had taken four and a half hours. But here I was atop the Matterhorn. Impossible. Ridiculous. I took out a granola bar and water and had myself a mountaineer's feast. We just sat on the snow with our arms around each other's backs, gazing out on the Alps as they stretched to France and Italy. Chris's words echoed in my soul.

I had done the impossible. I had pushed myself beyond my physical limitations. But that was the small part. The big part was the soul discovery I had made. I realized that I had found the power to reach the top of the Matterhorn only when I stopped listening to the frantic fear of my Self-Concept. When I replaced that fearful drive with the drive of love, everything had fallen into place. That's when I was finally able to get out of my own way. And that's when love reached back to pull me up the mountain.

What I discovered that exhausting, incredible day changed my future. I deeply realized that climbing our individual Matterhorns, whatever they may be, is never about getting to the top of the mountain, it is all about our reason for climbing.

SO WHAT'S DRIVING YOU?

It turns out our reason for climbing is all-important. As I see it, there are only two primary, deep-down motives in human life. Love and fear. Either we are moving toward love or away from it. Fear is really nothing but moving away from love. Fear is lack of awareness of our true nature.

That's why answering the "What Am I?" question is so important. If we are enduring souls with genuine purpose, then an act such as waiting for your friend and dad before you summit the mountain becomes a statement of love with deep and lasting meaning. If, instead, we are accidental blobs of biology, then such an act is just sentimentality. If Chris and Fun Boy had truly respected Darwinism, they would have let me die on the mountain to advance the human race.

If only getting to the summit matters, then saving the world, making a difference, and creating a sustainable, abundant future for our children is irrelevant. It's every man (and woman) for himself. But if life matters in a transcendent sense, then why we climb to the summit and *whom* we climb with matters more than the summit. In fact our purpose might even be to help other climbers rather than reach the summit ourselves.

QUALITIES OF LOVE

Love is an overused word. Its meaning has been diluted by misuse, familiarity, and Hallmark. Nevertheless, it is the word that best captures the pure energy that lies at the heart of human fulfillment. Love is more than brain chemistry. More than evolutionary impulses. How do we know? Intrinsically. We know it in our souls. In that peaceful place that exists deep below our insecurities.

Love leads to optimism, connectedness to others, joy, giving, meaning, and life satisfaction. Love is what drives our genuine Promise, both at home and in the workplace.

Fear leads to arrogance, greed, paranoia, isolation, self-protection, self-destruction, and extinction. It leads to a life built on accumulating, competing, striving, and anesthetizing the pain. It leads to a death marked by panic and regret.

If our main Drive in life is fear or any of its derivatives, we will lead selfish and ultimately meaningless lives. There's no way around it. Selfishness is the ultimate paradox. The more we care about "what's in it for me," the less actually ends up being in it for us. Selfishness can never be satisfied. It is the classic vicious cycle: Selfishness creates fear of loss; fear of loss makes us selfish.

Our Self-Concept, that empty mental piñata we've been taught to identify with, is at the heart of fear. The Self-Concept, on some raw, panicky level, knows itself to be an illusion. And a finite illusion at that. It is terrified of its own inevitable death. And so it lives in denial. It pretends it is solid and permanent. It erects a fortress around itself, proclaiming its importance and permanence by acquiring possessions, status, achievements and right opinions.

But fear is our perennial state when we identify with something we know to be finite, fictitious, and destructible. The Self-Concept.

Many common life Drives are distillates of fear. Some of these are:

- Certainty–the need to be right
- Security–the need to be safe
- Acceptance–the need for approval
- Significance–the need to be important

All of these are fear-driven motives and will fail us as life Drives. Think about it. Certainty? We can never be certain about anything. A piano could fall on our heads the next time we step out of a cab. Security? We will never find physical or emotional security in a world that contains nuclear weapons, terrorism, automobiles, and a stock market. Acceptance? We can't control how others regard us. Significance? To whom? Other insecure, competitive people?

These are all Drives of the Self-Concept. As goals in themselves, they can never be fulfilled. They are born of fear and give birth to fear in an endless cycle.

Remarkably, though, we do achieve all of these goals and more the moment we abandon them in favor of love! When we give up the need to be mentally certain, a deeper, soul-based certainty flows into our lives. When we stop looking for security in the outer world, we suddenly find unshakable security within. When we abandon caring about whether the world accepts us, we find the deep self-acceptance that had previously eluded us. When we stop pursuing significance in the eyes of others, we gain the admiration we no longer seek.

The only way out of the trap of fear and selfishness is to elevate our thoughts and actions to a higher plane. To stop thinking about the Self-Concept entirely. It is not *who we are*. So why let *it* run our lives?

Yes, and why let fear and the small-minded competitiveness of our Self-Concept dominate our society, our economy, our careers and our future? It's all terribly unsustainable.

CHANGE HOW YOU THINK ABOUT CHANGE

What drives you, fear or love?

CHAPTER 11

WHY ARE YOU CLIMBING?

limbing down the mountain was harder than going up. I came
down very slowly. Adam and Chris were waiting for me again
on the grass in front of the Hornli Hut. Adam was in shorts, lying
in the sun surrounded by a half dozen empty water bottles. "Ready to
go again?" he asked. By that time I was staggering about in an adrena-
line hangover. It lasted for days, producing a sweet buzz of well-being.
When it finally dissipated the lesson of the Matterhorn remained. Crystal
clear. It is so simple. No matter what we give our personal effort, time
and energy to we must ask ourselves, "Why are we climbing?" To get to
the summit is not an answer.

This insight changed the way I talked to business clients and students, and eventually led to the American Dream Project and a new
model of leadership for sustainable abundance called REALeadership.

For well over a decade I felt as though I was watching a train wreck
in slow motion. I saw our world's resources being depleted at an alarm-
ing rate as billions of us scrambled to reach the summit of consumer
Nirvana. My business clients were increasingly consumed with short-
term profits, stock options, and moving on to their next gig. It was as if
they were executive rock stars playing in city after city but never putting
down leadership roots.

We created a false economy complete with fake wealth. Wealth that
suddenly disappeared when reality punched a hole in the bubble of our
unsustainable excesses. The deep reason for this bizarre palooza of greed
is, I think, that not enough of us demanded to know, "*Why* are we climbing? *Why* are we madly racing to the summit of personal materialism?"
As I watched the *means* of business (profit) become the *ends* (purpose)

I became more and more detached. I almost retired. But as I spoke to younger people on the American Dream Project tour, my hope reignited. In city after city it became clear that tomorrow's leaders have a different agenda from today's. And when I looked at our research results, a new viewpoint emerged. A new order of priorities by which we can redeem our future.

GAIN, GROW, GOOD

Fear-based motives create a motive of Gain, Grow, Good. In that order. Unfortunately, this is the priority system of traditional careers and the model of enterprise taught in our business schools. First we Gain as much as we can, then we Grow our power and wealth, then (if there's any time, health, or surplus left over) we do Good for others. We need only look at wealthy philanthropists from John D. Rockefeller and Andrew Carnegie to Bill Gates to justify living our lives in this way.

Figure 11.1: Gain, Grow, Good

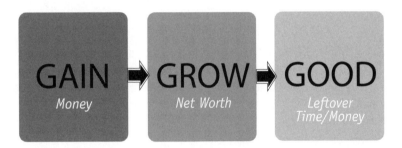

Philosophers like Ayn Rand and economists like Milton Friedman have actually offered a moral justification for selfishness, arguing that if you live a life of aggressive self-interest some mysterious balancing force will produce the most good for everybody. However, John Nash won a Nobel Prize for mathematically proving the opposite. Nash proved that working for the greatest good of all will actually produce the greatest good for every single person. In other words, a person's highest personal benefits occur in human systems where *all* people benefit the most. If you doubt this imagine a world where nearly all consumers are too poor or too in debt to buy what is being produced. It's what a Gain first mentality creates, and it's what we've created. While it may be convenient to think that ruthless self-interest creates good, it doesn't. Five thousand years of human history are very clear on that.

And yet, this is still the model of global business and the default model of most of our lives.

"It's time to create my legacy," says the old tycoon. "Time to give back." Okay, but when we live our whole lives from a love-based Drive we don't need redemption from the sins of our own avarice. We don't *need* to live our lives in linear chunks (Gain, followed by Grow, followed by doing some Good). Instead we can constantly weave as an integrated whole the good that we are designed to do into the tapestry of our lives. We don't need to hope we'll live long enough to care about our fellow human beings.

The model of Gain, Grow, Good is destroying humanity's ability to sustain itself. Emerging countries and aggressive entrepreneurs wanting to jump on the more-is-better consumption bus are extracting the Earth's resources faster than they can be replaced and fouling the air and water faster than they can recover.

The answer is not to tell billions of people not to enjoy the benefits of electricity and indoor plumbing or the Internet. Rather, it is for each of us to consider, *why are we climbing*? The only real answer is to help create a future where everyone has a decent chance to live the life we want for our own children. This turns the old priorities on their heads so we can see clearly a new future based on a reversed agenda of Good, Grow, Gain.

Figure 11.2: Good, Grow, Gain

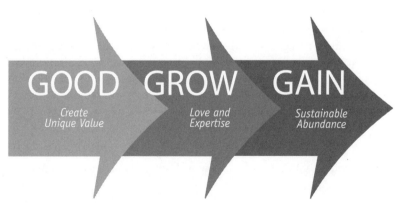

The Good, Grow, Gain model is the practical expression of a love-based Drive. It simply means that we think first of what we have to give, knowing that the more sustainable value we offer the world, the more we will responsibly Grow our enterprises and Gain the resources for everything we truly need. Just as our frantic need for certainty, security, acceptance, and significance are only attained when we stop seeking them, it's only when we adopt love as our motive that we continually ask the questions, "How much good can I do?" By putting good first, we gain more than we ever thought possible.

You see love is a much more creative motive than fear. Love is the motive of sustainable abundance.

GOOD, GROW, GAIN IN ACTION

I first met John Kontopuls when we honored him as the American Dream Project leader of the year. I had been teaching a class at the University of San Diego on leadership, and my students found John to be a local example of the kind of leader whose practice of Good, Grow, Gain had made him so successful.

John owns Elite Show Services, Inc, the largest provider of private security guards in his region. John is a former banker who stumbled into this very unglamorous business about 10 years ago. John has more than 2,000 full- and part-time employees. He provides security guards to the San Diego Padres and Chargers games as well as to banks, hospitals, rock concerts, amusement parks, and anyone else who needs security.

Elite Show Services Inc. is not only the largest private security company in San Diego, it is now almost the only provider in town. John dominates. The reason is simple. He's elevated the idea of rent-a-cops to positive, high-energy professionals who love his company, his customers, and the public they serve. I know that sounds impossible. How many times have you had dealings with a smiling, knowledgeable, help-you-with-directions, security guard? Me either.

John's secret to developing exceptional people is simple. First, it's not pay, perks, benefits, or even selecting the right candidate. The truth is, most rent-a-cops never aspire to the job; it's usually a last resort. John's business is different because his focus isn't on how much he can gain from his employees. His focus is on how much good he can do for them. He does this by providing education to his employees in any subject they want. John isn't just running a business. He's running a university of life for people who often have little formal education and few life skills. Many have disabilities, too.

He regularly asks his employees what they'd like to learn. This can range from how to manage a credit card to martial arts to achieving marital bliss. Whatever his people want, he finds a way to provide it––free. John also puts good first by teaching his employees that working for him is a stepping-stone to bigger, better jobs. His jobs are a way to learn responsibility, professionalism, teamwork, and management. But John's greatest satisfaction happens when an employee gets a better job in an industry with more upward potential.

Don't think for a minute John is a wimp. He expects a lot. He's demanding and disciplined. And by striving to do the most good he can first, he gains plenty of money and nearly total market dominance. But John doesn't educate his work force to make better employees. He does it to make them better people. John speaks at length how he doesn't give to gain. Good is not a business strategy; it's a core motive that animates value creation that results in prosperity. John's moral imagination is switched on high. He has made Good, Grow, Gain his business. John has found a way to save the world right where he stands. He is proof that when love is your Drive, you will gain more than you ever thought possible.

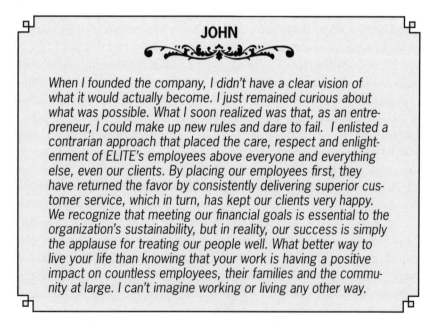

JOHN

When I founded the company, I didn't have a clear vision of what it would actually become. I just remained curious about what was possible. What I soon realized was that, as an entrepreneur, I could make up new rules and dare to fail. I enlisted a contrarian approach that placed the care, respect and enlightenment of ELITE's employees above everyone and everything else, even our clients. By placing our employees first, they have returned the favor by consistently delivering superior customer service, which in turn, has kept our clients very happy. We recognize that meeting our financial goals is essential to the organization's sustainability, but in reality, our success is simply the applause for treating our people well. What better way to live your life than knowing that your work is having a positive impact on countless employees, their families and the community at large. I can't imagine working or living any other way.

CHAPTER 12

INTEGRITY

If we intend to keep our Promise to do what we came for, it begins with putting our noblest Drive in gear. We must really *own* it at a core level of our being. A superficial attempt to think Good first will peter out before it creates any real value. Creating sustainable abundance in our own lives as well as for humanity's future requires moral imagination. This kind of thinking comes from a deeper, different place than most of our thoughts.

INTEGRITY IS ESSENTIAL

Most of us obey all kinds of rules, many of them unspoken and unwritten. We keep commitments, show up on time, answer our e-mails, deliver our deliverables, pick up the check for lunch—not necessarily because we *want* to, but because we feel we must. We keep our promises because we fear ugly consequences if we don't.

And that's okay. Self-discipline and trustworthiness are important. They are stepping-stones to something bigger. They build our inner strength.

But if we want to unleash our authentic Promise, we must realize that it can be empowered only by real integrity. Integrity means acting on purpose. Our purpose. A purpose that we own right down to our cells. That's where our real Promise comes from.

Integrity is not just honesty. It is more than good behavior. Integrity is doing the right thing for the right reason. Because we want to. Because we freely choose to. Even when no one is looking. This is one of life's deepest challenges. Genuine integrity means that our choices flow from the deep wisdom of our soul. Without integrity, we're just trying to summit some mountain and hoping to be admired for it. We're maybe even doing the right thing for the wrong reason. We're doing it because, on some level, we're afraid not to. Our true Drive is to seek approval, buy favors, avoid punishment, create a shiny self-image.

That's not integrity. And it will not create innovation and invention at the level we need. Real integrity is authentic to the core.

Imagine if all of your motives were completely transparent. Everyone else could hear what you thought. Now imagine that you absolutely didn't care if they did. In fact, you wanted them to. What if you were completely free of social fears, punishment and the judgments of others? What would you think? What would you do?

Or how about this? What if everything you really desired could be yours, free from the judgment of others? Suppose what you really love is to party all night, sleep late and lie by the pool all afternoon. Suppose your sole reason for not doing so is that you don't have the money, or that your spouse, children, or parents would disapprove. Okay, take away all those limitations. Just imagine it: you have all the time and money you need and no one's judgment to control you. The only consequences of your behavior will be natural ones. If you drink too much, you'll get hangovers. But no one will throw you in jail, or even yell at you or look at you funny. What would you choose?

Take it a step further. Often I ask my clients, "Would you never steal anything if you absolutely couldn't be caught?" "What if you could be unfaithful to your spouse and no one would find out?" That's a showstopper.

These are questions of integrity. Are we doing the right thing because we *choose* to? Or because we're afraid not to? Why do we even think something is right? Is it just fear? When we live at the level of integrity, we act for the *inner* reward, not an outer one. It's this kind of integrity that enables us to think new thoughts, create new value and solve the supposed unsolvable.

To really live at the level of integrity turns out to be one of the more formidable challenges of life. We can't just snap it on, like a switch. It turns out to have a great deal to do with maturity. We must grow into it. Integrity can only be lived when we are mature enough to take it on.

Let's take a look at how that works.

MATURITY

I remember as a child longing for the day I would reach adulthood and be free to make my own choices. I found it strange that adults would eat things like eggs and broccoli of their own free will. I pledged that when I became an adult, I was only going to eat dessert. It seemed very clear to me that this was a worthy ideal. In fact, when I was in college I even tried to live it out.

There was a local ice cream shop that offered an epicurean challenge called "Pigs in a Trough." Twenty-four scoops of ice cream. Yes, a 2 followed by a 4. The deal was, if any one person could eat it all in one sitting, he could come back for a free Trough and share it with friends. Yippee.

Driven by my high maturity level and lifelong love of ice cream, I took up the quest. About sixteen scoops into my personal quest for immortality, something I never anticipated happened. I felt my stomach begin to freeze. I didn't even know this was possible. My core temperature dropped. I felt as if I were slogging through a blizzard on Mount Everest wearing only a Speedo. I tried to fight back by eating faster—maybe the friction would create some warmth. But no. I went down in torturous defeat to mounds of uneaten, melting Rocky Road and Praline Pecan.

I lived to eat again another day, but something in me died permanently that day. My desire to eat only dessert. And that's a good thing; it turned out not to be my real Promise. Discovering that would require some growing up. Life is more than dessert.

OH, GROW UP

Maturity is essential to integrity. Maturity goes a long way toward revealing why some people live rich, fulfilling lives, and others suffer from one emotional train wreck after another. Building on the research of Dr. Lawrence Kohlberg, developmental psychologists have mapped out three distinct levels of maturity that shape the way we experience our desires, our dreams and ourselves.

In broad strokes, we all progress from (1) Pre-Functional (or Dysfunctional) to (2) Functional to (3) Fulfilling levels. Only at the final stage are we capable of making choices that spring from our soul's true desires. Sadly, over 30 years of research studies indicate that fewer than 10 percent of us make the full journey. Most of us never become a force for good and live lives of sustainable abundance because we are focused on the mountaintop instead of the reason for our journey. It's easy to get lost on the way.

THREE STAGES OF MATURITY

Figure 12.1: Stages of Maturity

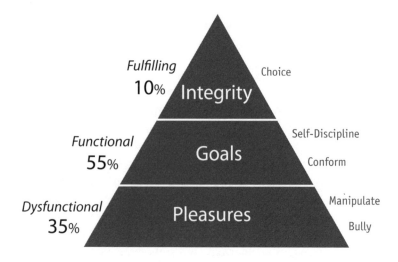

Dysfunctional

We begin life at a level of maturity that is Pre-functional. We are driven purely by our wants. All of our focus is on ME. We want what we want, when we want it. As babies we are impulsive tyrants. All we desire is a full belly and a clean diaper. When we don't get it, we scream.

As we get a little older, screaming doesn't cut it anymore. We learn that we must negotiate. We begin "horse trading" with our parents. You want peace and quiet? Fine, but it'll cost you. Two chocolate chip cookies and a juice box, to be precise. We learn our parent's emotional buttons. We figure out that we can train them by promising not to push those buttons if they will simply do as we wish. It's called manipulation.

Bullying and manipulating are natural stages through which we pass. In children, we call this Pre-functional. When adults fail to mature beyond these strategies, we call it Dysfunctional. Research suggests that as much as 35 percent of our adult population is Dysfunctional: still bullying and manipulating their way through life. Many of these characters end up in our prisons and social programs. Others are on the loose. We may work with them. They may even be related to us.

TYRANTS

Bullies and manipulators are tyrants. They use threats to get their way. They refuse to take responsibility for the problems they cause or the unsustainable world they create. Today, we've allowed too many powerful tyrants to make a mess of our future while they refuse to clean up after themselves. One way we can defeat a tyrant is to refuse to work for them or buy their products. We can consciously choose whom we work for and whom we buy from. We can choose carefully and deliberately.

Functional Level: Conforming

The Functional level of maturity unfolds in two stages. The first of these is Conforming. In our late childhood and early teen years we become concerned with fitting into a group. Instead of focusing only on our storm of wants and needs, now we begin to focus on our Self. This is not the real self, of course, but our Self-Concept and our Comparative Self––the way we want to be seen by ourselves and others.

No level of maturity can be skipped over. The Conforming stage is vital to our development. Conforming is the beginning of Self-Discipline. It teaches us to forego our immediate impulses in order to function within a group. It also teaches us to accept business-as-usual and life as it is.

While Dysfunctional adults focus on wants, Functional adults focus on goals and responsibilities. Duty is the theme of the Functional level. Duty to our tribe, duty to the ideals of our Self-Concept.

STUCK IN CONFORMITY

If we get stuck in Conformity we will never make or keep our unique Promise. We will only become drones for someone else. Organizations such as political parties, religious groups, governments, businesses, and even environmental and social action groups often insist we accept their dogma in every detail. Often they discourage personal choice, personal opinion, or even reflective thought. Conformists will never *save the world* and will probably be too scared to *be home for dinner.* Unless, of course, their boss okays it.

Functional Level: Self-Discipline

The highest plane of Functional maturity is Self-Discipline. At this stage we establish a tight set of rules and standards for our personal behavior. When we live up to these ideals we feel okay. But our Self-Concept keeps moving the bar up, so contentment never lasts for long. Self-disciplined people push themselves through life, propelled by a drive to attain ever more demanding goals. Whatever goal we achieve only brings brief episodes of satisfaction. We never have quite enough. Because what "enough" means is always changing.

Highly self-disciplined people tend to be leaders. We are driven to show up, do our work, and achieve the goals we've been given. We are the people that companies love to hire. We work hard to be accepted and respected. The world depends on us. Or so we think.

Many high achievers under-achieve at happiness, though. High achievers are prone to making goal errors and poor career choices. That's because at this level of maturity we are still motivated, on a deep level, to win approval. Though we may not be consciously aware of it, we aim for excellence mainly in order to please others, just as we did as children. In fact, my most driven clients are the ones that feel they had a parent who was impossible to please. And they're still trying to measure up.

At this level of maturity, we want to be seen as a great executive, a great neighbor, a great parent. We are so busy tuning in to what we are *supposed* to do that the signal of our true desires gets scrambled. It also explains how so many smart people have created a world that doesn't work. We've been great at achieving the wrong goals.

While it is certainly more admirable to be highly self-disciplined than a bully or a mindless conformist, it has a great cost—endless personal stress and anxiety and a world looking for real leaders.

It's important to know that Self-Discipline is only a base camp from which we make our final march up the mountain. It is essential that we make it to base camp, for there we gain trustworthiness, self-control, and reliability. But Self-Discipline is too exhausting, too empty to serve as a final destination. It requires us to constantly force ourselves to do things to achieve goals we've never carefully examined and to follow rules that keep us busy but unfulfilled.

Integrity is the real summit. It is the personal path to sustainable abundance. Integrity calls us to be true to our unique design and true to our soul's desires. Integrity provides its own fuel for life. It replenishes, rather than drains. Integrity is essential not only to keeping our Promise but also making sure it is our Promise. The one we alone are meant to keep.

Fulfilling Level of Maturity

The peak of maturity, which is reached by about 10 percent of the adult population, is one we call Fulfilling. At this level, anxiety ceases to run our lives because we no longer look to the external world to fulfill our psychological needs. We are no longer driven by cravings, responsibilities, or someone else's goals. Our focus is on I, the true I, the soul I.

Imagine a tropical lagoon. At the early maturity levels, our fears, needs, and wants create emotional storms that stir up a lot of wind and whitecaps. We can only see the busy surface of the water. So that's all we're concerned about. But at the highest level of maturity, the water becomes still and we can see deep down to the bottom, where all the beauty is—the treasure of our inner life and our real Promise.

The only hope we ever have of reaching the Fulfilling level is to see our souls clearly. To *fuse with* our essential nature rather than identify with our anger, our fears, our roles, our behaviors, and our achievements.

To attain this level of maturity is to live at the highest level of human volition. Here we become actively conscious of our individual free will and act on our highest Drive. We do not live to serve our emotions, nor are we frantic to fulfill fleeting needs and desires. We do not require the acceptance and recognition of others to feel worthwhile. We experience our own intrinsic worth and the intrinsic worth of others. Above all we are conscious choice-makers. We realize that nearly all choices do matter. Every choice helps fulfill our Promise or detracts or postpones it. When our fear evaporates and our habits are re-considered, we become freer than we've ever been. We become soul-aware choosers. The energy of personal fulfillment, clean, renewable human energy in its highest form.

The level of Fulfilling maturity comes from integrity. Integrity *can* be attained by anyone with a sincere desire to be, in the deepest sense, who they are. It provides an enduring sense of moral and emotional clarity. Though we may still be influenced sometimes by the emotional storms of life, integrity gives us a firm anchor to weather those storms

Figure 12.2: Drivers of Maturity

and remain calm. In integrity, all of our thoughts and actions are integrated with our Promise. We no longer question *who* we are and *what* we are doing on Earth. That alone cures 95 percent of life's anxiety.

HOW DO WE GET THERE?

Okay, so we can only get to integrity by maturing—does that mean we have no choice but to wait ten, twenty, or thirty years until it finally "kicks in"? No. The good news is that we can fast-forward the maturation process just by letting the *idea* of integrity grab us by the heart. We can read about it, think about and observe it in the people we fiercely admire. We can let them inspire us.

Once we are "hooked," we can begin to experiment. We can try––every now and then—acting on the highest motives we can imagine, *without telling anyone*. Then we can check in with our souls and notice the deep sense of inner satisfaction and fulfillment we experience.

Once we taste the inner rightness that comes from acting from a noble Drive, we will start to rapidly lose interest in acting from our smaller motives. Superficial concerns will begin to slough off like molted skin. And our maturation process will be kicked into warp speed.

Maturity, after all, is not a function of years. We all know twenty-year-olds who are vastly more mature than some sixty-year-olds. It's a matter of opening our eyes and our hearts and making soul-fulfilling choices.

Are you interested in knowing what personal/business level of maturity you/your company resides in?

Go to SavetheWorldBook.com and take the Personal Maturity Assessment and the REALeadership Maturity Assessment.

LOVE, INTEGRITY, AND OUR FUTURE

Integrity and maturity will have a big impact on our future and the world we are creating for our children. Our collective immaturity has led us to a world with too few natural resources and too much violence, poverty, sickness, illiteracy, and environmental destruction. Much of our world's imbalance is caused by the mad pursuit of our obsessive wants or our mindless obsession with achieving short-term goals without considering long-term consequences.

You see, business has no built-in moral compass. You can be very successful at business by taking short cuts of polluting, wasting resources and exploiting labor. If business is going to become an engine of sustainable abundance, WE have to make it so.

What's missing in our economic system is moral maturity. Just as there are three levels of personal maturity, there are three levels of business maturity, which are reflected in business ethics.

Figure 12.3: Business Levels of Maturity

On the first level are the totally self-absorbed businesses that use the excuse "If it's legal, it's moral." So if it's cheaper to pay a fine for polluting a river than to fix the source of the pollution . . ."Well, that's just good business." Wall Street firms average $1 million a day in fines for violating financial regulations. It's just a "cost of doing business." We all know what that's brought us.

The next level of ethics is self-discipline. At this level genuine morality is sought. The intention is to follow the Golden Rule. Leaders seek to produce safe products of good value. While profits are vigorously pursued, human and environmental harm is also consciously minimized. But it treats morality as a heavy responsibility instead of an opportunity to create unique value. That's why leaders often see it as a kind of tax instead of an advantage. The future of the world rests with Level Three.

At the third level of business ethics, integrity, we seek to create as much value as we possibly can. The Greatest Total Value for everyone we touch. In business, this goes beyond being a good corporate citizen, giving to charity and minimizing harm. It means developing products and services that actually heal the environment and promote genuine well-being. It means creating positive, healthy value for the world at large, beyond business-as-usual. In businesses of integrity, employees are respected, benefits are generous, customers are valued, service is extraordinary. And growth is natural, not forced.

Utopia? Not at all.

There are a growing number of high integrity enterprises around the world. More are being founded daily. It's a new level of business maturity. It's a new way of thinking about leadership. It's the model we must adapt if we want to survive and thrive amidst the daunting challenges of the twenty-first century. (For more on this see REALeadership.com.)

CHANGE HOW YOU THINK ABOUT CHANGE

What can you do to constantly live in the Fulfilling level of maturity?

CHAPTER 13

THE PAYOFFS OF INTEGRITY

When we live in integrity to our Promise, reality no longer frightens us. We embrace it with open eyes rather than winces of dread. It no longer has the power to topple us because we're no longer protecting a false Self-Concept. When we align ourselves with our soul, we align ourselves with truth, not with fearful pretense. So when crisis strikes like a tidal wave, we no longer feel that we're sitting in a house of sticks that we must frantically barricade or abandon. Instead, we ride the wave like a surfer until it plays itself out. We're in synch with the raw energies of life.

Consider these 7 "payoffs" of living from integrity.

1. **Integrity quiets the mind.** When the focus of our life goes beyond our Self-Concept, the noisy babble in our minds quiets down to an occasional background whisper. This profoundly transforms the way we experience daily life. We stop living in our heads. Suddenly we can admire a sunset without trying to analyze why it's beautiful. We can sit in silence without addictively reaching for the TV remote. In fact, silence becomes a deeply nourishing "soul food" that we insist upon building into our lives, rather than drowning it out with endless distractions.

2. **Integrity stimulates creative persistence to achieve our self-chosen goals.** When we are stuck in our Self-Concept, we are often paralyzed into inaction or denial when challenging events occur. But when we know our true goals,

we don't get sidetracked. Guided by our Promise, rather than our fears, we move steadily forward, unperturbed by setbacks or short-term failure. We know that obstacles will arise and that we will deal with them. Anxiety abates.

3. **Integrity gives us healthy awareness of our shortcomings.** When we live in integrity, we don't fear what we are not good at. We don't try to cover up mistakes or inadequacies. We welcome the input of others who have talents that we don't possess. We do exult in our gifts and manage our weaknesses so that they don't become fatal flaws. But we don't sweat our shortcomings. Instead, we invest the greatest part of our energies capitalizing on our true strengths.

4. **Integrity gives us a sense of purpose.** When we're aligned with our Promise, a delicious sense of meaning permeates our life. An inner theme informs every decision, large and small. We understand that the little things are the big things. No act of kindness, encouragement, teaching, or emotional support is seen as insignificant.

5. **Integrity means we're not afraid to ask for what we want.** When we live in integrity, we can ask for what our soul desires with a power and intensity equal to that desire. Whether we actually get what we want becomes secondary to the knowing and asking. Stating our desires unapologetically, without whining or begging, has spiritual power. It takes the internal pressure off. If we sincerely believe we deserve a raise, for example, we ask for it. If we believe our employer can make better, safer products or have more responsible policies, we stand up and ask for those changes persuasively. The chips may fall where they will, but we know that we have looked life in the eye and made our Promise known. We can sleep easily, soul-respect intact.

6. **Integrity means being patient and decisive.** A client-friend of mine loves to fly fish. Sitting quietly in his boat, he employs what he calls "gentle pressure." With graceful

ease and an unhurried rhythm, he snakes his line out across
the water, over and over, relaxed but watchful. The moment a telltale ripple breaks the surface, though, he yanks
back his rod and solidly hooks a trout. This is exactly how
he approaches his position as CEO of a multi-billion-dollar
company. Patient and decisive. He casts his line out and invites discussions. When he recognizes the answer, he makes
a clear decision. His people feel heard, yet the company
moves forward. Patient but decisive. That's a gift of integrity.

7. **Integrity strengthens our spiritual immune system.** Our
    own negative thoughts and those of others pass through us
    without infecting us. On the other hand, when our Self-
    Concept runs our life, we're susceptible to all manner of
    spiritual ills—doubt, disillusionment, jealousy, despair–
    –triggered by people and events. Only our soul can discern
    what is real and what is important. Having integrity in our
    soul is like taking mega-doses of spiritual vitamins. Events
    that "sicken" those around us lose their power to affect our
    health and well-being.

Integrity is not just a tool for inner sainthood. It's highly practical.
Even profitable. Integrity to our Promise clarifies choices through all of
these seven payoffs like Lasik surgery corrects myopia. Integrity actually helps us see beyond our present horizon to create abundance when
scarcity is the only thing in sight.

I honored an inspiring business owner at our American Dream Project Town Hall at the Center for Peace and Justice at the University of
San Diego. Matt makes uniforms for amateur sports teams in the U.S.
and for teams in 40 other countries. It's a good-sized business supplying
uniforms to 500,000 soccer, baseball, basketball, you-name-the-sport
teams. Matt's principle Drive is to do good first. His integrity to his
good-first vision has made him a bloodhound relentlessly sniffing out
how to create value for both his employees and his customers.

Leading a business from a good-first commitment has changed everything about his businesses. And it had to. Matt has huge, aggressive
global competitors, American big brand sports apparel companies as

well as crafty Asia-based factories all trying to destroy his grip on his customers through rock bottom pricing. Matt's business appears to be vulnerable. You see, he makes most of his uniforms in highly regulated southern California where his $14-15 an hour labor has to out compete 15-50 cent an hour labor in China. This is not a small problem. It is a daily, grinding challenge. And for Matt, all this is personal. For him integrity means responsible manufacturing, thrilled customers, and well paid employees. He has hundreds of people depending on his brain to make their jobs viable.

As competitors' price-cutting became more brutal, Matt saw his good-first quality and customer service with same day shipping advantage wither. Relentless price pressure was threatening to shrink his business and precipitate layoffs. So Matt re-invented his business. He combined new technologies in new ways to make one-of-a-kind customer designed uniforms on demand. He eliminated waste, reducing his carbon footprint. He set a new standard of customization and quality that reignited growth. What the iPod is to music, Matt is to sports uniforms. The inspiration for Matt's unconventional solution is his good-first mindset. It is his commitment to keep his employees employed and his vision for what he could do for his customers that stimulated his thinking to create this unique value exploded his *growth* and helped him *gain* new customers and higher margins. Matt told me that for him it was a matter of being true to himself and what he believes in. That's integrity. It's how Matt keeps his Promise.

LOVE AND INTEGRITY

When we live in soul-based integrity, we find ourselves effortlessly adopting love as our life's main Drive. Love that asks us, "How much good can I do?" Integrity-based love. Not saccharin niceness. Not guilt-driven kindness. Not clingy emotional attachment. Integrity-based love does not ebb and flow in response to other people's behavior. It has no expectations, including the expectation that the love will be returned. It is vibrant, limitless, fearless, and free. We love because we choose to, not because we think we *must* or else.

When we are living in our Self-Concept, the idea of devoting ourselves to love feels like a massive act of self-sacrifice. But genuine love arises from our own integrity's desire to give. It's not something we have to do. Giving the gift of our Promise is what we want to do. It's as if we're suddenly free from the cage of our fears and unleashed to finally do what we came to do.

The surest way to know that we're "in" love—soul-based love—is that we no longer seek credit or reward for behaving lovingly. We don't try to earn brownie points for being kind or generous. Giving itself is the reward. It does not look for thank-you notes. No response is needed. When soul-based love becomes our Drive, we never use it as a bargaining chip, giving or withholding it according to some inner scorecard. Soul-based love doesn't need. It just is. It is offered because it wells up from our true nature. Giving value ignites our energy because it is *Who We Really Are.*

That's what it's like to have integrity in our soul.

PRESENCE FLIPS THE SWITCH

I have made a fascinating discovery in my own life. That is, the integrity of love can be energized, anytime and anyplace, by the simple act of being fully present. Simply bring your awareness completely into the here and now and you will find yourself relating to others in a spontaneously loving way. What I mean by being fully present is that you are completely "with" the people around you. You listen to them without an inner agenda. Without formulating what you're going to say next. You appreciate and honor them. You allow them to be who they are without trying to fix them or change them.

And when you do this, you instantly find yourself relating to others on a love frequency and others responding to you on the same wavelength. Full presence is soul presence. It means you show up for every moment. This matters in virtually all circumstances from the family room to the conference room. Showing up is the key.

A surefire sign that you are not in integrity is that your mind is a three-ring circus. When you're sitting at dinner, you're pretending to listen to your spouse but you're actually having a second conversation with your boss in your mind. When your child is telling you a story, you're checking e-mails and saying, "Uh, huh . . . I'm listening. Go on." There is no such thing as true multi-tasking. There is only ping-pong focus. It is exhausting to play that game and never satisfying to any of the players.

When your life has true integrity, you *feel* your own feelings. You savor beauty, taste your food, and laugh easily. You are even alert in meetings. You have an interest in collaboration. As *your* agenda fades into *your* purpose, you think of creative new options and have more energy. And that only happens when you're driven by love instead of fear. When your first motive is to do good rather than to gain. Fear adds a layer of self-protective thinking on top of everything you do, eliminating the possibility of either presence or integrity.

Living with integrity to our Promise is not unattainable or unrealistic. In fact, it's the most realistic way to live. Integrity happens when what really matters most in *life* matters most *to us*. It's then that our truest life finds us.

It's then that we can clearly see how to save the world and still be home for dinner.

TURN ON THE POWER OF LOVE IN YOUR LIFE

Here are three ways to turn on the power of love in your life every day:

1. Ask yourself, in a state of relaxed silence, what you're most grateful for. Swim in pure gratitude for three full minutes. Then ask how you might be more loving to a specific person today. Choose someone to really "be" with for at least 30 minutes today. Picture yourself being fully present to that person and make a Promise to do it.
2. Bring yourself back to the here and now over and over again throughout the day. Get in the habit of spending time with nature each day. If you can't get to the woods or the shore, just put all your attention on a flower, the sky, or a puddle for a few minutes. Let the "natural" world teach you its powerful lessons of Presence.
3. Do good first. Each day, actively look for opportunities to use your unique personal gifts, your talent, knowledge, and insight to help another. Be prepared to be inconvenienced. In fact, revel in the "inconvenience" and recognize that this is where life really shows up.

If you do these three things, none of which require a monastery, you will find your Drive in life shifting from one of defending your Self-Concept to one of love. You won't have to force this change; it will be impossible to avoid.

CHAPTER 14

LOVE CHANGES OUR MENTAL LIFE

When love is our Drive, everything changes. Everything. And it all changes for the better.

When love becomes the driving force of our lives and doing good becomes the way to see opportunity, it alters our mental life in two very observable ways:

1. **Our minds are attracted to good ideas.** Twenty-first century life is a battleground of ideas, played out via the Grid. Fear generates bad ideas. It magnifies fearful selfish motives—defeating enemies, acquiring more than the next guy, obliterating the competition—and makes them seem convincing and justifiable. History is brimming with tyrants selling fear-based ideas. Every single shameful chapter of history was caused by fear-based thinking. As are all of today's global problems.

   When we operate from a place of love, though, we can see right through bad, fear-based ideas. They no longer "hook" us or draw us into debate. The test of a good idea is that it does not serve one person or group at the expense of another. We no longer view the exploitation of our planet or people as necessary for progress. When love is our Drive, our minds naturally give birth to ideas that move us toward sustainable abundance. These ideas call us to "higher" solutions and better answers.

2. **Our minds quiet down.** When fear dominates our lives, our minds are constantly buzzing. Our thoughts revolve around how we have been victimized, threatened, neglected, wronged, and bested. We worry about losing our money, our status and our stuff. We defend our mental positions. We plan. We scheme. We replay conversations, making ourselves come out on top. We worry, worry, worry. We form hardened attitudes.

When love takes root, this type of thinking evaporates. With our minds freed from competitive, anxiety-soaked chatter, the inner slate is clear to hear the wisdom of our soul. Intuitive messages reach us more directly, because they can—they're not buried under a din of mental noise. Stress levels plummet. Anxiety retreats like a wave to sea. We make good decisions and think thoughts outside that tiny box we used to be trapped in.

LOVE CHANGES OUR EMOTIONAL LIFE

When our core is filled with fear and dread, we are weak. We embody a negative, "empty" sort of energy. We need. We want. We seek to gain as our primary Drive. We are always looking to people and things to fill the aching void at our center. We are frustrated and angry when they don't.

When love is at our center, we no longer live a life of wants, demands and grievances. We start to care about the creative desires of the soul. We are more than filled up. We overflow. Nothing can crush us, because we're full inside. We have plenty to give.

Strong emotions no longer threaten us because we know that they are not who we are. We can fully experience grief, sorrow, pain, and disappointment without fear of "breaking."

Of course, when love is our Drive, our emotional life, overall, becomes powerfully "positive." Love feels good. Powerfully good. Every study I've seen on the subject confirms that giving and serving produce overwhelmingly positive emotions. The more we love, the better we feel and the longer we live. It's that simple. It really is.

LOVE CHANGES OUR RELATIONSHIPS

When Giving + Loving becomes our Drive, our day-to-day dealings with each other acquire a new dimension. We relate to people without the mask of our Self-Concept. We no longer think primarily in terms of how people can be *useful* to us; rather, we are able to relate to them intrinsically. We are able to sense their true nature below the mask of their Self-Concepts.

Love also gives us the vision to see clearly who is trying to bully and manipulate us. It gives us the courage to end relationships with unhealthy people. When we have the integrity to cease being "hosts," parasites go away.

Bringing genuine love into our intimate relationships, most particularly marriage, is one of the great cornerstones of human fulfillment.

It is shocking how many marriages are built and sustained on emotions that have nothing to do with real love. We settle for a "you scratch my back, I'll scratch yours" kind of arrangement. A mutual needs-meeting contract. We keep a running scorecard of who did what for whom and who owes what to whom. We blame the spouse for our own unhappiness. Our life becomes a sitcom between two love-starved rivals browbeating or manipulating each other to serve their own self-interests.

All of this changes radically when we adopt soul-based love as our Drive. Suddenly all that stuff we promised in our wedding vows but never really internalized starts to make sense. We recognize that giving really and truly is the key to a thriving marriage. We throw away the scorecard. We quit negotiating and start loving.

Of course real love, soul-based love, is not afraid to ask for what it truly desires from a partner. Soul-based love does not turn us into wimps or doormats. We can ask respectfully for what we want, but without being insistent, mean, or manipulative. We quit nagging and quit ignoring. It turns out love has a volume knob. We can turn it on whenever we desire to.

LOVE CUTS THROUGH RED TAPE

Love turns us into activists. When we're immature we are socially unaware. The only world we live in is the small cramped one of our insistent needs and wants. When we become socially aware we begin to feel empathy towards others' suffering. At least we can imagine what it might be like to be in someone else's tattered shoes. When love uncovers our integrity, our motive to do good turns us into activists. We can't help ourselves. We quit wringing our hands and get to giving.

My daughter, "Sissy," recently got a job at Starbucks. She noticed the very first day, when she was helping to close, that they were taking all of the food out of the food case—not just pastries, but sandwiches, etc.— and throwing it in the trash. She was appalled and asked why. They said that they had no place to put it and that nobody comes by to pick it up, so . . .

Sissy told her manager about a community center just three blocks from her house. She said she could drop the food off there every morning. Her manager told her there was a possible legal issue. "Starbucks is a big company and if someone got sick from the food, they might sue."

So Sissy said, "How about if I just dispose of the excess food every night? Once I take it out the door, I own it and it's my business what I do with it." The manager stopped for a minute and turned on the courage of her common sense. "Sure," she said. "Let's see how it works."

Now most nights, even when she's not working, my daughter calls the manager on duty to see if there's food that's going to be thrown out. Usually there is. My daughter swings by, picks it up, and takes it to her new homeless friends the next morning.

We can all do this. We just have to fire up our minds and our hearts and look for those opportunities to do good that are before us every day. If love is our prime Drive and giving defines our ethics, our creative minds will ignite in solving tiny problems and huge ones alike. If we simply change *our* world, the world changes.

LOVE CHANGES OUR MORAL LIFE

Love is the underpinning for all true morality. Merely *behaving* in a moral or loving manner is not enough. If my only reason for not smacking you in the head is fear of breaking the rules, then you cannot call my choice a "moral" one—it's only self-protection. "Good" behaviors are often spawned by fear—fear of social rejection, fear of jail, fear of damnation.

When we are motivated by love, though, our behaviors are naturally right, even if they may depart, from time to time, from what the rule book says. In fact, when we live in love, we can throw away the rule book because ultimately the only rule that matters now is the Golden one.

The rule-based version of morality most of us have been taught never leads to fulfillment. In fact, those who become really "good" at moral obedience inevitably become judgmental of those who seem not to be. And sometimes end up chopping heads off to make their point. Morality that is not refreshed by love can cause people to commit outlandish and unspeakable acts.

A lot of the world's morality is based on fear. Fear of being booted out of God's inner club. But true love is never withheld from us by God. It is only withheld by ourselves from ourselves. Universal love does not withdraw from us. *We* withdraw from *it*. As for love, it is always present, like air or the sun.

Does that mean we're free to commit whatever acts of depravity we want? Is it a license to misbehave?

Well, no. This is where things get interesting. The more we adopt love as a personal Drive, the less we *want* to commit acts that are harmful to ourselves or others. When our intention is love, it operates authentically within us and we spontaneously make loving choices.

The bottom line is this:

We don't "be good" to earn love. No. It's the other way around. We adopt love and then we naturally begin to radiate goodness. And then we don't need rules or the threat of eternal torture to make us do the right thing. Doing the right thing, the noble thing comes naturally when we move beyond duty to our persistent desire. To our authentic Promise.

LOVE CHANGES OUR CAREERS AND BUSINESS

All this talk of love is great for our personal lives, but does love belong in the boardroom and the retail outlet? Absolutely. Love can transform our work lives as well as our personal lives.

If we want loyal, energetic, creative, committed employees, the secret is to love them. That's right, love them. If we want loyal customers, love them.

Van, one of the most successful leaders I've worked with, recently headed a health care organization of nearly 40,000 employees. He is an amazing leader, loving and demanding, gentle and tough, universally respected. I have seen him end conflicts simply by entering a room, like Yoda wielding The Force.

I once asked him how it was possible to feel love for so many people.

"You can't love a statistic," he said. "Having 40,000 employees doesn't mean anything; it's just a number. I have to stay connected. So every time I visit one of our facilities, I try to spend 20-30 minutes with one of the frontline or mid-level employees. I ask them about their kids, their families. I try to understand their hopes, dreams, and concerns. After a half-hour of human interaction I have fallen in love with them. Every person has a story. Everyone's life is of critical importance to them. My job is to make their lives important to me. The way to love 40,000 people is one at a time."

The point is love does not fit into a compartment. Living in our soul's integrity invites us to look at every minute of life through the lens of love. When we do, everything changes. Everything.

LOVE, THE ONLY DRIVE WORTH HAVING

Love is the only operating Drive that will carry us to the fulfillment of our Promise. Being right, being best, being safe, being acceptable, being a winner—these motives are pale and hollow substitutes. They will run out of gas before getting us to the finish line. And they will create conflict, resentment, and discord along the way. When love is our Drive, we find ourselves incapable of choosing careers, relationships, and lifestyles that create harm and separation in the world. We stand for something. We make choices that contribute to the healing of the world whether we're a Starbucks barista or the CEO of a global enterprise.

Fear flies airplanes into buildings. Love heals us.

 For more help realizing if your life is driven by Love or Fear, and what you can do to help turn on love in your life, go to SavetheWorldBook.com and take the Love or Fear Assessment.

CHOOSE THE LIFE YOU ARE LIVING

Now that you understand that the journey to your true life is the journey of keeping your Promise, it's time to decide. Time to choose to live up to your Promise. Don't just think about it. Don't just wonder if you should go for it. Decide. Now. Keeping your Promise may seem hard. But in the end, *not* keeping it is even harder.

As author Joseph Campbell points out, there is only one life story. It is the hero's journey. This one story is the foundation for all great literature and film because it is the universal story of our lives. The hero's journey is simple. All of us, individually and collectively, eventually find ourselves faced with an immense challenge. A crisis. Life as it once was suddenly stops working for us.

This crisis presents a choice. Either we take the coward's way out or choose the hero's response.

The coward's story is driven by fear. It focuses on what we *don't want*. We invent excuses as to why we can't change or why we are helpless. We blame others for all that is wrong and rationalize that what we do doesn't matter anyway.

But the coward's story always results in more loss and pain, more confusion, a shrinking of vision, a path to making us invisible.

The hero's response comes from a vision of what *we do want*. It creates a higher-level solution. A hero's response demands open-mindedness and a willingness to change. It means looking for the grains of truth in all points of view, rather than trying to be the one with the right opinion. It creates unity, hope, optimism, and a new kind of equilibrium.

All of us have our own hero's journey to face. We all have a choice. Yes, every single one of us.

Adolf Hitler was raised by an abusive father, a man who beat him every day until at age twelve the boy told his mother he had ceased to feel anything. He had become completely alienated from his emotions.

Walt Disney also grew up in an abusive family; his father was so abusive that Walt's older brothers ran away at the ages of 16 and 18, never to return.

Hitler built Auschwitz; Disney built Disneyland.

We all have a choice.

And how do we play out that choice? By being true to our unique Designs . . .

PART FIVE

DESIGN

CHAPTER 15

WHAT'S YOUR SAUCE?

R ecently I went to a funeral. Mary was the 94-year-old grand-
mother-in-law of one of my best friends. Mary was a fearless
soul who left a big impression by simply being herself. Her life
was the great American Dream. Italian immigrant. Little education.
Came to San Diego from Chicago with her husband, Tony, in the 1940s
with zero money. Despite their lack of education, Mary and Tony did
what they shined at. Cooking. They opened and ran Italian restaurants.
Mary's secret was her sauces. They were so good you'd want to fill up
a hot tub with one and simmer in it. You think I'm kidding. Once when
she sold a neighborhood restaurant, the residents forced her to take it
back because the new owner couldn't get the sauce right—even though
he was using her recipes!

Tony and Mary saved, bought apartment buildings, and built a comfortable life from nothing but their own work and mystical cooking talent.

Mary's funeral was not a memorial to her cooking or her real estate
prowess. It was instead a celebration of a fearless woman. A woman
unafraid to be who she was. To say what she thought, with love and
warmth, and to live with gusto. She understood how to create rituals for
family and friends, especially around food and talk. No one ever left her
apartment without coffee, a homemade pastry, and a spirited conversation.

Our lives, I find, are often a tapestry of small things that end up being the big things.

What I reflected on at Mary's funeral is that so many of us are frustrated by our big ambitions: to be rich, influential, famous, or even just

get promoted, recognized, and appreciated. But life seems to have its own plan for us. I'm sure Mary didn't consciously think about the difference she was making. What Mary did was take the time to live her life in her way, at her pace. Her personal style was reflected in her total lifestyle. Mary was powerful and inspirational because she was unafraid. She knew there was one thing she could not fail at unless she chose to. And that was to be herself. Her best self. The big loving self that comes from our deepest part.

And, of course, to make her special sauces.

When I work with powerful executives, the biggest problem I find is that they are afraid to be like Mary. There are so many external expectations to meet. It's so easy to lose track of our secret recipe.

Perhaps our big ambition should not be to achieve someone else's definition of success, but to live minute to minute more authentically. Surely at that we cannot fail. As those authentic minutes add up, the Promise that is within us will surely be kept.

So, I ask you, what's your sauce?

EACH OF US HAS A UNIQUE DESIGN

Although we share more than 99 percent of our DNA structure and pretty much 100 percent of our spiritual nature with other humans, there's still an amazing amount of room for individuality. Recent brain and personality research suggests that each of us is more unique than perhaps we ever imagined. Turns out that our one percent DNA difference leads to tens of millions of physical, psychological, and personality differences. The way we think, the way we learn, and the way we excel are extremely idiosyncratic.

Many of us feel frustrated and anxious when we're not allowed to do "our thing our way." This is not stubbornness, but our Design trying to shine through. Design is the second of the big three D's that lead to the fulfillment of our Promise. When our motivational Drive is expressed with integrity, a powerful force is released from deep within. That force is our Design.

Our very uniqueness holds our personal key to our Promise that is built on discovering, or re-discovering, our authentic Design. While goodness comes from following the highest Drive, *greatness* results from being different—being original. No one can be better at being you than you. Our lives are our anthem. And in order for that anthem to be heard, we must pick up our microphone and belt it out. And turn up the volume!

A few years ago my friend C.J. was attending a summer concert featuring a Beatles tribute band. They were dressed up like a 1965 version of John, Paul, George, and Ringo. They had the Fab Four's looks, accents, and music down cold. They were an amazing group of musicians, perfectly imitating genuine rock stars.

And they were fake. After twenty minutes, C.J. couldn't handle it. They were fake. He actually left his family sitting on the grass and spent an hour walking home. He couldn't stand listening to "fake Beatles." To this day, C.J. tells me that if he were a musician, he would rather spend his life playing his music in small bars and clubs than playing someone else's music to crowds of Baby Boomers trying to re-imagine their past. C.J. is an original. He is not about to sing someone else's song. Neither should we.

UNLEASHING YOUR DESIGN
My experience has led me to conclude that each of us has a one-of-a-kind "spiritual DNA." Our inner dreams and longings are the urgings of this spiritual DNA to fulfill its unique patterns here on Earth.

Most of us ignore our deep inner longings because they are quiet. Subtle. Gentle. Patient. Ignoring them is easy. At least for a while. It's much easier to dance to the tune of the Grid instead, because it is loud and catchy and attention-grabbing. The Grid's tune is something we all hear, together. So we can all watch one another do the same dance steps.

But the urgings of the soul are unique. Each of us has a different drummer inside. What if instead of looking *outward* for guidance and inspiration in our lives, we looked inward? What if instead of drawing meaning from the Grid's consumption-obsessed, fame-crazed game plan, we listened to our own souls?

We cannot fulfill our Promise until we discover our authentic inner Design. Fortunately, surgery is not required. We discover it by becoming aware of our persistent traits, talents, and track record. Our "Design" is the intersection of traits and talents that we bring with us into the world. Our track record is the expression of these traits and talents in action.

Talents are skills that you perform exceptionally well and with natural ease. They are the way others see and experience you—the outer you.

Traits are the inner you. They're the way you *experience* the world, what you pay attention to, what you derive deep satisfaction and value from, and how you like to engage life and others.

Those things that you both value (traits) and do extremely well (talents) are what you were Designed to do. They constitute your calling. Activities that are aligned with your Design *give* you energy rather than sap it. You never tire of them. In fact, you often have to be told to *stop* doing them. You do these things when you should be eating lunch. You would do them even if you didn't get paid. They fire you up. When you are expressing your Design, you have no longing to do something different. Something better, yes. More opportunity, of course. A bigger stage, more impact . . . sure. But you don't yearn to do something fundamentally different. You know you're doing *What You Came to Do*.

Life was not meant to be a constant uphill battle, endured with gritted teeth. It was meant to be lived with ease and grace. When we do the things we were Designed to do, we're no longer in a state of friction with our world, but one of lubricated flow. Life becomes easier and more satisfying all at once.

WHAT GIVES YOU RENEWABLE ENERGY?

I grew up near the beach. I was body-surfing by six and riding surfboards by 13. The Pacific Ocean flows in my veins.

I graduated from high school in 1967. By 1974, I had a degree and a family. What I needed was a job. That's where Xerox came in. I had spent three years floundering around. Then I was offered a great opportunity to work as a Xerox salesman. In the early '70s Xerox had a lock on the copier market. Copiers were known only as Xerox machines. Every business in America had one, wanted one, or needed a bigger one. In the pre-Kinko's world, a job at Xerox was an on-ramp to the good life.

Getting my job offer hadn't been easy—tests, interviews, letters, resumes—but I'd done it. In three days I was due to board a plane to Rochester, New York to start my Xerox sales training. It was about that time I started to get nauseated. I felt a burning in my stomach. Nothing I could do would put the fire out. The day before I was supposed to leave, I announced to my young family and to Xerox that I simply couldn't go through it. My psychological antibodies were freaking out. Not about Xerox, but about "corporatocracy" in general. I just couldn't do it.

Passing up this opportunity was not an easy decision. It meant my family and I would have to move in with my parents. But nobody could change my mind. Six months later, a friend and I bought a start-up sandal company named Beachcomber Bills for one dollar. We made flip flops that were the softest things anybody had every walked in. Unlike my Xerox experience, buying Beachcomber Bills brought me euphoria. I loved Mondays and hated Fridays. The company took off like a comet. Soon we employed 200 people bound together in a tribe of audacious fun. Our sandals were spectacular, our workplace clean, and we played basketball in the parking lot and sponsored the first International Professional Surfing Tour.

It burned out two and a half years later, consumed by the heat of its own growth. The victim of the late 1970's 20 percent interest rates.

Fortunately the failure was so spectacular it led immediately to more opportunities. In fact, it was my on-ramp to the opportunity highway I have traveled for 30 years. So why Beachcomber Bills? Why not Xerox? I'm convinced it's just part of my spiritual DNA. I am a starter of things. I'm sure I would have been competent at selling copy machines. Financially, I would certainly have been better off—it doesn't take much to be better off than flat broke in two and a half years, but that's just not my Design. My Design is to start good things and help others to start good things. That's what I've spent my life doing.

Knowing your Design is a foundation of your Promise. It is the equipment you've been given to change the world. Once you are clear on what you are Designed to do, doing it becomes the fun part.

Are you interested in knowing what you are Designed to do?

Go to SavetheWorldBook.com and take the *My Design My Promise* Assessment.

CHAPTER 16

APPRECIATING YOUR UNIQUE TALENTS

A talent is simply a natural skill. Talent yields spectacular success without painful and stressful effort. Tiger Woods had a knack for hitting a golf ball that was evident at age three. Yes, he had to practice for years to develop his skills to their highest potential. He had to fight through performance plateaus that would have left him good but not great. But Tiger had extraordinary natural skill from day one.

Each of us has talents. Talents are externally geared; they reveal themselves in our interactions with other people and the world. Talents are almost infinite in their variety. Some of us are talented at building things or solving logical problems. Others may be talented at communicating with children, motivating others, cleaning and organizing, impersonating famous people, telling jokes. Some talents have clear economic value; others do not. Not all talents need to be turned into jobs, but nearly all can be expressed in one.

Understanding our own talents is vital to fulfillment. A true talent is something that we do well and that gets results without headache-filled efforts.

ASK OTHERS

The best way to understand our talents is to ask other people. Why? Because typically we have blind spots regarding our own natural talents. That's precisely because they are natural. They come easily to us. So much so that we think everyone can do them. We undervalue them. What we ourselves notice are the skills we work hard to acquire. These seem to have more value to us because we've had to consciously master them. They've been hard-earned through effort.

We often see this in famous people who switch careers. An athlete becomes an actor. A comedian becomes a singer. They tend to value their second career more highly, while the rest of us wish they'd go back to doing what they're naturally great at. Remember Michael Jordan playing baseball? Most of us have forgotten that his first retirement was spent trying to hit a minor league curve ball.

When I am asked what my talents are, I like to think of my strategic thinking abilities, my organizational creativity, my branding and leadership expertise, etc., etc. But I once asked several clients of mine what they valued about me. They gave answers like, "I don't know, I just like talking to you," and, "It helps me when you listen to my ideas." "When I talk to you I feel encouraged to do my best. You really enlarge my vision." Or even worse, they said, "Inspirational speaking."

I was crushed. "Talking? Listening? Those aren't talents! Anyone can do those things! Are you kidding?" I thought. "And inspirational speaking. That's for showboat artists. Mickey Mouse stuff."

What I *wanted* them to value about me was my strategic work, my breakthrough growth plans and my Big Vision, not theirs. I wanted my clients to value these things because it took great effort for me to produce them. But that's not what my clients cared about, at least not as much. No, it wasn't the stuff I found hard that they valued. It was the stuff that came easily to me. Talking, listening, encouraging, motivating.

I dug deeper. "What exactly do you value the very most about talking to me?" Many of them said something to the effect of, "You help me think about what's most important, and you help me make the changes I need to make to live what's most important."

As I reflected on it, I realized that the abilities to talk and listen and help others to become "clear on what's most important" *are* valuable and underlie everything else I do. I also came to see it was their vision that excited them, not mine for them. Big learning. If I hadn't asked my clients, I would never have seen these native abilities so clearly. And now, recognizing these talents has led me to turn up the volume on helping people act on what's important to *them*.

You can do the same. Conduct your own Talent Inventory. Ask people you trust what they value most about you, what they think you do best, what they wish you would do more of, and what they think you should stop doing. Be sure to ask people who are on your side, who want you to succeed and be happy, but who will be ruthlessly honest, too.

You probably won't be excited by what your "Talent Team" has to say. That's because we generally admire others' talents and take our own for granted. It's time to change that.

FILMING THE FUTURE

I met Michael, Nick, and Jim doing the learning documentary for the American Dream Project. They are a multi-award winning team of producer, cinematographer, and director. In fact, nearly every documentary, public service announcement or film project they create wins Emmys. Lots of them. What struck me about them is how much they love the process of their work. Before they shoot, the hours run into days of conceiving, planning, and storyboarding. Filming days are spent improving, refining and creating something better than they originally imagined. Then they hole up in Nick's mountaintop edit suite for weeks, orchestrating teams of editors, and working with sound and music experts, periodically refueled by relief supplies of food and coffee. The beauty, pacing and impact of their work speaks for itself. What struck me most about Michael, Nick, and Jim, though, is their effortless effort. They seem to have boundless energy. They love to work so much they have to be told to stop.

A second thing they showed me is what "hungry learners" look like in action. These guys constantly read, attend seminars and tap their network for all the latest and greatest techniques and gadgets to help make them better. They know it's not enough to have talent; one must be eager to develop it.

Finally, Michael, Nick, and Jim only do projects that matter. They are not so much storytellers for hire as they are chroniclers of the many ways we can save the world right where we stand. More than anything, they are social-change agents, leveraging their talent and inexhaustible energy to make their difference.

So can we.

PUT YOUR TALENTS OUT THERE

Once you have input from people who know you well and care about you, think thoughtfully about what YOU think your talents are. What makes you most valued by your working associates or customers? What makes you a great friend, husband or wife, son or daughter, parent? How do you create fun and meaning for yourself and others? Then let these

MICHAEL

My first major in college was geology and, man, was it tough. What had started out as a boyhood hobby tested my still-forming manhood as I endured a seemingly endless barrage of classes in physics, calculus, and other stupefyingly incomprehensible subjects such as crystallography and crystal chemistry. It was so trying for me that I was a senior until I figured out that geology was all about rocks! What can I say? I can be a slow learner sometimes. Fortunately, though, I was aware of my own design and desires enough to realize (just in time) that I wasn't likely to find happiness spending nine months with a handful of scientists out in the wilderness scouting for oil and mineral deposits (which was where all the jobs were back then). Faster than you could say "igneous" I decided to pursue my first love – media production – and switched to majoring in film and television. Sure, I had to sort of start over, but I've never looked back. Suddenly I found myself getting straight A's...in nearly all my subjects. Everything seemed so easy for me as my new calling suited my naturally curious nature and desire to entertain and educate others perfectly. In fact, my senior project won a regional Emmy Award...thanks in part to the efforts of two fellow students Jim and Nick. Sharing the same design, desire, and drive, we three have been working together ever since. We eventually formed our own television production company and have enjoyed much personal fulfillment and professional success making documentaries and other programming for years now. Heck, we might even do a program about geology some day. The lesson in my little tale? Never underestimate the power of aligning your work with who you are at your core. It works for us!

qualities shine. Shout them from the mountaintops. Flash them on the Goodyear Blimp.

It's important that your family, friends, and working colleagues understand your Design. And that you understand theirs. When there is mutual support for friends, family members, and coworkers doing what they do best, *the way* they do it best, opportunities are amplified for everyone. When people are constantly being nagged to do what they have no natural gifts for, life is a stressful grind for everyone.

When we work together contributing our unique gifts, we can save the world.

CHAPTER 17

BUT TALENT ISN'T EVERYTHING

In the early 1960s, Art Miller, Jr. was hired by NASA to sort through thousands of resumes the agency was receiving from people who wanted to help put astronauts on the moon. Through this experience, he developed a whole new way of assessing people's Designs.

Art discovered some things that challenge conventional wisdom. Most people, for example, say that they like working with people. They claim, "I am a people person." Well, not so fast. Art found that people's true interests tend to be fairly evenly distributed among these four areas:

1. Data—numbers and facts
2. Physical things—machinery, tools, or materials
3. People—individuals or groups
4. Ideas

Most of us, it seems, like ideas, things, and data more than people. People factor in only because we need to convince others that our ideas and data are worth acting on.

Unearthing our real interests is essential.

When we think only of what we can do (talent), we miss half the point. The other half is what are we *wired* to do? What floats our canoe? What grabs our interest and won't let go? What makes us shine? If competition doesn't grab us, we won't respond to a contest. If cooperation doesn't light our candle, we won't be thrilled to be on a team.

There's more to our Design than talent. Something even more basic. To discover it, we need to ask such questions as, "*What ignites my passion?*" and "*How do I love to interact with the world?*"

The answer is found in our *traits*. Each of us has them. Traits are persistent and will not be ignored.

DISCOVERING YOUR ENDURING TRAITS

Traits are the way we engage the world. They are also the means by which we want the world and other people to engage us. When we find ourselves stuck doing a job we can do but aren't motivated to do, it usually means we've ignored the invisible aspect: our traits.

A trait is a persistent quality of our essential identity. Optimism, caring, courage, enthusiasm. Traits shine through in diverse circumstances throughout our lives. On a mountainside, in a boardroom, in a funeral parlor, or in the family living room. Where talent shows itself externally, traits are an internal phenomenon. They shape the lens through which we view our lives. They dictate the way we engage with the world.

Our traits, like our talents, are wired into us. They color the way we filter and internalize our experience. They create a pattern of interests and attitudes that endure throughout our lives. Doctors Christopher Peterson and Martin Seligman, in a book called *Character Strengths and Virtues: A Handbook of Classification*, list 24 human traits found to persist across time and culture. Each of us has a few of these traits that stand out in particular. These "signature strengths," as Peterson and Seligman call them, continually shape what we pay attention to and how we experience life. *For a trait assessment, visit the Authentic Happiness website at www.AuthenticHappiness.org.*

24 Human Traits

(From *Character Strengths and Virtues: A Handbook of Classification* by Chris Petersen, PhD and Martin Seligman, PhD)

Curiosity	Integrity	Humility
Love of Learning	Kindness	Appreciation of beauty
Judgment	Loving	Gratitude
Ingenuity	Citizenship	Hope
Social Intelligence	Fairness	Spirituality
Perspective	Leadership	Forgiveness
Valor	Self-control	Humor
Perseverance	Prudence	Zest

What are your top five traits from this list?

THE INTERSECTION OF TRAITS AND TALENTS

Design lies at the intersection of our talents and our traits. Our talents are energized by our traits. When we marry the two together, we unleash our Design.

When a talent for working with one's hands is combined with a trait of expressiveness and creativity, a Design for sculpting, woodworking, or knitting is born. When a talent for motivating people is combined with a trait of optimism, a Design for coaching, teaching, or grass-roots organizing may emerge.

When a talent for accomplishing goals is combined with traits of empathy and enthusiasm, a Design for sales, consensus building, or leading shows up.

UNDERSTANDING YOUR TRAITS

If one of your top five traits, for example, is curiosity, you're a natural learner. You're interested in knowing things for the sake of the knowledge. You love to make linkages between knowledge, theory, and personal experience.

What does this mean in the real world? Well, people who are curious don't do well in jobs that require routinely following an established process. They want to continually reinvent the process or pursue side tasks where they can learn something new every week. They hate doing the same thing over and over again. Jelly Bean Inspector would not be a dream job. On the other hand, people who thrive on consistency may find great satisfaction in following a set process—trying to perfect their performance by making fewer errors and getting better results over time.

There is no right and wrong when it comes to traits; there is only the need to understand your own.

CLIMBING UP A "CLIF"

Gary stared at a check made out to him for sixty million dollars ($60,000,000!). Clifbar was a leading brand of the new "food group" called nutrition bars and a giant food conglomerate was stepping up to buy him and his partner out. What a day this was going to be! Indeed.

Gary went for a walk before signing the papers and on his fateful stroll he decided not to sell after all. The reason was that he couldn't imagine finding anything more fun or rewarding to do with sixty million smackers than what he was already doing with his own company. This was a monumental decision. Not only was he walking away from a trainload of money, he was going to have to borrow tens of millions of dollars to buy out his partner. Gulp. But once Gary decided, that was that.

So why would a bootstrap entrepreneur keep his company, now saddled with huge debt, instead of sell out and move on? Because he was expressing his Design, and he knew it. He was doing what he came to do. In Gary's book, *Raising the Bar*, he recounts his Eureka moment of deciding to make a great-tasting, mostly organic nutrition bar. It was a completely natural decision for him, since he was a long distance bike racer and his mom was a professional baker. He had grown literally sick of the "carbo-power" bars he was eating on a 75 miler when his passion grabbed him.

He tells of another Eureka moment biking in Switzerland when it dawned on him that the object of bike touring is not getting to your destination but rather to savor the sights and experiences of the bike ride. Once he recognized this obvious but profound truth, he sought out the smallest, winding country roads instead of the fastest, straightest ones. His new goal was the quality of the ride.

That experience led him to create Clifbar in ways that expressed both his deepest Desires and his inner Design. From now on his business would be focused on the quality of the ride, too. First, he would have only the best tasting, highest performing, most natural product. Next, he would use local ingredients and minimal packaging. Third, he would create a nourishing work environment set on a verdant campus, with yoga and workout classes and three-day weekends for his employees every other week. He also erased his company's carbon print before most of us even knew we had one.

Gary's whole idea was to create a job he'd never want to retire from. Imagine that as your goal. Well, the only way to achieve that is for your work to express your Design. Now how about an entire life that expresses your Design?

Our talents are energized by our traits. When we marry the two together, we unleash our Design. And with it the courage to not sell ourselves out, even for $60 million.

HOW GREAT DO YOU WANT TO BE?

Figure 17.1: How Great Do You Want to Be?

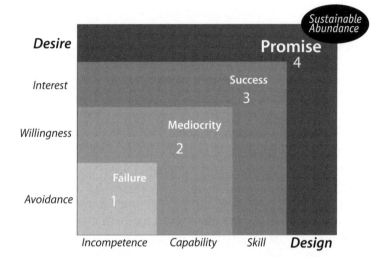

The chart, "How Great Do You Want To Be," shows that when we do things in life that use little of either our talents OR our traits, anxiety and dissatisfaction are the result. But when we do things that maximize both our talents AND our traits, we live our authentic Design.

In Zone 1, the lower left side of the graph, we find things that we (rightfully) tend to avoid because they are very difficult for us to do well *and* not enjoyable either. In my case, for example, anything having to do with gardening falls within this zone. From the time I was a boy I have avoided interacting with things that are naturally green. I seem to have a black thumb. When my mother asked me to care for our lawn or the flowerbed, inevitably, plants would perish. It was hard and I hated it. All of us have things we avoid because they are difficult and inherently unsatisfying. When we are forced to do these things, we suffer.

In Zone 2 are things we can do competently, but with great effort. These are activities in which we have to use the full focus of our energy and summon our untalented abilities to achieve. For me, this is anything to do with numbers, especially things like Quick Books, Quicken, or Turbo Tax. Don't ask me why I seem to be able to screw up even the simplest instructions. I've actually balanced my checkbook perhaps three times in my life. And I have lived over five decades. In order to be successful with numbers I have to make a superhuman effort. Perhaps with enough time and teeth-grinding effort I could get good at these things, but I have no interest.

Zone 3 is where most of us find that our life settles. This is where we're able to be successful. We have natural *ability* in these activities and we have put in the time to acquire the skills to succeed. This, however, is not necessarily where our greatness is, because our heart isn't truly in it. It isn't where our traits and talents really converge. We're in the top 20 percent, but not the top one percent. It's called the Competency Trap. Doing what we can do, even though it's not what we *should* do.

I have found as many as 50 percent of the professionals I work with in this zone. Doctors, accountants, lawyers. These people are often extremely bright, even multi-talented, but 20 or 25 years after making their calculated career choice, they are not *the best* surgeon, *the best* tax adviser, *the best* litigator. They are merely competent. Good enough to create the financial success needed to support the lifestyle they are now trapped by.

This syndrome, of course, is not limited to professionals. There are many of us in all careers that have fallen into the Competency Trap.

Finally, Zone 4 is where we are doing what we are truly Designed to do, where we become one of a kind and indispensable, where we make a unique contribution, where we provide a benefit or service that simply would not be available if we weren't doing it. This is where we amaze ourselves by our success because the return on our effort is so great. The success we experience is disproportionate to the time and effort invested. And that's the point. Getting into Zone 4 is, in fact, how we save the world and are still home for dinner.

When we act from the intersection of our traits and talents, we accomplish much more in much less time, with much less pain and stress. Our success never becomes a grind but feels like a natural process.

Of course, even in Zone 4, there are times that we must persist through difficulty and discouragement. Not everyday is successful and not every decision works out. But when we're operating in the place where our traits and talents gel together, pursuing our path feels like an invigorating hike through clean mountain air. It takes effort, but it's the kind of effort that makes us breathe more deeply, strengthens our muscles, and jacks up our emotions.

SOMETIMES OUR PROMISE IS SIMPLY TO EXPRESS WHO WE ARE

In the many years I have spent coaching people to unleash their Promise, I have noticed an interesting phenomenon. Some people have a very powerful Design, but do not have a single, dominant career Desire. There is nothing they greatly want to accomplish, no recognition they want to achieve, no experience that is critical to making their lives complete. They simply live out their Design.

One woman I recently helped has a role that I can only describe as Tinkerbell. Maria seems to come into people's lives at just the right time to offer a single bit of insight or encouragement that changes everything. She is highly intuitive and has the ability to see the deep truth of what is really going on. Maria also has the uncanny gift of seeing people's strengths as if they were fully realized. She often says to people who are suffering or worrying, "It's going to be fine." Those five words, spoken with her confidence and conviction, act like emotional balm, offering both instant healing and powerful resolve to get a better life in gear.

Maria doesn't "work" with people in a conventional sense; she just expresses what is obvious to her. She does not provide this service professionally. She is not a coach. She is a wife, a mom, and a volunteer. Meals on Wheels, Hospice, Children's Crisis Center, but only one thing each week. Maria is no Mother Theresa; she lives a full, enthusiastic twenty-first century life, enjoying HDTV, a sports car, and an occasional Margarita. Every day, she lives her Design. She focuses on living in the present moment with her attention fully attuned to the people around her minute to minute. When she intuitively feels the call to express her Design, she responds. Her Design is turned on in high, beautiful volume. This is how she is keeping her Promise to make her difference.

CHANGE HOW YOU THINK ABOUT CHANGE

What are you wired to do? What ignites your passion?

CHAPTER 18

WINNING BY DESIGN

I once spoke to Bill Russell, the legendary basketball center who starred on teams that, within 13 months, won the National Collegiate Championship, the Olympic Gold Medal, and the NBA Championship. Professionally, Bill played for the Boston Celtics under Red Auerbach. Bill's Celtics won a record 11 NBA titles. He said the key to winning a team sport was setting everyone up to win.

Coach Auerbach was a master at it. Virtually every player traded to the Celtics during Auerbach's tenure became statistically more productive and successful than they had been on any other team. The reason, Bill said, was simple: Auerbach always coached his players to amplify each other's strengths. He made sure everyone knew everyone else's success patterns. Playmakers always made sure great shooters were open. Great defensive players were matched up against opponents' best offensive stars. Bill emphasized that Auerbach never asked a player to do more than he could. He simply enabled everyone to maximize their strengths by putting them in the right position and situation to do that.

Wouldn't it be great if our lives worked that way? Our families, our jobs? Could it all begin, perhaps, by understanding our own Design and learning the success patterns of those we love and work with?

My three decades of guiding people toward their purpose gives me the conviction that we are perfectly designed to fulfill our authentic Promise. Most of us search for a purpose outside of ourselves. But I have found the clearest clues to be within. How we are designed to succeed. This is profound personal knowledge. Our Design has purpose in our own lives and in the world at large. When we understand our Design, we can unleash it and magnify its positive impact. This is how we free ourselves to save the world and still be home for dinner. But for that to happen we must "see" ourselves in action. We must understand our own track record of success.

TRACK RECORD OF SUCCESS

When Art Miller was doing his NASA recruitment work, one of his great discoveries is that our talents and traits are called forth *under specific circumstances*. We step up with our best stuff only when properly motivated by the situation at hand. Some of us respond to *need*—when we see a problem that needs fixing, it pulls us in. Others are motivated by *process*—when the steps to success are in place, we are energized. Some are motivated by *risk*—we thrive on obstacles and perform best under pressure. Still others are motivated by *being visible*. We like to be the center of attention, get up in front of others, and move the show along.

Miller's work gives us a good picture as to why some people thrive under pressure or risk, while others wither. Why some of us are bored by having a process to follow, while others are energized. The *conditions* under which our traits and talents thrive are as unique as the traits and talents themselves.

Over the last 40 years, Miller and his colleagues have conducted "motivated ability" interviews with more than 50,000 people. They ask each person to write down four or five significant achievements from his/her life—short Success Stories of a hundred words or so. Participants select one achievement from childhood, one from the teen years, and two or three from adult life. These must be achievements that the person both (1) really enjoyed and (2) felt s/he did exceptionally well in.

Miller has found Success Stories to be the surest, sharpest way for us to learn how our traits and talents are called forth in real-world circumstances. These stories help us see how and when we perform at our best and the conditions that turn us on. Most importantly, our Success Stories reveal what we're doing when we're at the top of our game. Here's an example of a Success Story from a client of mine.

Dan's Success Story

"I was a sophomore on the wrestling team and wanted to get a varsity letter. Few sophomores ever did. I had to beat a senior who had been wrestling for three years. He hated me. The first time we wrestled, he rolled me all over the mat. I thought I was going to throw up. But, over

the months, I kept challenging him for his varsity spot. We ended up in a key match. In the final period he was ahead by two points with five or six seconds left on the clock. He had me in a hold that I had always tried to escape by standing up. I knew that even if I was successful at that maneuver, I'd only get one point. He would win. So I did what I'd never done before in a match. I launched myself around him, got him in a reversal, and threw him on his back. He was shocked. The whole team just stood there gawking. They couldn't believe I'd beaten him in the last seconds. The cheers flew. It felt great."

Three of Dan's other stories revealed a similar pattern. Dan is an executive highly motivated by pressure. If ever there is an opportunity to save the day, pull things out of the fire, come from behind for the big win, Dan is there. Pressure brings forth his creativity and focus. Business as usual is a drag to him.

For years Dan had wondered why he couldn't get interested in the "regular" parts of his job. He was always pressing for some big new opportunity. One that would require concentrated energy and skill. One that would make a big splash.

As I helped Dan to recognize the themes of his stories, he came to see that he is at his best when the goals are clear. (Nothing like a wrestling match for goal clarity.) Dan also responds to challenge. Stress brings out the best in him—his best focus, his best motivation, his best creativity. And finally, he thrives on social recognition. One of life's big payoffs for Dan was to beat his nemesis in front of his fellow wrestlers, earning him the ooh's and ahhh's of his colleagues.

Another key to Dan's stories is that almost all of them described solo achievements. Wrestling is not a team sport like basketball. Individuals perform one at a time. Dan likes the spotlight on him.

I asked him where these themes showed up in his work as a high powered-consultant. He said that pitching clients on new business deals was a lot like a wrestling match. There was usually a measured time allotted for making the presentation. The "victory" was getting the green light. The deal.

The bigger the deal he was selling, the more Dan liked it. He also liked being the main presenter, supported by a few others who could give him feedback, preferably positive, after the meeting. Dan really thrived on being told how awesome he was.

One of the things I want to stress here is that there's nothing wrong with Dan's need for recognition and playing in a big arena. Some might say that Dan has a big ego. That's just slapping a negative label on the way Dan was designed to succeed. Everyone is different. Our Designs are not good or bad. They just are. Any Design can be put to good or bad purposes. Dan feels great about the value of the consulting he sells. He's deeply committed. In fact, he has told me that he couldn't sell services he didn't believe in. Dan is a person of honor who has a very useful Design for his career.

Dan used his track record of success to discover that he created the most value and enjoyed his work the most when he was delivering big pitches to important clients. The rest of his job felt like filler. Once Dan understood his Design in action, he arranged his work to maximize what he did best.

If we can organize our work so that we are spending at least two thirds of our time expressing our best stuff, our highest gifts, we will have outstanding success and will make our maximum contribution to the world. Most of us fall far short of this. At most, we spend 20 percent of our time doing what we do best. We spend the bulk of our time doing things we're not good at to get a chance to do a few things we are great at. What a waste.

To shape our lives so we spend most of our time realizing our Design, we need clear awareness of how we work when we're at our best. Understanding our own Success Stories is a powerful tool in this process.

MAXIMIZING YOUR DESIGN

Remember Van, the health care CEO who loves all of his 40,000 employees? He learned the hard way the importance of living his Design. His leadership responsibilities involved 23 hospitals and scores of other business entities that had independent leadership and boards. As CEO he traveled constantly, attending board meetings and strategic leadership meetings all over the health care system. He easily put in 80 to 90 hours a week. His days often started at 6 a.m. and ended at 11 p.m.

Then it happened. A stress test revealed that he needed a quadruple bypass. After the surgery, his physician told him he had a couple of options. First, he could keep working at his current pace and die. Second, he could retire. Or third, he could find a new way to work that would reduce his time on the job to no more than 50 hours a week. That, said the physician, would give him the chance to finish what he came to do as a leader and still have some life left to live when he retired. In other words, he could save the world and still be home for dinner.

As I sat down with my friend, I said, "Remember your Promise. It's to bring the best health care to the most people. So my questions were, what is it that you do that no one else can do in the service of your Promise? Going to every meeting doesn't really qualify. What do you *need* to do that no one else can?"

I asked Van to tell me stories of how his greatest achievements happened. What were the circumstances? What did he do? How exactly did he feel when he succeeded? As he told me his Success Stories his track record of success revealed itself. And with it the elements of what he was great at as well as what was deeply satisfying showed up in brilliant high definition. As I pointed out, Van's greatest strength was his integrity, sincerity, and judgment. He had an innate wisdom combined with a sense of virtue and purpose that amplified his leadership's extraordinary power. His integrity and sincerity was the engine of his success. Many times I had seen him walk into meetings of bickering administrators and doctors and cause a hush to fill the room. He would sit down, listen to both sides, get the gist, and make a decision. His decision always sounded like a suggestion, but everybody knew he meant business and almost always people were satisfied. He has that much integrity. That quality, I pointed out, was invaluable. It was a quality no other leader in the organization had. At least not at his level.

So as we mapped out his future, we determined he needed to make some organizational changes in order to strengthen the executives around him and release him from work that wasn't essential. He sent rapidly developing younger leaders to many of his meetings in his place. After his bypass he created a new life for himself, one that involved evening walks with his wife and dinner at home.

He found that his new "inaccessibility" made him more powerful than ever. When he *did* come to a meeting, people were delighted, listened intently, and really wanted to know his opinion. His greatest successes came *after* his decision to save his life by working less.

That's the power of truly understanding your Design and maximizing its impact. For my friend, he learned how to save the world *by* being home for dinner. For him it was a matter of life and death. It is for us too; we just don't realize it.

HOW TO VIEW YOUR TRACK RECORD

I strongly encourage you to write *your* Success Stories to become aware of your own track record. In your stories you will find your own signature style of success—the way you approach and complete things when you are at your most successful, by *your own estimation.*

Analyzing your Success Stories is simple. What you're looking for is the expression of your traits and talents in real-world conditions and circumstances.

As you learn to see your own signature approach to success, communicate it to those around you. Why? Well, we all succeed in unique ways. If your track record shows that paying attention to details is not the way you achieve results, let others know that. Tell them you are not a detail person and that you probably need detail people around you to keep surprises from popping up. There are plenty of people whose path to success is all about the details. They need you and you need them.

To save the world and still be home for dinner requires that we spend a majority of our time and effort doing what our track record reveals we do best. Working on things we value, using our most natural talent, is the only path to keeping our Promise. Otherwise we will end up doing what we think we *should* be doing or what others expect of us. If we just work hard to save the world any way we *can*, we'll burn ourselves out, destroy relationships, and possibly even become obsessed with our cause.

Instead, we must aim to provide the *Greatest* Total Value we can by doing what we, and no one else on Earth, were designed to do.

CHANGE HOW YOU THINK ABOUT CHANGE

What is it that *you* do that no one else can do?

PART SIX

DESIRE

CHAPTER 19

WHAT DO YOU REALLY WANT?

Adopting love as our guiding Drive answers the question, "Why do I climb?" Knowing our true Design is a torchlight in the darkness that guides our choices toward a life of sustainable abundance. It answers the question, "*How* do I uniquely reach my summit?"

There is yet another question we need to answer in order to fulfill our Promise—to save the world and still be home for dinner. That is: "Which mountain do I choose to climb?" This brings in the third big "D": Desire.

In my consulting work when I am trying to find out what someone's Promise is I often hit pay dirt when I ask, "What do you really want. What does your soul long for?"

AGAIN, IT'S A SOUL QUESTION

It is vitally important that we put the question of Desire to our *souls*. And that we do so with patience, care, and seriousness of intent. Because when we ask the question quickly and casually, it is our fear-based, over-striving Self-Concept that replies. And we get a very different set of answers. We mistake a young blonde and a new Ferrari for our true desires. Or we think that hours in the gym, plastic surgery, and an extramarital affair will create bliss.

Not so. Our soul does not scream for superficial self-indulgence. It does not long for a journey back to the impulsiveness of "I want, I need" found in the earliest levels of maturity.

Nor does our soul want what our self-disciplined minds often think we *should* want. Many of us are tempted by our religious, political, and cultural leanings to believe that we truly *want* things that hold no real interest for our souls. We confuse our ideals with our Desires. For example, if we have a strong belief in renewable energy and green communities, we might misguidedly believe that we truly desire to move to Vermont and open a solar panel store. But this, in fact, may be a career path that our soul will find numbing and unfulfilling.

Listening to the charismatic leaders of the day can also fool us into making choices born out of idealistic, rather than genuine, desire. It's important to separate what Bono or Angelina wants from what *we* want.

When we listen to our soul's Desires, they guide us to our real Promise and our deepest values, not just relief from pain or political correctness.

WHITNEY

Whitney is the 25-year-old founder of Girls for a Change (GirlsforaChange.org). She created an acclaimed program that helps inner city 13- to 17-year-old girls gain confidence and self-direction by turning them into givers.

Whitney's story is the journey of someone who listens to her soul and keeps moving toward opportunity. She graduated with a degree in art from a small college in Pennsylvania, then drove to California in her beat-up car, with $150 in her purse. Why? Well, the previous summer she had worked with inner city girls at a summer camp. Those girls, she said, made her feel "more alive" than she'd ever felt. The light of her Desire was lit.

So after graduation she headed back to California to seek, not her fame and fortune, but her soul's Desire. She started by working in a social-services program and within a short time was bringing Girl Scouting to juvenile detention centers and the county jail in Silicon Valley. Remember, Whitney is an Art teacher, not a social worker. She just did what she deeply desired to do and followed her common sense.

Soon she had a powerful insight. She discovered a big reason why young urban girls get into drugs, promiscuity, and stealing: they feel powerless.

So Whitney asked these girls a life-altering question, "If you could change anything, what would you change?" It may surprise you that the answers she got had nothing to do with bling, fame, or street cred. Instead these young girls expressed dreams of having safe neighborhoods, graduating from high school, and keeping their little brothers out of gangs. Whitney says her brainstorm came suddenly. "These girls feel powerless, but they aren't. They can discover their own possibilities by fulfilling their dreams of creating a better world." And the key, she discovered, is to do the same for others!

So each girl in Whitney's programs develops a social impact project with the help of a mentor. They complete the project, measure their results, and report on it. These teenage girls then go out to neighborhood schools and conduct programs that they have designed to teach 7- to 9-year-old boys how not to be sucked into gang culture. Or they help establish tutoring and mentoring services for struggling students.

The key is that they are finding their own new possibilities by bringing new possibilities to others. Wow. Girls for a Change now operates in Baltimore, Philadelphia, Phoenix, Richmond, VA, Silicon Valley, and even internationally. Whitney is pursuing her happiness by bringing happiness and hope to the hopeless.

So who does Whitney think she is? Who told her she was qualified? That's the point, isn't it? She was completely unprepared for this. She had no idea how to start a non-profit, how to raise money, or whether her program would succeed. She just chose to do it, and did. She declared her Promise and acts on it every day. She is truly changing the world right where she stands because it's what she desires most of all. You see, it really is a choice.

THE ENERGY OF TRUE DESIRE

Fortunately, nature has designed an elegant and simple system for revealing our true Desires. Simply put, our Desires are those pursuits that *generate* energy in us rather than drain it. They are the things that *yank* us out of bed in the morning,

A few years ago I was working on an assignment for a large organization that owned over 200 country clubs and 70 business clubs and had a prestigious membership of nearly 250,000 business leaders and executives. They hired a top company to do market research on what their members desired most in order to gain greater life satisfaction.

The overwhelming number one response was the need to connect to something bigger than themselves. The need to find meaning in their lives. And these were 250,000 of the most successful people in the world. The assignment I was given was to help the organization develop its own "great and noble cause," as their CEO had termed it, to help their members find deeper meaning. This led me to a search for experts who had helped successful people find deeper meaning in their lives. I wanted to know if there was a science to the quest of discovering our authentic Desires.

I discovered the work of a brilliant psychologist, Dr. James Loehr, who has spent his professional life helping athletes, Special Forces units, and executives reach distinguished levels of achievement. He is one of the pioneers of what is sometimes called Performance Psychology. Jim's work revealed that satisfying achievement has two components: success and meaning. No matter how many trophies, medals, or dollars one might win, without meaning there is no internal sense of success. And meaning, he confirmed, was as individual as our fingerprints.

Jim knows what he's talking about. He's coached 16 athletes to become number one in the world in their sports, no small achievement. Jim is also a cofounder of an organization now known as the Human Performance Institute. He has distilled his research and experience into a human development framework that is fueled by an exciting principle: he helps people link their deepest purpose to their achievement goals.

Jim's research with more than 100,000 people, ranging from stay-at-home moms and executive assistants to SWAT team members, navy seals, accountants, and CEOs, has found that we are driven by four sources of energy. First, the *quantity* of what we can effectively accomplish is determined by our *physical energy*. This is something we have a lot of control over by how much sleep, exercise, and nutrition we get. Second, the *quality* of our energy is driven by our emotional energy. Positive emotions spawn creativity and collaboration. Third, the *focus* of our energy is determined by the amount of concentrated and consistent *mental energy* we put on personally meaningful goals.

But none of these sources of energy compare with the power of the fourth source; this is what Jim calls *spiritual energy*. He doesn't mean spiritual in the religious sense, but in the sense of personal values and meaning. What I call our Promise. What he has found is that when human beings are fully engaged in fulfilling their deepest spiritual desires in their work, relationships, and lifestyle, their life takes on a force *many times greater* than normal. Jim recently coauthored a book on this subject called *The Power of Full Engagement* in which he describes how the combination of these four sources of energy are the engine to human fulfillment.

Needless to say, I became fascinated with Jim's scientific approach to understanding the forces that create a fully engaged life, a life that is the true expression of a person's unique Drive, Design and Desire. The reason I was so struck with Jim's research was that it seemed to directly validate my own 30 years of experience in helping people fulfill their Promise.

I believe—and Jim's work backs it up—that the true power-key for unleashing our Promise is to tap into what our souls deeply Desire. Real Desire can't be faked and it can't be substituted. It's not something we *choose*, so much as discover within. It's something we listen for, recognize, and then act upon. We can *think* we want to be a doctor or an artist or a businessperson, but unless we *truly* want it, deep in our souls, that choice will never gain real momentum. Because spiritual energy is real. And without that crucial source of energy, our Promise will run out of fuel before it gets to its wondrous destination.

One of Jim's most encouraging findings is that people who discover and fulfill their soul's Desires have little doubt about whether they are doing *what they came to do.*

CHANGE HOW YOU THINK ABOUT CHANGE

What is it that you *truly* aspire to be/to do?

CHAPTER 20

DISCOVERING WHAT YOU TRULY DESIRE

Many people I have tried to help discover their Promise are rich on motivation but impoverished in their focus. "What should I do? What? What? What?" This confusion, I assure them, is normal because to understand our soul's Desire it takes real insight. And insight most often comes by awakening to our own wisdom. Most of us need to be jolted awake so we become alert to our deepest most persistent longings.

The mental espresso needed to understand our soul's Desire begins with what we've begun to explore: unplug, ask, and listen. Silence is the key. Turn off the Grid. Turn off the inner chatter. Just listen. Silence stops the chatter in our minds so we can experience what wisdom lies beyond the noise. It enables us to hear our souls.

Our minds and emotions are continually swimming in a roiling river of other people's desires. This river is fed by all of the various tributaries of the Grid—TV, the Internet, radio, iPods, videogames, cell phones, and whatever else we'll soon invent to distract us.

The only way to become clear on what our souls truly Desire is to unplug from the Grid and listen. Every day, at least for a little while. First thing in the morning is an ideal time for many people. Before we fire up the laptop and switch on the morning news.

Getting in a daily habit of reflective silence is not easy. We are so used to being over-stimulated, the idea that we would voluntarily spend more than 15 minutes doing nothing but sitting in silence seems downright monkish. But silence is not only the simplest way to access deep wisdom in our lives; it is the ultimate static cleaner. It wipes away the noisy buzz of the Grid's desires and allows us to catch a glimpse of our own.

Yes, I'm talking about self-reflection. Soul-reflection might be a more accurate term. It's a way of unplugging, asking and listening that enables you to know what was hidden inside you all along.

JENNIFER

I met Jennifer during the American Dream Project tour. She had big ideas about translating some of the things I was talking about into a course students could learn from. Jennifer immediately impressed me as smart, organized and self-aware. She wasn't always that way. Jennifer grew up in a small rural town about 20 miles from nowhere. At an early age she knew one thing. She wanted out and she wanted up. What that meant, in her mind, was a big important career in a big important city, New York. She looked at the power women on TV and in movies and thought their lives looked fabulous—the clothes, the prestige, the expensive cars, the important dinner meetings, the respect, the sense of "I have arrived." That was the life she wanted. She was sure of it, and she set out after it. Marriage? Kids? Not a chance. What was glamorous about that?

Jennifer was a star student. Valedictorian of her high school class. Voted most likely to have "success in the city." But even as she focused on this dream, there was always a small part of her that wasn't so sure this was what she truly wanted. She fought against this nagging doubt. Of course the big city dream was what she wanted, she kept telling herself. Look at the amazing life she would have.

But by the time she was a freshman in college, the lingering doubt had grown into a strong voice deep inside her. "Are you sure this is what you really want?" it asked over and over again.

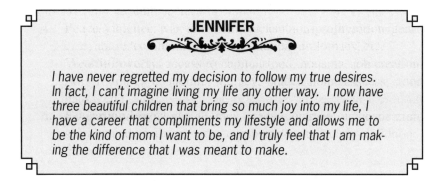

JENNIFER

I have never regretted my decision to follow my true desires. In fact, I can't imagine living my life any other way. I now have three beautiful children that bring so much joy into my life, I have a career that compliments my lifestyle and allows me to be the kind of mom I want to be, and I truly feel that I am making the difference that I was meant to make.

Finally, so bothered by this nagging doubt, she decided it was time to get some answers. She started going for long solitary bike rides in a nearby canyon. She even found a favorite spot she called her "thinking spot"—a comfortable rock by a creek where she would sit for hours just listening to the water. She kept asking herself that most vital of questions, "What do I really want?" She did this every day for months.

One afternoon during one of her "think sessions" she had the idea to go to the career guidance center at her university. She got on a computer there and found a program that provided a detailed analysis of almost every career imaginable. She first looked up lawyer, her present career goal. As she read about the projected salary, average hours worked per week, locations where most of the jobs were, etc., her inner voice got louder. "Are you sure this is what you really want?" Okay, okay she admitted to herself. Maybe not a lawyer. She looked up several other prestigious-sounding professions, and she had the same feeling every time. Maybe not. Her soul was speaking to her.

Suddenly it struck her like lightning. This wasn't the life she wanted. This wasn't the life she was meant to live. This wasn't who she really was, deep down inside. She realized that she had been letting her Self-Concept script her life.

She made a decision that day and never looked back. She changed her major and went into teaching. Her friends and family wondered what had gotten into her. Many told her she was selling herself short. But she felt that by teaching she could make a real difference. Her difference. She also felt that teaching would allow her to live the kind of life she wanted, with plenty of time for her other passions, meaningful relationships, and yes, marriage and kids. That day on the computer she realized that just maybe her most important role in life would be as a mother, where she could make the greatest impact possible in the lives of her children. She discovered her true desires.

After that inner realization, Jennifer says she felt light. The fog of her confusion lifted. So she did become a high school teacher and a wife and mother. She is also a blogger striving to influence the world in ways that matter to her. Blogging didn't even exist when she made the choice to follow her soul's wisdom. Interesting.

Meditation is Not Weird!

Modern medicine has finally caught up with why people of wisdom have practiced meditation throughout the ages. Studies using the latest brain scanning technology have revealed that regular meditators perform better at nearly all kinds of mental and emotional tasks. Meditators have more physical energy and can sustain their attention longer, enabling them to learn faster. Meditators are also healthier, thinner, and less likely to engage in risky behavior. They are emotionally happier. They miss fewer days at work and are more productive. They are also more collaborative, creative, and solution-oriented. So, how can this be?

One answer might lie in what meditation physically does to our brains. According to studies at Massachusetts General Hospital, meditators have more developed cerebral cortexes than hyperstimulated multi-taskers. The cerebral cortex helps us with decision making, attention, memory tasks, and emotional judgment. It is our internal flame of wisdom.

GETTING TO TRUE DESIRE—A RECOVERY PROGRAM

We are so addicted to stimulation, it's as if we are chain-smoking mental noise, and the interruption of that flow feels a little frightening. To break away from it, we need nothing short of a personal recovery program. It's a way to recover our innate capacity for insight. A way to switch on the light of our soul and see our deepest, most noble desires. This recovery program doesn't involve signing up for a retreat, heading for the nearest monastery, or checking into a detox center. But it does require a commitment, like beginning a serious physical exercise program. Think of it as aerobics for the soul. It's simple and free, and after the first 24 hours, extremely satisfying.

Many of the exercises are inspired by Jim Loehr's research that helps us convert stress energy into clean renewable human energy. It helps our brains connect with our soul. It's a great way to jumpstart a lifelong habit of meditating and detaching from the Grid.

Here's how it works.

6 Steps to Getting Clear on Your Soul's Desire

This Aerobics for the Soul Program can be done for three days, six days, thirty days—whatever you can honestly commit to. Take it seriously and it will pay serious dividends.

1. **Shut off the Grid.** No TV, movies, novels or news, and that includes newspapers. Also no music. With one exception. Instrumental music that is soothing and sets the stage for contemplation is permissible. Some neuroscientists believe that Baroque music creates brain waves that promote relaxation. Any kind of music designed for quiet reflection is good. No lyrics, though. If this sounds like deprivation, just try it. In time, it will feel like *liberation.*

2. **Eat only healthy food and only when you are hungry.** Don't overeat. It is wise to eat five small meals instead of three big ones. When you eat, focus exclusively on the taste and texture of your food. Sit down, really taste the food, and eat it slowly, bite by bite. No sweets or manufactured snacks, alcohol, sodas, or energy drinks. Just water and tea and healthy food.

3. **Get some solitary exercise everyday.** Walks, yoga, dance. Focus on how your body feels. Your muscles, your breathing, your movement. It's all right if you go to a class or have an instructor, but forgo competitive sports like tennis for now.

4. **When you work, put all your attention on it.** Do it mindfully, enthusiastically. Take 10-minute breaks every 90 minutes. When you take a break, physically get away from your workstation, desk, or office. Listen to pleasant music, go for a walk, sit on a bench, or stare at some flowers. Return refreshed and throw your creative energy back into your work. Start to shed filler work that doesn't produce value. Treat the value-producing aspects of your job as sacred and significant. Don't work more than eight hours. When work is over, unplug. No cell phones or e-mails. Give yourself fully to your non-work life: your family, hobbies, friends. No multitasking. Get eight hours of sleep.

5. **Be intensely present with people.** Plug into the power socket of the present moment. Engage others in significant ways.

Minimize trivial conversation. When you are in a conversation, put all your attention on the person you are talking with.
Consciously look at their eyes, the structure of their face.
Notice their energy and voice, their concerns, their hopes,
and their happiness level. Don't allow your mind to wander.
Keep bringing your total concentration back to the conversation. Ask questions as they arise in you and look for ways
to offer help. Do this with everyone. Not only members of
your family, but incidental people such as cab drivers and
cashiers. Just watch what happens when you do this.

6. **Practice presence with your senses.** From time to time put
all your attention on how the air feels against your skin. How
your chair feels against your back and legs. What you smell.
Listen carefully to all sounds, even those you normally ignore. Look for light and shadow. Just keep paying attention.
As you do this, thoughts of gratitude are bound to creep in.
Gratitude for being alive, for being in this moment, for beauty. Give thanks. Your emotions will become elevated, your
thinking will become acute, and your sensitivity to your essential self—the part of you that is beyond your brain—will
begin to become more obvious to you.

Do everything else that's part of your daily life as necessary.

TROLLING FOR ANSWERS

As you walk about in this unplugged state, simply ask, from time to
time, "What does my soul want?" kinds of questions. Our goal is to begin to vividly imagine living and doing our soul's desires. We spark that
by asking ourselves small inspiring questions. These are questions that
connect our mind to our soul.

Dr. Bob Maurer is a favorite professor at UCLA's medical school.
One of his goals is to teach medical students how they can encourage
recovering patients to make behavior changes to improve their recovery.
You know, how to help cardiac patients stop intaking vast quantities of
French fries and ice cream. From his decades of studying human change
Dr. Maurer has found that it is insight driven. The insight we often need,
however, is the first small, even tiny step we might take that will lead us
to our big beautiful future. The engine of these kind of step-by-step in-

sights are the questions we ask ourselves. Dr. Maurer suggests questions like "If health were my first priority, what would I be doing differently today? How might I incorporate a few more minutes of exercise in my daily routine?" Or, "Whom could I ask for help or suggestions about my career?" These are questions that inspire practical action.

It is particularly important to ask questions that address the areas of your life that are most confusing or are causing you the most suffering to small first steps of change. Simply ask, for example:

- What might be a first step I could take to find out what my soul desires for my work?

- What does my soul desire for my relationship with my seven year old?

- What might I do today to get me closer to her?

- What does my soul desire for my marriage?

- My health situation?

- My friendships?

Only ask questions that can lead to real answers and first steps. Destructive questions are those that bring forth upsetting emotions. Questions that generate fear and frustration discourage us from trying. They are problem-focused rather than solution-focused. Questions like: "How did I get myself into this mess?" and "Why am I so miserable?" will almost always lead to more suffering and more mistakes. Breakthroughs come when we quietly ask for our soul's direction regarding the dilemmas of our lives.

We now know through brain research that your mind will not let your questions rest. If you're consistently asking yourself questions that matter to you in ways that make change seem possible, your mind *will* seek to resolve those answers. The point is that our minds will work like a 24-hour idea factory if it isn't scared, overwhelmed or confused. By "mind" here, I don't mean the busy, anxious and analytical "top" part of the mind, but the deeper, unconscious recesses that have access to the soul. Often in unexpected moments, such as standing in line at the grocery store, sitting on a plane, or cooking dinner, you'll suddenly recognize your answer with startling clarity.

As you're asking about your soul's Desires, pay particular attention to answers that represent a new direction, an unusual approach.

Perhaps the question that gets at the truth of the soul more than any other is, "What do I already know?" Often we already know what we need to do to fulfill our Promise, but for some reason we don't like the answer. It makes us uncomfortable. It calls us to do things that may require change or learning, or may involve talking to others about things we believe they don't want to talk about. So we pretend not to know.

But if you really want to know your soul's desire for creating personal sustainable abundance in your life, you might simply ask yourself, "What do I already know?" Write down the answers in a journal. A place that you can come back to and reflect on. Listening to your soul also calls for minute-by-minute attention. Putting attention on what is actually happening in your life. Looking for both green lights and red lights. Noticing meaningful coincidences and timely opportunities that may arise.

Don't be deceived that a passing flash of a bright idea is necessarily the truth. When you uncover real answers, they will persist. They will not be one-time "light bulb" ideas that later seem foolish. Rather they will lead to ever-deeper knowledge. One idea building upon another. People and strategies linking up in powerful ways. A course of action that makes greater and greater sense as time goes on.

After you practice the five steps of Aerobics for Your Soul for three days to two weeks you can have an ice cream cone and take it down to 20 minutes a day. You can power up the Grid again. However, you will probably want to set aside three days or a week every six months or so to repeat the "program."

Two weeks to a month every year without TV and junk food and with a conscious effort to maintain personal presence will bring clarity to your Promise and reveal your authentic Desires. And maintaining a daily ritual of 20 to 30 minutes of soul reflection will make you an expert on the purpose of your own life.

But don't take my word for it. Try it.

EVERYONE HAS A PATH TO INSIGHT

Daily soul-reflection is an essential habit if we are going to live an inspired life. But not all of us are designed to become Dali Lamas. The
majority of us will also need to tap into our soul's wisdom through three
other paths to insight. While I believe *all* of us need regular self-reflection, most of us will grow faster by also traveling the three active paths
to insight as well. They are:

- Learning
- Doing
- Serving

Learning

When we are seeking to really understand our Promise it is often necessary to seek new possibilities. New options. Some of us look at all our
present options to save the world and say "none of the above." Then we
are stuck so we do nothing. But new knowledge is the garden of insight.
And it is astonishing just how much new knowledge is out there. We just
have to open our eyes. Most of us, for example, are still living in a world
where the ideas of Newton and Descartes rule the roost. But for the past
century, science has been evolving in shocking new directions. The very
essence of reality is nothing like what we've been taught to believe it
is. Yet few of us know anything about these "new" century-old ideas.
Learning about them can dramatically activate insight in our lives.

If we wish to have supple minds that are capable of insight, we need
to work at removing the blinders of our own ignorance. We do that by
opening ourselves to learning. That means constantly Looking, Listening, Re-thinking, Re-imagining.

Make a commitment to read a book about something completely
new to you once per month. If it helps, join a book club. You'll make
new friends and read more. Commit to watch at least two documentaries a month about subjects you would normally bypass. When doing
this, try to choose important ideas rather than trivial ones, though even
a trivial idea, if new, can open doors. If you lean toward psychology,
read a biography instead or a layperson's physics book. If you love non-
fiction, read a novel.

What's the point? The more we know, the more dots we connect.
And making new connections between ideas and experiences leads to
insight. Insight we may never have gotten without learning that one

new idea. It's especially helpful in finding innovative solutions to "unsolvable" problems. Once we begin to focus on an area of expertise by linking previously unrelated ideas in brand new combinations, we'll experience bursts of insight through blue sky stimulation. You see, to be really free to follow our soul's Desire, we must enlarge the scope of possibilities beyond what we already "know." That's one vital thing Learning does.

Doing

We can also expand insight through work or play. When we are "in the zone" of effortless mastery—singing, sculpting, rock climbing, playing basketball, preparing dinner, giving a speech—we sometimes merge with something that can only be defined as spiritual energy that guides our efforts effortlessly. We experience this "force"—sometimes called Flow—as a form of super awareness. A state where the doer and doing become unified. This takes our minds out of the driver's seat and lets life operate *through* us rather than *by* us. When the world is working through us in this way, we often receive direct and powerful insights. A blast of self-evident truth may burst upon us in a great "aha" moment.

Inspiration, or creative insight, is another manifestation of the same force. When the right words appear from the tip of the pen, when the music leaps from the piano on its own or the finished painting appears in our minds before we dip our brush, we can feel our souls connecting with a transcendent reality far bigger than our limiting thoughts.

When we have these sorts of experience often enough, we no longer need to *believe* in a reality that's deeper than our thoughts. We *experience* it. It becomes a river of insight we can rely on to help run our lives.

Serving

Many of us open ourselves to new insight through unselfish behavior and personal expressions of love. When we serve those who are suffering, when we help a stranger or respond to someone in crisis, we experience a force that is greater than the mind. This kind of experience can be more powerful than life itself. It is certainly more powerful than a mere chemical reaction in the brain.

In times of catastrophe, when ordinary people risk their lives for others they don't even know, we witness something superhuman. We discover first hand that life in all its difficulty is sacred at its core. It breaks down old mental barriers and lets in powerful new insights.

Devoting ourselves to our jobs with an attitude of service to mankind rather than an attitude of "What's in it for me?" can have a similar effect. When we subtract our ego from our work, we are able to drop all the self-protective, stress-driven thinking that constricts us so much of the time. When we open ourselves to pure service, we open ourselves to the most profound insight a human can have. And when we truly experience insight, we find the wisdom that leads us to our Promise.

CHANGE HOW YOU THINK ABOUT CHANGE

What can you do daily (learning, doing, serving) to increase Insight?

CHAPTER 21

DISCOVERING YOUR DESIRE
THROUGH WISDOM

I am convinced we are designed to fulfill our soul's authentic Desire. We come equipped to succeed on our climb, but our navigation system must be switched on. Reflection, learning, doing and serving all make that system more accurate. But it isn't enough to *discover* our path. We must also *travel* it. And good travel requires constant decision-making. It's our decisions that help us fulfill our Promise or keep us from it. And good decisions require wisdom.

I started climbing the Matterhorn at 4 a.m. I wore a climbing helmet with a powerful light just above the brim. In that morning darkness, the light was essential. Otherwise I could've fallen right off the edge. Wisdom is a super halogen high beam that lights up our trail when darkness surrounds us. All that's required is that we turn on the bright light of our brain and become a fully conscious climber.

You see inspiration and courage are not enough. That's why I depended on a light to see the best path and stay connected to my climbing guide. Every dream, every insight, every yearning of the soul must, at some point, be illuminated and interpreted through the mind. And our undisciplined mind can mess things up. Big time. I have seen many, many well-meaning people pursue what seemed to be a noble idea only to trip on the rocks of reality. They believe that if their motive is pure the results will take care of themselves. They don't. I believe wisdom is our soul's guidance system. It illuminates the path to our true Desires.

Wisdom is the clear light of human thought. It enables us to keep the big picture in mind as we make day-to-day decisions. It lets us see the best path *and* the dangers at the same time. It lets us satisfy the demands of our minds and our souls simultaneously.

Turns out, most of us are not very good at thinking. We tend to use only one of our thinking abilities primarily, while under-relying on the others. That creates distortion and bias leading us to make mistakes and foolish judgments that put us on dangerous ledges.

But the great thing is that wisdom is learnable. It comes down to using all of our thinking abilities to test out our new ideas, insights and decisions to see if they hold water.

MARTYN SAVES THE RAINFOREST

Martyn grew up near Liverpool when the Beatles were all the rage. But it wasn't John and Paul's music that captured Martyn's attention as a boy. It was toads. You see he was fascinated by nature. Not just the way most children are. He was seized by nature. For instance, a certain species of toad near his house was endangered, so at age eight Martyn decided to save the toads by bringing them to live in his bedroom. Fortunately his mum also loved animals so his idea to create a toad habitat, complete with slugs and dirt, under his bed was gently re-directed.

Martyn didn't have a hard time following his inner voice or understanding his Design. He earned a Ph.D. in ecology and went to work for a global company to develop technologies and strategies to promote agricultural productivity. For years his work took him around the world, enabling him to grow his expertise like a well-fed tomato plant.

Then he went to Brazil. Wow. Brazil. Nature, beauty, passion. Martyn soaked it in. He had a full plate of business development duties for his company but also began to partner with a non-profit to develop rainforest conservation strategies and ideas for sustainable agriculture. This side job soon took over his heart and mind like background music he

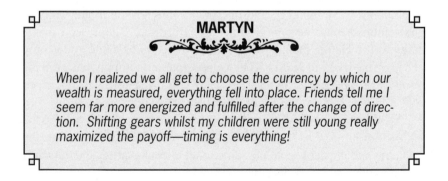

MARTYN

When I realized we all get to choose the currency by which our wealth is measured, everything fell into place. Friends tell me I seem far more energized and fulfilled after the change of direction. Shifting gears whilst my children were still young really maximized the payoff—timing is everything!

could not shut off. Martyn returned to England where he found himself frustrated with the endless corporate meetings, politics and bureaucracy of his full-time job. In time he was assigned to work in Japan where his oldest son was born. Suddenly the clear question of what was he doing to create a world he would be proud to pass on to his son was hounding him. What he had previously accepted as business-as-usual became increasingly unbearable. The voice of his inner wisdom was constantly chanting a mantra that there was something more. His years of learning, doing and serving were giving birth to a new song of change.

Being a scientist, though, Martyn refused to be impulsive. So he sought professional career counseling, took some career assessments and engaged in serious reflection. Finally his head and heart united in clarity. He knew what he had to do.

He got his finances in order, lowering his monthly overhead, and then he made the call. Pro-Natura, the Brazilian organization he had worked with conserving rainforests ten years earlier was his target. Might they need someone like him? Could they pay him as a full-time executive?

Of course they could. In fact, Pro-Natura's founder said Martyn's timing was "inspired". They needed a CEO of the Americas to direct all of their innovative sustainable projects throughout the western hemisphere. He was hired straightaway.

One more thing. It turns out Pro-Natura is deeply committed to life balance so their organizational structure favors a "sustainable family life." Sounds like save the world and still be home for dinner to me.

Martyn is an exciting example of how integrating a worthy Drive with your Desire and Design leads to an extraordinary life. Martyn's way of fusing his inner calling and expertise with sound decision-making is a model of how to follow your passion without creating upsetting drama in your life. It's wisdom in action.

THINKING UNMASKED

Dr. Robert Kinsel-Smith is a brilliant scientist who has been researching human thinking for over 25 years. He's developed and refined a thinking assessment that reveals our individual habits of thought that guide our decision-making. Hundreds of thousands of people have used his assessment to understand what they need to do to make better choices. Kinsel-Smith concludes that we have three fundamental thinking dimensions: **(1) Reason, (2) Common Sense,** and **(3) Intuition.**

Wise people use all three thinking dimensions in both their outer and inner lives. They run all of their decisions through a three-dimensional process. Most of us, sadly, are not wise. We don't do this. Most of us aren't even consciously aware that we think in three dimensions. That's why we learn by trial and error, the clumsiest and most brutal way to navigate life.

When all three ways of thinking are used, our risk of making bad decisions is low. When we make choices based only on only one or two of these thinking dimensions, we leave ourselves wide open for massive blunders. Not using all of our thinking capacities is like walking through a minefield blind-folded, with a metal detector sitting in our backpack.

We *have* a brain. It is only wise to use it.

THREE FUNDAMENTAL WAYS OF THINKING

Figure 21.1: Three Ways of Thinking

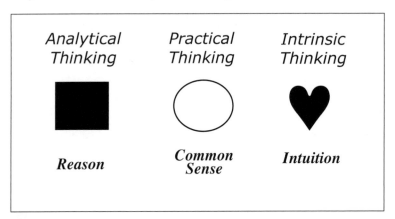

Reason

The symbol for Reason is a box. The box represents order and structure, boundaries and rules. The stuff that falls within the box is certain—the known facts, the way "things are done around here," the rules by which our family or business is run. When we tell ourselves to "think outside the box," this is the box we're talking about. It's the box of rules, facts and judgments that we have agreed not to critically examine. It's our ground rules, our assumptions about how things are supposed to work.

Reason is analytical thinking. It is important because it helps us solve specific problems and create order and predictability. It narrows our focus in chaotic circumstances. Reason gives us rules, accounting, math, science, policies, procedures, hierarchy and order. It produces right vs. wrong morality and ethics. The Law. Black and white thinking. It's the way we measure people and decisions against standards and facts. Reason leads to contracts, guarantees, schedules, programs, "shoulds," and "musts."

Reason looks at the pieces, not the whole. Reason's main tool is logic. It is an excellent means of testing whether a plan has major flaws, whether a contract covers all the bases and whether an idea holds water.

Reason is an important part of a sound decision-making process. Martyn was professionally trained to rely on reason. Thus his career change was careful and thought out. He resisted the urge to leap until he had a landing zone.

Questions We Might Ask When Using REASON
(analytical thinking)

- *Does this decision make logical sense?*
- *Does it follow good, established rules?*
- *Is it in line with my plans?*

You can see from these questions that reason is an excellent tool to improve what you are already doing or reduce risk. You can also see that using reason alone can trap you in a logic box that suffocates your imagination.

Common Sense

The symbol for Common Sense is the circle. Where Reason is linear, Common Sense is holistic. It attempts to get a 360-degree view of what's going on around us so we can make a quick, practical decision and keep moving forward.

Common Sense is practical thinking. It focuses on what's happening here and now, on which decision will bring about the result we want right now. It is not about logical principles or moral principles; it is about getting the job done.

Common Sense cues us on the best time to try a new method or strategy. For example, if profits just took a nosedive, the air conditioning is broken, and the boss's teenaged daughter just ran off with a rock musician, this might not be the ideal moment to ask for a raise.

Common Sense is flexible and dynamic. Though a speed limit may be posted, we further adjust our own speeds to the vehicle we're driving, the load we're towing, the weather conditions, the time of day, the odds of getting a ticket. Common Sense recognizes that not all of reality can be reduced to a fixed set of instructions. It employs the genius of conditional thinking; given a certain set of circumstances, this is the best choice. Martyn had the common sense to start his new job search where people knew him and with people he knew. Thus he got the job he most wanted and has deeply enjoyed.

Questions We Might Ask When Using COMMON SENSE (practical thinking)

- *What has worked before in a case like this?*
- *Will my plan work in the real world?*
- *Will my proposal be seen as the best one compared to others?*
- *Does this job or project involve work that I am skilled at?*
- *Am I better than the competition?*

Common Sense is an amazing tool for taking action now. It focuses on the next step on our path. That's great except it doesn't challenge us with the question, where is this path leading?

♥ Intuition

The third thinking dimension, Intuition, is represented by a heart. The heart stands for feelings, passion and compassion.

Intuition is that mysterious faculty that perceives the unseen elements of a situation. It is not really *thinking* at all, per se, but a deep form of receptivity. Those of us with highly developed Intuition find it a reliable barometer for correct decision-making that enriches our lives in incalculable ways.

Intuition is intrinsic thinking. It enables us to experience connections among people and events that our logical mind does not see. It takes into account intangible factors that may be critical to the success of a decision. It can often tell us that there is a hidden "bomb in the basement," even if it can't give us specifics on exactly where the bomb is located. Intuition runs far deeper than lists of pros and cons. It is the place from which internal hunches and inspired gut feelings are born. Should I take this job or not? Should I marry this man?

Intuition allows us to find work and relationships that connect with our hearts and souls. It is the tool of passion and purpose. When we think intrinsically about our work, we give it meaning beyond its paycheck-producing powers. It challenges us with questions of meaning. When we think intrinsically about other people, we see them as individuals with unique worth. Most of us, for instance, love our children intrinsically. We don't judge them against models or calculate their economic value. We wouldn't trade one child for another (at least not most of the time), nor for one who is smarter, more athletic or more beautiful. Our child is irreplaceable. Our intrinsic thinking is always on a quest for purpose and gives us the ability to turn our thinking into love. Martyn followed his intuition in Brazil to work on eco-projects that he loved because he loved them. His time was squeezed with his many business responsibilities, but he could not resist expressing his Design in the service of the environment. Look where it took him.

Questions We Might Ask When Using Intuition
(intrinsic thinking or gut sense)

- *Is this choice right for me?*
- *Does it express my true nature?*
- *Do I love my job?*
- *Is this plan what my soul desires?*
- *Do I have any bad gut feelings?*
- *Beyond my pros and cons list, what do I really want to do?*
- *Will this action or decision serve the world?*
- *Does this plan have a higher purpose?*

Our intuition can be a powerful tool if it is refined and informed; however it's easy to mistake emotion for wisdom and feeling for truth. That's why all three dimensions of thinking matter.

Does God Have a Special Purpose for You?

Millions of believers say that God has a plan for each of us. I happen to agree. But for many of us, this idea doesn't work too well in practice. We never know for certain that we've keyed into "God's will." So we pray and we study and we meditate and we strain to listen for a divine voice. When we don't hear it, we beat ourselves up. We become anxious and think we're unworthy of answers or that we're doing something wrong. Or we look for divine direction to be revealed through chance events, random opportunities and spontaneous "good feelings."

The problem with this approach is that there is simply no way of being sure when events really are meaningful. Sometimes stuff just happens. Are we hearing messages from the Divine or only the voice of our emotions or inner fears or wild hopes?

While the greatest limitation to imagination is our over-reliance on rational thinking and its inability to provide insight, we can also go too far the other way. We can glut ourselves on what we think are "insightful" feelings and make terrible decisions. I've counseled many people who had "good feelings" about opportunities that led them to bankruptcy and immense suffering.

If you believe God has a plan for you, use the tool he gave you to succeed. Wisdom. We are all well-equipped to fulfill our Promise.

WISDOM INVOLVES USING ALL THREE THINKING DIMENSIONS

Most of us don't employ our three thinking dimensions—Reason, Common Sense and Intuition—in a balanced way. Almost all of us rely heavily on just one or two. This is a huge problem when it comes to making important decisions or setting the course of our lives.

If we're heavily **analytical thinkers** (reason), for example, we believe that we can "figure out" our life's purpose based on reason. We look at charts and statistics and, after making careful lists of pros and cons, choose the career, the mate, the house, the lifestyle that seems the most Reasonable. Then we stick with it. Even when we start to feel hollow and anxiety-ridden, we stick with the plan, reasoning that life is not fun for anyone. We dwell in the box of our Self-Concept, trying to live up to its relentless demands. Life is exhausting, but we consider this a given.

If we tend to be **practical thinkers** (common sense) we are more flexible, more able to change course when the wind changes, more able to see our place in the system. But our decisions are always based on "getting what I want now." We have no clear overall vision, no sense of greater purpose. We are slaves to the demands of the moment.

As common sense types we want immediate results, we want to get things done right now. We think in terms of "can," not "should."

If we're overly **intrinsic thinkers** we can have our share of problems too. We can be easily manipulated. By refusing to see the truth about others and only seeing their imagined "potential," we may give people opportunities they don't deserve. And uninformed intuition will only echo our deeper biases. For instance, if we tend toward optimism our intuition will tend to be whispering, "This will all work out." If we tend toward pessimism, our gut will tell us "no" all too often. Becoming genuinely crazy is another danger of too much intuitive thinking. Some people become so intoxicated with the idea of mystical guidance that they begin "seeing signs" everywhere, reading significance into the most mundane occurrences. Or, in the name of "following their bliss," they leave their families, quit their jobs and run off to Mexico to find themselves. Remember Martyn. He had the patience and discipline to make his life-changing decision carefully. When he gained the confidence that is wisdom's gift, he acted boldly.

If we want to live the life of our Promise we need to carefully apply wisdom to all of our choices and decisions. Because our choices *do* matter, not only to ourselves but to the other 7 billion people on the planet.

Every choice born of wisdom creates ripples that touch all of humanity.

PART SEVEN

SUSTAINABLE ABUNDANCE

CHAPTER 22

OUR TRIPLE BOTTOM LINE

W hen we learn to listen to our souls and uncover our truest Drive, Design, and Desires, we find a new sense of balance coming into our lives. We activate our connection with the rest of humanity and discover that we truly don't want to live lives of wastefulness, selfishness, competition, and one-upmanship. In our souls, what we really want is sustainable abundance.

Sustainable Abundance. We want it for the whole of humanity. Everyone should have the chance to live a decent life, and to do so in a way that doesn't destroy that same chance for others—now or in the future.

But we can only get there with an inner GPS system programmed for the correct destination. If we punch in an address of a penthouse on Fifth Avenue, the abundance we seek will only be material. And material abundance is never enough. First, it's only comparatively satisfying. We can make over $100,000 a year, but if we are the least wealthy person in a very wealthy neighborhood, we'll still feel small. If, on the other hand, we're the richest people in a modest neighborhood, we can feel pretty inflated. Second, we'll never have enough of what money can buy to keep us stimulated. A steady diet of luxury will still leave us hungry for more. Fifteen minutes after buying the Dream Car or The Sailboat, we're busily trolling for the next thing on our "want" list.

Sustainable abundance is found by looking closely at our triple bottom line. The term, triple bottom line was coined over twenty years ago as a way to measure whether an enterprise was operating in a sustainable manner. It turns out a single focus on measuring only one bottom line, money, ends up driving business decisions that are unbalanced and often destructive to our future. Triple bottom line business thinking asks us to account for our impacts on people and the planet, as well as profit. Likewise our personal triple bottom line urges us to view all our decisions *simultaneously* in all three principle dimensions of life: relationships, lifestyle, and career. We have Promises to keep in all three dimensions if we wish to live lives of sustainable abundance. Weaving a rich tapestry of satisfaction in all three areas is the triple bottom line of our lives.

OUR TRIPLE BOTTOM LINE

Relationships

Humans are social beings. We long to connect. Healthy relationships are more than convenient living arrangements. They are our greatest sources of trust, intimacy, and validation. They require attention, nurturing, and *time*. Time to communicate, to touch, to engage, to enjoy meaningful conversation. Time to just laugh and be stupid. Time to develop enough rapport whereby honesty flows freely even when there is no time to talk. Relationships are primary; they are not just for whatever time is left over.

We all know this. Relationships are *primary*, not just for time left over.

Lifestyle

The healthiest lifestyles promote positive emotions and reduce stress. People who live at a human pace, rather than a digital pace, are invariably more content in the long run than those who wear themselves out through an aggressive, goal-driven lifestyle. Play is vital. A playful lifestyle includes spontaneity, creativity, stimulation, joy and meaning. Recreation is literally *re*-creation: a process that restores our energy. And regular time for reflection should be our way of life. Long commutes and overstuffed schedules with too little time left for play are not lifestyles; they are life-killers.

Career

We all want careers that genuinely interest us and are not just the means to pay the interest on our loans. An ideal career stimulates us and enables us to make our difference. It is challenging and rewarding and provides variety and opportunity for growth. It leverages our traits and talents. A healthy, sane career offers a reasonable payoff for the amount of effort we put in. It calls us to use our gifts, but also *gives* us the gift of time leftover for life and love. In an ideal career we can clearly see how we are making a meaningful contribution to the world. We feel it.

BUT SOMETHING'S OUT OF WHACK

Unfortunately, many of us develop goals for each of the three dimensions of our lives independently of the others. We take jobs that demand our attention night and day. Soon our quest for a rich family life with time for bedtime stories, long walks together, and spiritual growth slips away. We start living life as it shows up, using our energy to put out fires, rather than powering up continuous joy and meaning from all three dimensions of life. Stress-cracks begin to crumble our inner foundation. We become numb to dissatisfaction. We accept anxiety as normal.

Many of us attack our triple bottom line in sequential order. Following the Gain, Grow, Good model, we invest several decades in developing our career, with the hopes that the later years can be devoted to enjoying life and giving attention to our loved ones. The trouble with the sequential approach is that by the time we're ready to engage with our spouses or children, they may no longer want to spend time with us. And by the time we are ready to indulge our passions, the passion has flickered out.

Creating a life of sustainable abundance begins with understanding our Drive, Design, and Desires and weaving them together in the here and now. When we're doing things *in all three dimensions of our lives* that reflect our Drive, express our Design, and satisfy our Desires, we feel both deeply content and constantly energized. We are living our Promise.

When almost every day is a celebration of our unique Design and deepest Desire, we live in sustainable abundance.

Okay, so how do we do that? Well, one of the surest ways to know if we are living in sustainable abundance is to listen to the rhythm of our lives.

 If you intend to live your dream life and a life of sustainable abundance, the *Dream Life Assessment* at SavetheWorldBook.com will illuminate which parts of your life are bringing you great satisfaction and which parts are causing you stress.

THE RHYTHM OF OUR LIVES

The operating system of our personal GPS is the rhythm of our daily life. By rhythm, I mean its pace, its flow, its balance of stimulation and relaxation, challenge and satisfaction. A life of sustainable abundance has a sane and graceful rhythm. It is not marked by panic, anxiety, and stress. It is not filled with endless appointments and a frantic rush to tick off items on an ever-growing "to do" list.

The key word here is "sustainable."

I was deeply affected by Matthew Kelly, a young Catholic from Australia who has the gift of inspiring others to become the "best version of themselves." He discovered his gift quite by accident in his early twenties by giving a short talk to a church group. In an amazing series of rapid-fire events he became an international star in Catholic circles, leading retreats and giving inspirational weekend seminars all over the world.

He was so successful he started to burn out. His lifestyle was not sustainable. He became depressed and anxious and unable to fully function.

In desperation he took his ragged self to a monastery in Austria to unplug, ask, and listen. Pretty big step. But then, monasteries are built for a reason. In the Alps he hiked himself out of his depression and had a powerful spiritual epiphany. The insight he gained was that all life is designed to thrive *in its own rhythm*. And we all have our own personal pulse.

The rhythm of our lives is the sustainable pace in which we live the totality of our lives in all three dimensions. We each have a psychological and physical rhythm that is sustainable because it enables us to maintain a positive, creative, friendly mood and have the vital physical energy we need to feel both light and powerful. If we over-rev our rhythm, our inner engine will overheat and drive a piston through our soul.

What a beautiful discovery. In my own work with others and in my personal life I can attest to rhythm being the metronome of personal sustainability. We know we're in rhythm when we are fully present in our work, love, and play. When we are overloaded in any one of these dimensions, we become numb and anxious.

When we're constantly planning, worrying, and multi-tasking, we've lost our rhythm. We've become the person who's never really there. We lose intimacy. We become isolated. Self-alienated. Misunderstood. Anxious. Our temper gets shorter. We feel less connected. All of these things happen when we lose the rhythm of our life.

Here's how we know we're in a sustainable rhythm. When we're having a conversation with a loved one, we're fully present. When we watch a sunset, we're not thinking about our accounts receivable. We actually *listen* to music and *taste* our food. When we're in the rhythm of life, we have the mental and emotional space to be wherever we are. So when we're at the movie theater or out to dinner we're not thinking about our work. We're not thinking about the repairs we need to make on our house. We're enjoying whatever experience we're having, with the people we love. Period. We're either *in* rhythm or *out* of rhythm. If we're honest with ourselves, it's easy to tell which is the case.

The encouraging news is that our personal rhythm is not fixed. The more attention we give to integrating our life, work, and love into one sustainable whole, the more natural and sustainable our rhythm becomes. Life confirms that we're on the right track by bringing us feelings of inner calm and "rightness."

Attending to our triple bottom line is how we are designed to live abundantly and sustainably.

SUSTAINABLE ABUNDANCE IN REAL LIFE

Gary loves helping people. He loves his family. And he loves football. He played football in college and what he wanted to do more than anything else was coach high school football. But being a high school teacher really didn't work for him. He wasn't interested in teaching history

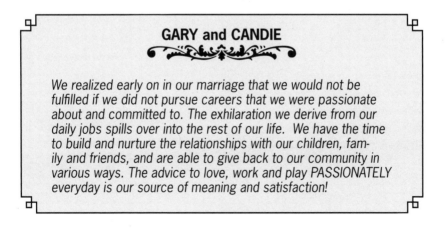

GARY and CANDIE

We realized early on in our marriage that we would not be fulfilled if we did not pursue careers that we were passionate about and committed to. The exhilaration we derive from our daily jobs spills over into the rest of our life. We have the time to build and nurture the relationships with our children, family and friends, and are able to give back to our community in various ways. The advice to love, work and play PASSIONATELY everyday is our source of meaning and satisfaction!

or driver's education, just coaching football. Gary has a passion for all things male. He loves the feeling of a locker room, of being on a team, of hanging out with the guys. He found a career that was perfect for him as a firefighter. So he works 48-hour shifts and is able to be home with his family 20 days a month. And he has plenty of time to be the assistant coach of the local state champion high school football team. Gary is saving the world his way. Every time he responds to a fire or emergency, he's making his difference. Every young boy that is inspired by his coaching is a life changed.

Gary's wife, Candie, works from home. She has her own web and graphic design company. Her major client is me. You see, Candie is insistent on using her talent to make the world more sustainable. A better place for her children. She doesn't just worry about the future. Every day she puts her time and talent to use by communicating ideas to save the future. Together Gary and Candie fashion a life that mixes love, work, and play together in a delicious home-cooked stew. It is hard to see edges between their family, career, and lifestyle. It is all one complete thing.

You don't have to be Bill Gates to live your abundant life. You just need to be intent on what you value and enjoy, and design a life to support it. That's what Gary and Candie do. They are living their abundant life every day.

CHANGE HOW YOU THINK ABOUT CHANGE

Are you in *rhythm*? Why or why not?

PART EIGHT

RELATIONSHIPS

CHAPTER 23

DO YOU WANT TO BE HOME FOR DINNER?

Our quest to save the world and still be home for dinner is fulfilled largely through the power of relationships. Deep life satisfaction requires us to do more than commit to developing our best selves. We must also engage in meaningful relationships. If it's true, as is often said, that most of us will become acquainted with about 1,000 people in our lifetime and that those 1,000 will do the same, that means a million people are two degrees of separation away from our influence. Our impact, just by being alive, is far broader than any of us can imagine.

For the vast majority of us, the way we change the world is through our impact on our widening circle of human contacts—at home, at work, and in the community. One sentence uttered at the right time and circumstance can change the entire course of a person's life. Often we have no idea how our example is leaving an imprint on others. Sometimes the smallest kindnesses have profoundly magnified effects. Some days the way we change the world is to change a diaper.

"Being home for dinner" is all about building healthy relationships. That's why relationship is a crucial element of our triple bottom line. If we don't make a conscious investment in our important relationships, it is unlikely we'll change the world in a way that matters. And we'll never, ever be home for dinner.

RELATIONSHIPS FIRST

The single greatest determinant of human happiness is great and lasting relationships. I'm not making this up. This fact is revealed in study after study, survey after survey. We are simply wired to seek bonded, rewarding, love relationships.

Perhaps this is explained by the theory of consciousness that says human connections occur mainly on a spiritual plane. That when two people connect in a deep way, it isn't primarily through our words but through our *meaning*. The way we share that meaning is by creating a new joint consciousness.

Picture two people talking. Between them and above them there's a bubble. And in that bubble there's a mingling of two souls in a shared consciousness. This shared consciousness creates a feeling of understanding and love that transcends definition.

This kind of interpersonal melding is a pinnacle of human experience. It is even more powerful when this love or shared consciousness endures over years, decades, or a lifetime. Then it deepens and richens like a fine wine. I believe it to be the most powerful of all energy because it connects us not only to each other but also, in some mysterious way, to *all* others.

Without connection, what's the point of anything?

Why, then, do so many of us put career first? Well, because we're told over and over that it's the responsible thing to do. If we have security, money, and resources, we tell ourselves, everything else will work out. But it doesn't. A career-first priority accelerates divorce rates, starves friendships and turns lifestyle into a word that describes the size of our living rooms and the number of cars in our garage.

Life's priorities need to go in this order: Relationships, Lifestyle, Career. That's not to diminish the value of career. But, really, what's the point of career success without the love of our spouses, families, and friends?

If relationships are the greatest source of meaning, joy and satisfaction in life, then doesn't it make sense that we must consciously put them first, rather than giving them whatever time is left over? Healthy, meaningful relationships are the foundation of our Promise. So we must thoughtfully create the lifestyle and career conditions that support the relationships that really matter. Not the other way around. All three life dimensions are important. But developing thriving intimate relationships must be the driver of the other two.

FRIENDS MATTER

Putting relationships first means having deep, long-lasting friendships. So how are we doing at that? Recent research tells us that in our overly busy, hyper-caffeinated lifestyles, nearly 25 percent of us don't have a single friend we can really confide in. How sad is that? Research also tells us that, on average, all of us have fewer friends than we did a couple of decades ago.

That seems to be a course of pathology. A trend that will not only leave us individually empty but deeply wounded as a society.

No amount of good we do in the world, no amount of world-saving activity can replace the deep human connection of trusting friendships. Friendships encourage us to *be who we are* and *do what we came to do*.

Our lives are simply too rough, too painful, too filled with suffering to travel alone or with only a superficial pack of drinking buddies. We are designed to thrive through caring relationships. We simply need to truly know others and be known. Yes, we can fill our lives with stuff, work, and even adventure, but it's not enough. None of us can be truly happy without friends.

MAKING FRIENDS AS IF YOUR LIFE DEPENDS ON IT

The first winter after my graduation in the early 1970s I decided to go to North Shore, Oahu. It is every surfer's proving ground. The powerful waves of Pipeline and Sunset Beach thunder over sharp coral heads, taunting every surfer with the question, "So you think you're good, do ya? Prove it."

In spite of the fierce surf I was comforted by something entirely unexpected: deep friendships. You see, the North Shore's best waves only break from December to March, attracting a traveling tribe of surfers from around the world. This winter was no exception. Nearly all of us who had gathered there had one thing in common. We all loved the feeling. That unexplainable thrill of joyriding high-speed waves.

Hawaii added a dimension that bound us together even more. Danger. Hawaiian winter surf brings drownings, injuries, coral cuts and just plain over-the-top fear. So in the water everyone is a lifeguard. Everyone. That winter we all looked out for each other. One day my surfboard broke in half out at Sunset Beach and someone I barely knew made sure I safely reached the beach. Another sunny afternoon I wiped out on an offshore reef and was attempting to swim to shore when I got caught in a rip current that was carrying me out to sea. I lost my judgment and was unable to swim across the rip. Just as that terrible sense of exhaustion and panic began to overtake me, someone I had only met the night before saw me from the beach, grabbed his board, paddled out and rescued me. Yeah, I know, I was an idiot. But living in a community of people who you could depend on with your life…that was awesome.

So I survived that winter and four years later I went back. It was a different place. The North Shore "tribe" had disintegrated. Now there was high tension. The traveling Australians were challenging the local Hawaiians for dominance. The Australians claimed they were the best surfers in the world. The Hawaiians were angered by the Australians' arrogance. Fights were happening, both in the water and out. Paradise had deteriorated into a mad circus of bad vibes and violence.

So what happened? Cable TV, that's what. You see, during my first trip to the North Shore television was non-existent. At night we all walked from house to house rented by members of our worldwide fraternity. We talked, played cards, and swapped stories. Most of all, we got to know each other. Beyond the games and conversation, we heard each other's life stories, learned about faraway girlfriends and, of course, shared our hopes and dreams. Some of us made lifelong friends but nearly all of us felt connected by our common interest and an unspoken mutual promise of "you can depend on me."

But four years later cable TV had infested the North Shore. The sense of community had been redefined to include only friends living in the same house. At night, instead of walking down the old Kam highway road to drop in on the new arrivals, we watched the tube. That's when war broke out. The Australians lived in fear of the Hawaiians and moved to condos in a private compound. Our community degraded into a hyper-competitive every-man-for-himself surf war.

My experience on the North Shore seems to mirror what's happened to our whole society. Every year TV viewing time rises. Today the average American watches more than 4 hours per day. The people who watch the most have the fewest friends. We used to watch TV shows as a family. Now each of us watches TV in our own room or we're on the Internet doing our dance with the digital world. Yes, in some ways our constant cell phone conversations, texting, and social networking on MySpace and Facebook has increased communication but mostly in trivial ways. In fact today we speak in terms of digital identities or even *personal brands* in which we manage how other people experience us as if we're all Paris Hiltons.

Yet for all our "mediated" communication we've become more socially isolated with fewer vital friends, looser family ties and more fragile marriages. As a society we're watching our social capital erode, but we don't have to. The good news is the number and quality of relationships we have is completely within our control.

FRIENDSHIP 101

There are two levels of friendship. The first level is based on mutual benefit. These are friends who get something they value from the relationship. That could range from companionship to access to new people to date or business opportunities. Friendships based on mutual benefit only work when the benefits are pretty evenly balanced. Both friends are getting what they want.

Many people who primarily engage in this level of friendship do so because they overvalue independence. According to Dr. Chris Peterson, about 30 percent of the population falls into this trap. These folks don't feel secure in being vulnerable so they avoid intimacy. They have difficulty trusting friends, business associates, or spouses, so they don't wholly connect. With this kind of person you can only have a friendship based on mutual back-scratching. That can stave off a certain amount of loneliness, but most of us long for friends at the second level.

The second level of friendship is based on intrinsic respect. Friends at this level not only know our secrets; they share our values and give us respect, compassion and caring. Recent social research has uncovered the hidden magic of Level Two friendships. Healthy, happy, mutually supportive friendships contribute to three important things we all desire:

1. **Life satisfaction**—the abiding feeling that life is good and will stay that way.
2. **Character strength**—virtuous personal behavior.
3. **Wellness and long life**—feelings of energy and vitality.

It turns out that people with trusted friends also tend to be enthusiastic, resilient, and self-disciplined, as well as able to solve problems and achieve goals. People with genuine friends attract supporters, advocates, mentors and new opportunities.

Level Two friendship is also vital for a happy long-term marriage. The nature of romantic relationships is that they start with the heat of a raging fire but endure at the temperature of a warm, comforting bath.

When we first fall in love it's passion first, friendship second. Passion ignites a volatile pool of brain chemicals. That fire burns on its own fuel for about one to two years. But for a romantic relationship to last, the connection needs to reverse to friendship first and passion second. In fact, the friendship constantly re-kindles passion through deep emotional and intellectual intimacy.

Who knew we could get all that by having friends?! Well, it's more than *having* friends. We all need to *be* friends as well. When someone we value can trust us with his or her most vulnerable feelings or off-the-wall thoughts, we both feel connected at the core. It's the mutual feeling of being valued intrinsically—beyond our behavior, looks, or social position, beyond our quirks and bad habits—that makes a great friendship so irreplaceable. There is nothing more affirming than being deeply known, accepted and treasured.

Level Two friendships require the one thing we often "hoard" the most—our time. Friendships deepen by spending time together. Time to play Scrabble, go for a hike, or wander around a farmer's market. Time where the only payoff is a closer relationship. Yes, genuine friendship takes time. But consider this. What investment of time are we now making that could possibly bring us a more satisfying payoff?

CHANGE HOW YOU THINK ABOUT CHANGE

How much time do you spend nurturing genuine friendships?

CHAPTER 24

A GOOD MARRIAGE MAKES US HAPPY

The next relationship ingredient that is vital to a life of sustainable abundance is marriage. Research across seventeen countries has found that the happiest people are married. (The second happiest people are those who have never married but have several close friends.) In fact, married people are twice as happy as any people in any other relationship category. Nearly three times as happy as people just living together. Turns out, living together without a formal, legal commitment is very stressful. "Cohabitating" couples have a 75 percent breakup rate. They are twice as likely to abuse alcohol, smoke, be victims of abuse, suffer chronic pain, and miss days from work. Conversely, married partners live the longest, are the healthiest, have the most money, and enjoy more sex than any other category. No wonder they're happy.

So if marriage is so great, how come all of this divorce? How come 50 percent of us who are married often wonder what it would be like to be married to someone else or not married at all?

Well, because only 5 to 10 percent of marriages are marriages of sustainable abundance. There are lots of reasons for this, to be sure. But the main ones are that most of us invest too little, expect too much, and think we're right about everything. We simply don't nurture our *friendship* or re-ignite our romance.

These failings certainly aren't new. These bad habits have been ruining marriages since the dawn of history. But they've been greatly accelerated by the Grid. The Grid trains us to think of marriage like a business deal or, even worse, like a consumer purchase.

One of our biggest problems in marriage today is a tendency called maximizing or "re-optimizing." As author Barry Schwartz reminds us, consumers are constantly on the lookout for a better deal. For instance, if we buy a Honda, we keep wondering if we would have liked the Toyota better. We love our big-screen television until we see our best friend's bigger and better one.

When it comes to relationships, the Grid shows us lots of alternative options. Pretty soon we start to say to ourselves, "My wife's okay, but I wonder what it would be like to be married to . . . ?" A great saboteur of marriage is the habit of comparing our spouse to a fantasy. A character in a TV show, a celebrity, or, worst of all, the high school sweetheart we didn't marry.

When marriage becomes tiresome, it's easy to tell ourselves we made a selection error or that our mate has changed and is in need of replacement. What's missing is genuine Level Two friendship.

MY TRUE PARTNER
Not too long ago I had a pretty severe "Mohs" surgery on the left side of my face. It turns out that a lifetime of surfing comes with a downside. Having your face exposed to the sun for five decades is a bit like sticking your head in a microwave. When I started surfing in the 1960s, there was no such thing as sun block. Coppertone was for sissies. So I contracted non-malignant skin cancer on my left temple, which, if untreated, would take over my face like a wine stain on a linen napkin.

"Mohs" surgery is a lot like "mowing" the skin off your face. My doctor explained that the surgery would take place in several rounds. Each time 2 millimeters of skin is removed and examined in a lab. The face scraping continues until all the bad-boy cancer cells are removed.

The lab time between each "mowing" is two to three hours. The doctor said three to four rounds of surgery are common. So the actual surgeries are brief, but the waiting time in between is eternal. They told me to pack a lunch. Since this was virtually an all-day commitment, I showed up with a briefcase full of work to pass the time and boundless optimism that all of this would be nothing more than a flesh wound. I felt like Jack Bauer. No problem.

Round One went as expected. But two and a half hours later the lab results revealed that the cancer was much bigger under the skin than on the surface. A nickel-sized "lawn" to be mowed turned into a silver-dollar size cancer estate, complete with potential nerve damage, skin grafts, and sagging eyebrow. As my doctor's concern rose, I turned from Jack Bauer into Napoleon Dynamite.

Fortunately my wife was sitting next to me. I had insisted she not wait with me. I had my work, you see. This was nothing, I had told her. "I'll call you when it's over." She knew better. When she senses things my logic doesn't see, she doesn't argue; she just does what she must. With or without my permission. So she waited with me. When I came out of the surgery room, armed with the bad news and a big pressure bandage on my head, she gave me her "love look" and closed her eyes and took my hand. I could feel her prayers. I could feel her grace. I could feel her confidence.

We went outside and went for a walk. In her powerful, quiet way, she reassured me. I am lucky to have a wife whose fierce loyalty is irrational. If my face sagged like a bag of sand and I became clinically depressed, I know she would be at my side. Not out of duty or guilt, but out of grade-A, 100 percent pure love. She is my constant compassionate cheerleader.

Unexpectedly the second round of "mowing" managed to cut out all those pesky, perverted cells. I was clear! But the real gift, of course, was the love of my wife and best friend. That kind of loving partnership is only born of a commitment that says, "No matter what happens, we're getting through this together." I am very lucky. Yes, about my cancer results, but about much more. I am lucky to have a wife who loves me not only as a hunk of a husband but even more deeply as an irreplaceable friend.

HOW TO CREATE A BLISSFUL MARRIAGE
Here are a few other things I have discovered to be vital to a marriage of sustainable abundance.

Choose a Mate Well
Wise selection of a marriage partner is critical. Design plays a role in this. Traits, in particular, should be honored when considering a mate. In most cases, two people who are compatible tend to have some commonality in their traits, without being too identical. When two people are curious, for example, they constantly stimulate each other's minds and teach things to each other. They delight in the sheer joy of sharing knowledge and ideas.

And yet, we also benefit from the gentle pull of traits in a mate that we do not possess strongly ourselves. Optimists can benefit from the gentle restraint of the prudent. However, if your prudent boyfriend is overly cautious, he may drive you nuts as a husband. We need to ask: Is there enough mutual ground so that we can enjoy life together and not drive each other crazy? Are there enough differences so that we can spur each other to growth and "fill in" for each other's blind spots? Remember, our traits don't tend to change over a lifetime. For love to last, we should be in sync with the main traits of our mates, right out of the starting gate.

Maturity Matters
If we marry a pleasure-centered, immature bully, or a victim-manipulator, healthy marriage is pretty difficult. If you can't trust your partner, intimacy is impossible. So it's essential to avoid the 35 percent of people who are at the dysfunctional level of maturity. The happiest marriages are between partners who are functionally mature. That means each has enough emotional intelligence to be capable of commitment, intimacy, and intellectual honesty.

But as for finding the perfect person, well, as author John Ortberg writes, "Everybody's normal till you get to know them." Everyone has personality defects, inexplicable moods, and irrational opinions. We're all imperfect. Our quest is to find someone whose imperfections are perfect for us.

If you are already married, then accept your mate's imperfections, work around them, joke about them, deal with them. Fuming about what is missing, instead of enjoying what is present, is a poisonous prescription.

Give Continuous Loving Attention
Respected marriage researcher John Gottman tells us that the strongest predictors of happy marriages are: 1) small continuous acts of loving attention, and 2) handling conflict with respect.

Continuous loving attention simply means being fully present with a loving heart. It means looking your spouse in the eye with genuine affection when she enters the room. It means turning away from the computer and giving total attention when he asks you a question. It means giving her loving touches whenever she is close. Small moments of presence and caring accumulate to create a powerful love engine.

Miserable couples treat each other like someone to manage, control or even to defeat. Happy couples treat their spouses like their favorite person on earth.

Have Healthy Rules and Boundaries

All healthy relationships have critical boundaries and rules. Breaking them results in ending the relationship. No one should tolerate abuse, violence, serious addictions, or seriously self-destructive behavior. It's impossible to have a healthy relationship with an unhealthy person.

Not all relationships will work out. Forgiveness is vital, but relationships of trust are earned through mutual respect, responsibility, and faithfulness. Learn the difference between loving and trusting. Love everyone. But use wisdom in extending trust. Let go of relationships where trust is not a palpable presence.

Finally, and most importantly, if you really want a happy marriage, I suggest adopting what I call the Three Pillars of Love:

1. **Understand**
2. **Involve**
3. **Affirm**

The three pillars aren't just for romantic partners. They work for all relationships. In fact they are the same pillars that produce deep lasting friendships. And the payoff is nothing less than life's jackpot.

THREE PILLARS OF LOVE

Pillar 1: To Understand

A prime need we all have in relationships is to be understood, to be truly known. We can only provide understanding when we value our partners intrinsically. This means we don't value them for how they please, fulfill, serve, complete, or satisfy us; but for who they are in and of themselves. We don't appreciate their good qualities alone, but the whole package. We treasure both their gifts and the quirks that others may find annoying. We taste the spice that makes their entire dish unique. Only when we value our partner intrinsically can empathy flow.

Empathy means that we acknowledge and validate our loved one's feelings. Positive or negative. Joyful or despairing. A universal human need is to have our feelings understood, not judged, not fixed, not negated, or dismissed.

Conversation is vital to understanding. Happy couples talk a lot. Little conversations throughout the day. They talk in bed in the morning and at night before they go to sleep. Dead-end couples, on the contrary, seem to get their entire talking life "over with" when they're falling in love. During those hormone-enhanced early days, they talk all night. They sit down for dinner at seven and don't leave the table until midnight. The restaurant closes around them. When they're fifty, though, they're sitting in the same restaurant in silence. We've all seen couples like this.

Amidst the struggles of life, conversation frequently devolves into functional topics: fixing the car, cleaning the house, paying the bills, getting the kids to school. Or trivia: the latest celebrity scandal. Talking about these things has its place. But lasting romance requires soul conversation. Without knowing the depth of our beloved, there is nothing real to love. All we see or hear is the superficial, the practical. We lose sight of the good stuff, the soul stuff.

The kind of talk that fosters intimacy is talk about the things in your life that intrigue or challenge you right now. Delights and dilemmas. Not topics of earth-shattering importance, but important topics for this day, this week, this month in your soul's journey.

We need to understand our mate's life as it is unfolding, day by day, week by week, and to have our own unfolding life understood by them. We need to talk and listen. All the time.

Pillar 2: To Involve

A blissful marriage requires hands-on involvement. It is not enough to tolerate the interests of our loved ones; it isn't even enough to support them. If we want love that lives and breathes, we must involve ourselves in our partners' interests. At least some of the time.

This fact was vividly illustrated to me recently. I had given a speech on this subject to a large organization. Three months later I was stopped by a woman who had been in the audience. She said that when she heard my speech she thought I was an unrealistic romantic. But when she got home she saw her husband in the spare room sorting his precious baseball cards. She'd never understood how a grown man could spend money on old bubble gum cards with badly printed pictures of dead baseball players. It was just stupid. But she said, "That night I was different. I went into his baseball shrine and asked him what made a certain card special. With that single question he lit up like a Christmas tree and spent the next 20 minutes showing me his favorite cards and why they were special to him. Then I topped myself," she went on to say, "I told him I wanted to go to a baseball card expo with him at the end of the month. You would have thought I had suddenly transformed into a Playboy bunny."

We don't have to be involved in *everything* our spouse does, but we should try to be involved in some of the special things. The best thing the woman with the card-fanatic husband told me was that *he* suddenly got more supportive of *her* interests as well. Research says that intimacy grows when people are willing to invest at least 7 hours a week on each other. This means seven hours of communication and experience-sharing, not seven hours of watching TV. Not seven hours of solving household problems. Seven hours of talking to each other, sharing "alive time," and being involved with each other's passions.

Pillar 3: To Affirm

One of the most powerful things we can do to amp up the wattage on a relationship is to constantly affirm, rather than negate, our partner or our friend.

Affirming is simple. As soon as you notice your partner doing something well, being kind or thoughtful, expressing her gifts, or looking good, you mention it. Say it as soon as you notice it. The habit of affirmation is one of the most powerful loving skills you can develop. Why we keep our positive thoughts a secret is a great mystery.

Learning the habit of affirmation takes practice and awareness. Luckily, it's a habit that quickly grows. Turns out, it feels as good to confer affirmations as it does to receive them.

Dan Baker, founding director of the Life Enhancement Center at Canyon Ranch, cites research confirming this. "When we affirm others, we use parts of our neo-cortex that generate positive moods. Affirming stimulates neurotransmitters that are mood elevators. Those who affirm and love others are making themselves happy." It's simple. Want to feel better? Make someone else feel better.

All of this takes conscious commitment. But what a payoff. It's the true nourishment that comes from being home for dinner.

MARRY YOUR BIGGEST FAN ON EARTH

I have two clients who are senior executives for the same company. They are unusual co-executives because they have been married to each other for more than 10 years. The company they work for is a high-pressure, multi-billion-dollar Fortune 500 organization. When I first started working with Chad, I couldn't help noticing his enthusiasm when he talked about his wife. He was wild about her in every way. He thought she was a brilliant executive—creative, compelling, able to get things done quickly. On a personal level, the raves were even sweeter; he called her an amazing wife and a gifted mother.

Carole spoke about Chad as if he were a god. The most brilliant, visionary leader she had every seen. A sensitive husband and a loving father. She freely used words like adore and admire and she meant them. To hear two people separately talk about each other with such affection and idealism is exceedingly rare. For husbands and wives in business together, it is virtually unheard of.

As I continued to work with Chad and Carole, I discovered two things. First, they use something called Active Advocacy. That is, they are each other's greatest fan and they aren't shy about making that known. Genuinely advocating for your loved one in the real world, in front of others, is a bold statement of love.

Second, they spend time together. Whenever they aren't working, they are together. When one of them travels, they keep in constant contact by phone and e-mail. It isn't just about keeping each other up to date, it's about what they are both feeling, it's about their hopes, dreams, and frustrations. They invest at least an hour a day in nothing but personal communication with each other. They have no secrets.

What is a relationship that is both sustaining and abundant? Well, how would you like to be married to someone who is your biggest fan on earth? Who makes your mother look like a wimp? What does it feel like to be with someone who is always interested in communicating their thoughts and feelings candidly and completely? That's a definition of true intimacy. It's the deepest connection human beings can have.

PART NINE

LIFESTYLE

CHAPTER 25

HONOR YOUR DESIGN IN YOUR LIFESTYLE

Let's look at the second element of our triple bottom line—lifestyle.

Our lifestyle consists of where we live and how we live. Lifestyles are either stressful or energizing. Stressful lifestyles suck energy out of us. Sustainable lifestyles give us energy—that "rip off the covers, can't wait to get out of bed and live this day" feeling.

Our personal Design is a key element in making sustainable lifestyle decisions. The activities in our "leisure" life that have the power to elevate our moods and passionately engage us are those that embrace our Design most fully. We never tire of them. They always give us juice.

Many of us have lost our sense of what brings us joy for its own sake. Life has become one big dulled-down, generic blah, punctuated by stress. To rise above the blah and anxiety of life-as-usual, we must learn to do things that turn up the volume on our joy, things that are healthy, uplifting, and restorative to our sense of well-being. And we must do them regularly.

I recommend creating a "Life List" of things that engage your Design. To make this Life List, pay attention to your true feelings. What activities consistently bring you joy, passion, and energy from the inside out? Write these activities down in a list, and then do them regularly. It's that simple.

But in addition to doing things we enjoy, we must also do things that we value. Things that have meaning to us and are consistent with our noblest Drive.

In short, all of our lifestyle choices need to be guided by the twin criteria: Value and Enjoy. If we consciously fill our lives with things we both value and enjoy, we can save the world and still be home for dinner.

Value = Save the World
Enjoy = Be Home for Dinner

VALUE AND ENJOY: BOTH + AND

Remember Both + And thinking? Well, it is important for our lifestyles as well. Both + And thinking enables us to say I can live where I most want to live, have a rich personal life and make my difference. It pushes our imagination higher to live our whole dream instead of a fraction of it. How? By choosing Both + And everyday.

The big Both + And question we must answer is how we integrate being a force for good (saving the world) and living our good life (being home for dinner). Our daily insight into achieving this whole comes from being quietly aware of what we both value and enjoy.

For instance, if we volunteer at a homeless shelter (what we value) doing something we have low interest or genuinely dislike, we'll become cranky and our service lousy. If we enjoy counseling and talking and encouraging people but all we do is wash dishes, we wilt. Or, if we love sports but only spend time with our children helping with homework or discipline, instead of going to games or coaching, our parenting will become pretty brittle.

Volunteer to do things you value by doing what you enjoy. Your discovery is that you enjoy the things that express your talents and your traits. If you enjoy communicating, make sure you can engage the homeless you are volunteering to serve in inspiring conversation. If you enjoy creating cleanliness and order, help keep the shelter clean and the dishes put away.

If you love the arts and your children, help with the school play. If your commute is drudgery, sucking your life energy out of your brain cells, use your commute to plan your best career move, to improve your mind, develop your talents, or network with people who can help. Above all, don't resign yourself to an exhausting, stress-filled life of draining self-discipline, disconnected from your design.

So, go for Both + And in your life. Create ways to do what you value AND you enjoy. Through it, you will find your Greatest Total Value to your family, your community, and your life. Your energy will grow as both your positive impact and your joy expand.

WHERE YOU LIVE

One of the most important lifestyle decisions we make is about where we live. The place we choose to call home can have an enormous effect on our ability to live in sustainable abundance. Too often, though, this choice is made passively—out of convenience or perceived economic necessity. We pick a home because it's near our job and affordable. Period.

Or, worse, we let our Self-Concept make the choice. And of course, it chooses a place based on the statement it wants to make to others. It cares about approval, not fulfillment. So it will often pick a place we can barely afford. And we end up working our lives away to pay the mortgage on a chunk of dirt and bricks that our souls don't even want.

Where we live ought to be a genuine source of enjoyment, stimulation, and deep soul satisfaction. If we are always coping with the down sides of where we live, whether that be a long commute, a too-expensive community, or a place that just doesn't "fit," we are not living in sustainable abundance.

Of course, for some of us to fulfill our Promise we may choose to live in the middle of suffering and trouble. Kent, a friend of mine who also teaches leadership, recently moved with his wife to an inner city neighborhood in the Northeast. He wants to help this community get back on its feet. He still travels around the world to work with corporate clients, but his real Promise is to transform his neighborhood by using his leadership wisdom in a roll-up-your-sleeves, face-to-face way. He figured if he was going to save the world right where he lives, he ought to live in a place that really needed saving.

On the other hand, it's all a choice. Even paradise needs saving. Consider Mark and Patria. Mark is a 31-year-old father and Patria a 28-year-old mother of two. Mark and Patria met and got married during college in Hawaii. Patria went on to get a master's degree in social work at Columbia University. After working in New York and Northern California, they followed their dream to live on the ocean in Hawaii. No, there was no inheritance or IPO. Just the will to really live as they wanted to. They moved to Hawaii's northeast shore. Patria is a social worker who helps battered souls regain their dignity. Mark is a stay-at-

> ## MARK and PATRIA
>
> We are consciously making decisions to follow our dreams and fulfill our life promises here in Hawaii. Nothing fancy—just on our own modest incomes. We feel lucky everyday. When we look back on various decisions we've made over the years, the pattern is that we've avoided making decisions based on money—or acquiring materials; our choices have been around pursuing our passions and dreams. We've taken to heart the advice that if you follow your passion, then the money needed to live will follow. The sense of community we enjoy here, is one of the things we love the most.

home dad and professional photographer. They rent a modest home on a beautiful beach with a slide from their back yard to the sand along a coral-fringed lagoon. They do all this without financial help from parents or permission from The Grid. They do it because they've been very clear on what they most value and enjoy. They choose to do what so many of us wish we could.

Know this: Wherever you would most like to live, there are people living right now who make no more money than you do, are no smarter than you are, and have no more skills than you do. Think about any resort area you've ever visited, every beautiful small town or exciting city anywhere in the world. Think about the remotest villages in Africa or New Guinea. People just like you have just figured how to live in these places to do what they value and enjoy. They, too, are keeping their Promise instead of just waiting for the right time.

THE LEADERSHIP PROFESSOR

I met Dave when I was teaching leadership and entrepreneurship at the University of San Diego. Dave was born in England where he learned to love golf and hate the cold. He became a toy inventor and created a highly profitable enterprise inventing and developing toys he licensed to the big toy companies. Eventually he began to feel the restless urge to fulfill a deeper Promise. He wanted to teach college students leadership. Not just a list of leadership skills and competencies but LEADERSHIP that leads to a better world. Dave is into it. He's won teaching awards everywhere he's taught. He also wanted to live in a place where he could golf year around. He first chose the University of San Diego and has since moved to Clemson University in South Carolina. Dave looked for a smaller town with the vitality of college students, warm weather and nature's beauty. He integrated his lifestyle, his family life, and his passionate career into a rhythm of personal sustainable abundance. Dave's life didn't just happen to him. He chose it.

LIVE ABUNDANTLY NOW
Part of living in sustainable abundance means living in a place you can afford in a way you can afford that our planet can afford, now. Not twenty years from now. There are lots of small towns and medium-sized cities away from America's crowded coastlines that offer a high quality of life at a reasonable price. It's often possible to buy a terrific home in one of these towns for a half, a quarter, a sixth of what you would pay for the same home in a more prestigious zip code.

Ask yourself this: How much does your zip code really contribute to fulfilling a life of sustainable abundance?

If you are buying a house, make sure it really supports your desires and values.

Many people buy homes they can afford but which are 60 to 90 minutes away from their job. So they spend three hours a day burning gas to commute from a bedroom they only sleep in to a job they don't like to pay for a house they rarely enjoy. The hope is that the price of the house will climb enough to pay for another house that is also going up in price in still another place they don't really like but that looks like a promising investment. They spend their lives trading up for more expensive mortgages. So how well has that worked?

A home is a home, not an investment.

Many of us don't even ask the most important question, which is: How will buying this house serve my noblest Drive (Value) and fulfill my soul's Desires (Enjoy)? Twenty-one percent of all CO^2 emissions come from the houses we live in and the energy it takes to run them. Living in a house with rooms we don't regularly use and in a place that makes daily travel a necessity maybe not be contributing to our happiness and may actually be keeping us from our Promise. Consider this. Have the people who have made the greatest contribution to the world always owned their own homes? Some have. Most haven't. And for many of us, the obsession of owning and paying for a home may be standing directly in the way of keeping our Promise.

If you can't comfortably afford to own a home, the stress of trying to own one will only make you focus on the money you don't have, instead of the gifts you do have. You might consider this strategy: travel light. Don't buy a home. Mass home ownership is a relatively new idea. It's great when homes are affordable, but we live in new times. The cost of rent in many parts of the country, even for nice homes in great areas, is often much lower than the cost of mortgage, insurance, taxes, and maintenance.

Real estate is wonderful as long as you own it and it doesn't own you. Don't give up living your abundant life by choosing a home and location you can't afford.

Life is the experience, not the stuff. We come with nothing. Leave with nothing. Ask your soul where you long to live and where you most want to keep your Promise and then go live there.

CHANGE HOW YOU THINK ABOUT CHANGE

If you could live anywhere in the world, where would it be? Why?

CHAPTER 26

HOW YOU LIVE

How we live, of course, is just as important as where we live.

HOW WE LIVE

Our lifestyles impact not only ourselves, but everyone else on "Spaceship Earth." Today we find ourselves on the verge of running short of everything because we are so terrific at turning things into money. But as the world's population continues to explode to 9 billion, in a few decades there are simply not enough resources to support our accelerating consumption. Today we have a world in which every 20 minutes, a species of animal or plant life disappears from the planet. More than 80 percent of the Caribbean coral reef cover has vanished since the 1970s. Fifty percent of the world's wetlands have been destroyed since 1900. Twenty four billion tons of fertile soil disappears each year. One-third of the planet's land surface is threatened by desertification....

I could go on for pages, but do I really need to? We know the world is in rough shape, due to the choices we've been making individually and collectively.

But we can do something. We can make simple and easy choices in our lifestyle that will collectively add up to a big difference.

A lot of us feel discouraged about trying to do anything. Sure, we might go out and get a hybrid car or recycle our garbage or buy fluorescent light bulbs, but then we hear they're opening a coal plant a day in China and we think: "There's no amount of light bulbs we could buy or gas we could save that would make a dent in even one new coal plant." So it seems hopeless.

But I encourage you to think about it differently. One way to look at it is that every time you make a choice, you're doing something that affects both the outer world and your inner world. And when you make a love-based choice, that choice adds to a chorus of other choices that are pro-planet, pro-civilization, and pro-future.

And that chorus of voices is rapidly growing. Just a few years ago people thought global warming was for tree-huggers and idiots. Now there is a general consensus that global warming is really happening and that if we don't do something about it, terrible things are going to happen. So now millions of people are demanding that our leaders pay attention and that businesses create products that don't abuse the environment.

As we're painfully aware, financial pressure is a major driver of stress. There is nothing you can buy that is worth the price of peace of mind. We live in a society "consumed by consumption." Our economy is driven by messages convincing us we don't have enough of what we need. But if we spend and behave intelligently, we have the power to feel content about our lifestyle. We can experience "enoughness" and abundance, even if we're not wealthy. We can do that by having the unique things that we truly value, we truly enjoy. Cool stuff that is cool just for us.

How do you know what your cool stuff is? Well, what are the things that you consume, buy, or use that you never get sick of? If you include these things in your life and cut out all the waste and filler, you can feel rich without a six- or seven-figure salary.

Americans waste gobs of money on fast food, for example. We eat faster than anyone on Earth. We don't taste our food; we inhale it. (We also have sex faster than any other people on earth. Go figure.) Instead of wasting money on overpriced, nutrition-free "food," you might ask yourself: "Do I really enjoy eating that much? Or is it simply a source of energy for me?" If that's true for you, load your cupboard with nutrition bars and your fridge with salad, and save your money for something you really love—like new music or an evening at the theatre once or twice a month. If, on the other hand, you really savor fine food, stop wasting your money on fast food, save up and go to truly excellent restaurants a couple of times a month. Celebrate food; it will make you feel rich. The same thing can be said about TVs, stereos, furniture, clothing, shoes. If it's something that has the power to sustain your emotional attention, save up for the best and buy it without guilt. But if it's just filler or for show, let it go.

If you want to live rich, pay close attention to what you really value and enjoy, and spend your money on those things. Minimize everything else. Then you can feel rich no matter what your income is. And when you feel rich, your unique gifts will glow.

ANDREW

Andrew is a young father with three small children. He and his wife read *Omnivore's Dilemma* and *In Defense of Food* by Michael Pollan. They got pretty alarmed about the quality of the average American's food supply. Andrew has always been a lover of great food. Even though they are a one-income family, they made an agreement that they were going to eat like kings. So a couple of times a week they go shopping as a family for the freshest locally grown food they can find. Andrew is extremely selective about the meat, vegetables, fish, and fruit he buys. Then each night he involves his family in food preparation. This includes his two girls, ages 10 and 7. Andrew is the chef and he makes exotic dishes that include wine reductions and soufflés.

He says he's part of the Slow Food Movement, a movement that started in Italy. It entails fresh locally grown food, great tasting recipes, and conversation during both the preparation and the eating of the meal. Andrew has brought Italy to his home. His home is modest, but his family eats gourmet-style and has lots of fun, interaction, and conversation as well. The point is that a high-quality sustainable lifestyle is possible. It's all a choice. And choosing how to live is the most important choice we make.

WHAT YOU BUY

In order to save the world and still be home for dinner, what you value must also be reflected in your day-to-day choices. Andrew advised me to be a more careful consumer of food. For instance, buy local. There are a number of reasons for this. First, local food is fresher and tastes better because you're getting it while it still contains all of its nutrients. Second, it reduces carbon dioxide emission because it doesn't have to travel as far. Small local farms are also generally more environmentally friendly than large-scale industrial agriculture operations and tend to utilize sustainable farming techniques. Third, buying local keeps your money in your community, supporting local farms, creating local jobs, protecting open spaces and natural ecosystems. Fourth, it's the easiest way to cut out processed food. (*A great resource to help you find local farms is at www.LocalHarvest.org. Also, consider growing your own.*)

What we buy makes a huge difference in the world. As consumers we wield great power to make an impact via the things we buy and the companies we support. And because consumers now have access to so much information, we can make informed decisions in everything we buy. Every time we buy a product, we are casting our vote for that product and company.

Make your vote count. Become a conscious consumer. Car companies built gas hogs because we wanted them (well, they told us we wanted them and we believed them). A consciously led life means rewarding companies that make things that are healthy and environmentally responsible. These products and companies are on the increase. Voting with our wallets is the surest way to convince business to create sustainable products.

Find out where a particular product comes from. Learn about the working conditions for the person or people who created it. Find out if the raw materials used and the production methods are environmentally friendly. There are great resources available that can tell you where to go for "green" products. One of these is the Conscious Consumer Marketplace, provided by The New American Dream at newdream.org. Co-op America also has a National Green Pages directory at coopamerica.org/pubs/greenpates that is a complete guide to eco-friendly products.

Research the companies you buy products from on the web. Often company websites carry information about the good they do under headings of Corporate Social Responsibility. There are a lot of great companies that are making a difference. Support them. Just the other day in a workshop I was teaching I mentioned the water purification processes Procter & Gamble has developed to try to eradicate water-born diseases and death by diarrhea in children. A student said, "I didn't know that. Do they make water filters for tap water?" And I said, "Yeah, they do." She replied, "Well, I'm gonna buy theirs"

Purists complain that most companies are doing more harm than good and their small-time good deeds are just for P.R. Maybe so. But

A Few Suggestions for Saving Energy

I could fill this book with ways we can make a difference, but then I wouldn't have room to talk about anything else. Here, just for starters, are a few simple suggestions for saving energy that you and your family can do, starting today:

- Move your refrigerator away from the stove, dishwasher, or heat vents. Make sure the door seals are airtight.
- Wait until your dishwasher is full before you run it, but don't overload it.
- Use pots that fit the size of the burners on your stove. Use lids so you can cook at a lower temperature.
- Match the water level and temperature settings on your washer to the size of your load. Don't run the machine for just a few items.
- Clean your dryer lint filter before you put in every load.
- Make sure your water heater is set to 120 degrees. Some thermostats are preset to 140 degrees, which isn't necessary.
- Use compact fluorescent bulbs. These bulbs provide as much light as regular incandescent bulbs while using just one-fourth the energy.
- Replace or clean furnace filters monthly.
- Install ceiling fans. They'll cool you off in the summer and promote heating efficiency in the winter.
- Turn off the TV when no one is watching it. The same goes for computers, radios and stereos—if no one is using it, turn it off.
- Turn off all the appliances at the surge protector/control strip––that four- or six-plug extension chord that you plug all your computer things into. Some devices, like modems or other networking boxes are drawing small amounts of power all the time.
- Unplug cell-phone chargers from the wall when not in use. They consume the same amount of electricity, whether they're charging a phone or not.

These choices pertain only to energy conservation and are only a few of the hundreds of things we can do. We can make similar choices around issues of waste, pollution, poverty, racism, health, education, etc. etc. If everyone made just a few conscious choices, like these, every day, imagine the difference we could make.

many companies are doing more than ever before, and a new generation of leaders is coming up that will turn their Corporate Social Responsibility into core corporate strategy. I know because I work with these young leaders. If you want to accelerate the process, call or e-mail the companies you buy from and congratulate them on their good works and ask them what their plans are to clean up their total act.

It matters. Consumers rule the future.

Are you interested in sustainable tips and thoughts on ways to make a difference in your lifestyle, career, and relationships?

Go to SavetheWorldBook.com and subscribe to the SAVE THE WORLD daily email. It truly is a daily dose of world saving inspiration.

OUR CHOICES MATTER

Change does happen when each of us stands for the future. Never believe you are alone. Our choices and our voices create change. There is a collective consciousness and YOU permanently change it every time you make a conscious choice!

There is another reason to live in a more thoughtful way. It is the internal peace that comes from making good choices. Of course you could say, "With so much waste and pollution, what difference does it make if I do a little of that?" Well, it makes a huge difference, not only to your children and the people in your circle, but to you. Every human being must answer the question, "What do I stand for?" At the end of our lives we want to look in the mirror and say, "I did what I really believed in." This is integrity. And so every time we choose to do something that is sustaining and life-affirming, it really matters. Deeply and truly. Never forget it.

CHANGE HOW YOU THINK ABOUT CHANGE

What do you stand for?

PART TEN

CAREER

CHAPTER 27

IS THIS THE BEST I CAN DO?

The final element of our triple bottom line is career. Career is essential because it is perhaps where we can make our greatest impact on the world. Humans are wired for work. We long to be productive. To matter not only for who we are but also for what we do. In fact, our work is so important to us that we too frequently let it define us instead of us defining our work. But this is backwards. The opportunity of our career in today's world is to determine for ourselves the Greatest Total Value we can provide. This means that using our individual talents and traits in a combination that is virtually unique, creating value that no one else can. When we do this, we simultaneously *create* work that is most personally satisfying to us and offers the most value to the world.

Most of us work between 2,000 and 3,000 hours a year. That's a lot. Over 40 years it means 80 to 100,000 hours of work. That's either a lot of time to fulfill our Promise or a lot of time to waste.

So what are we trying to accomplish with all this time? That's the question we must ask.

The challenge is to take the time to deeply consider our choices. Who do we work for? Does the work we do produce real value? Do we work in a place that is psychologically healthy? Does the organization produce more value than it consumes? Is it building or destroying the future? Are we proud of our workplace, our company, our industry? Would our children or our mother be proud of us? Is our work the expression of our deepest and most noble longings? Could it be?

When it comes to career, there are basically three kinds of work we can do. First, there is work that is destructive to people and the planet. This is work that exploits human weakness, preys on insecurities, greed, and addiction. It poisons people and pollutes our environment. This kind of work is actively destroying our future. Lots of nice, talented people do it. Mostly without thinking about it.

Second is work that doesn't really matter. Making and selling products and services that are generic. If they disappeared, no one would notice.

Third, there is work that genuinely contributes to the quality of life on our planet. This kind of work opportunity exists in every field. If we consciously choose to make our difference, we can turn entertainment into inspiration, law into justice, and janitorial work into disease prevention.

My experience is that if we get clear on our highest, love-based motives, opportunities to work at this level will appear everywhere. Perhaps they'll appear where we already work. For example, a software engineer I taught works at Hewlett-Packard and got his colleagues to volunteer to help small non-profits with their databases. I recently had breakfast with a young Intel executive who is helping implement technology in hospitals and homes to reduce medical errors and medical costs. After a recent training session for Nike, I learned that their famous LIVESTRONG cancer cure campaign they support through the Lance Armstrong Foundation was the big idea of Ron, an inspired web marketing professional whose pure personal motive has resulted in nearly 70 million dollars raised for cancer research. Who is Ron? He's just a guy with a noble idea. He's *you*, he's *me*; armed with wisdom and passion.

The world is asking all of us the same question: What can you do right now, right where you are to save the world? Answering that question today and everyday will lead us to the career we most desire. Building a sustainable career begins with an awareness that we are all responsible for how we invest our talent and energy. It's something we all need to think about every day. When we look in the mirror, we must ask our soul, "How much good am I really doing? Is this the best I can do?"

SAVING THE WORLD

Parker is one individual I know who settles for nothing less than working at the third level of work value. The first time I met Parker at the Beach Grass Café in Solana Beach I was stunned by his energy and enthusiasm. In his late fifties, Parker really has his hands full. He's a marketing manager at the University of California San Diego's extension program.

The program offers classes to adult learners not only throughout the San Diego region, but throughout the world. Parker told me that virtually all the corporations he knew in the San Diego region were clamoring for education on Corporate Social Responsibility and sustainable business practices.

The interesting thing about our meeting was that it took place at a café in which Parker had just made a bakery delivery. You see he and his wife are also social entrepreneurs. His wife owns a gourmet bakery and is up in the wee hours of every morning leading her teenage workforce in making healthy, delicious goodies for store customers and area bistros. And it isn't just the organic ingredients that their bakery uses that make them social entrepreneurs. The primary motivation of Parker and his wife is to educate young high schoolers, many of whom are recently immigrated Spanish-speaking students, on the joys and responsibilities of owning one's own business dedicated to healthy products and improving the community.

After fifteen years, the business has scores of successful "graduates" who are pursuing their Promise. Parker and his wife are drawing up the legal papers to donate their business to three local area churches: a Jewish synagogue, a Protestant church, and a Catholic one. Church leaders will have to agree to continue to run the bakery as a sustainable business to help feed the indigent, employ the unemployed, and teach students sustainable abundance. What an idea.

Nobody could have created this career for Parker and his wife; they simply invented it. But that's just the half of it. Parker's day job led him to create the Responsible Enterprise Forum for UCSD's extension. He, along with other UCSD leaders, have a vision to help San Diego become a leader in community sustainability within the next decade. They've gotten me involved in leading executive seminars bringing together CEOs, non-profit leaders, marketing directors, HR directors, and corporate philanthropy specialists. Together we hope to stimulate community collaboration around strengthening San Diego's sustainable economic base and helping to create solutions to our environmental and social issues. The result will be a cycle of enrichment where the lives of the students as well as those of executives and employees of area companies are energized by a common vision.

So what is it that makes Parker special? It's simply his tireless will to fulfill his Promise through his work. He will settle for nothing less.

He didn't ask anybody's permission to invent these ideas or to live his incredible life; he just does it.

FOUR IMPORTANT QUESTIONS

The quest for each of us in giving our Greatest Total Value through our career is to continually seek out places where our unique talents, traits, and experiences enable us to become *one of a kind*. If we are going to both succeed and be happy in our work, we need to leverage our unique gifts to their highest potential. There is nothing to be gained in being average. We must define our greatness and then deliver it.

To do that, it helps to answer four questions:

1. What is my Promise, the greatest value I can imagine creating?
2. What is unique about my work? What's my secret sauce?
3. What am I doing now that's wasting my time or getting in my way? What things must I stop investing effort and attention on?
4. What is the one thing I need to *over*-invest my time, effort, and energy in so as to leverage the full value of my traits and talents?

Then, as Mr. Nike says, "Just do it." No one can be better at being you than you. And when you go big on who you are designed to be, your Promise will ignite.

BECOME AN EXPERT

To "go big" on our Design in our career, we must become experts. When our traits and talents are linked to specific knowledge and experience, that's when our value is turbocharged. It takes about ten years to truly become an expert in a field, so it's important that we choose our focus of expertise carefully and with sound self-knowledge. We must not only be *willing* but *excited* to invest the time and effort necessary to become an expert. We must have a burning desire for mastery in our chosen field.

The good news is that the world values experts in nearly everything. Even a dog trainer has his own TV show (*The Dog Whisperer*). For that matter, so does a bounty hunter (*Dog, the Bounty Hunter*). How about becoming an expert in something that directly contributes to the future of humanity?

ANYONE CAN BE AN EXPERT

The role of grocery checker is quickly becoming an endangered species. More and more stores are using automated self-checkouts. Soon electronic tags will be put in product packages so that you can fill your cart, swish your credit card, and your whole cart full of purchases will be checked out in a matter of seconds. No lines, no waiting, just get the stuff and head for your car.

It's all great unless you're a grocery checker. So what's Whole Foods' big idea? Turn their front line staff into nutritionists and meal planners.

The Food Network on television has proven to be a huge success because people are fascinated by food. People are always looking for inventive, nutritious recipes and novel foods they haven't tried before. But rarely can you find this information at the place you buy food. It almost always has to come from the Internet, from a book or from some famous TV chef.

That doesn't make much sense in the opinion of Whole Foods. Their idea is to put food experts right there in the store—in the veggie isle and at the seafood counter. Food consultants at the point of purchase. Of course, this is going to require checkers to become experts on nutrition and cuisine and unleash their friendly personalities. But that sounds like a far more interesting and satisfying career to me. Does it to you?

THE QUALITIES OF EXPERTISE

There are several important qualities we need to embrace if we want to become experts in our specialized field of one.

First of all, we must be willing to engage in disciplined *practice*. Get busy pursuing what you want and practice it to a point of failure. When I first started public speaking 25 years ago, I was horrible. My first paying client was Aetna Insurance. They asked for their money back. I stunk. My failure motivated me. I spoke for free whenever I could, I taught free classes and I got a speaking coach. Now public speaking is an effortless joy, but it was a climb. We only grow more competent when we push ourselves to the absolute limits of our current knowledge or expertise. Practice, in time, can lead to *learned intuition*, an unconscious feel for our "game." An accomplished professional athlete seems to know where everyone is on the field or the floor. They can adjust their swing in imperceptible ways that allow them to hit the ball further and more accurately. That's the kind of thing a true expert can do. Practice is what makes it happen.

Second, becoming an expert demands that we are open-minded and creative. The world needs new solutions. What the world needs is genuine new ideas, not just old ideas in new costumes masquerading as innovation. True creativity seeks a way to leapfrog over current limits to create new, unexpected value. We must be willing to challenge our own prejudices and opinions with new data. We must be constant learners seeking cutting edge concepts from mentors, books, and the web. We don't have to be creating iPods to be innovative. A psychologist can be innovative. A housepainter, a teacher, anyone. It all depends on whether we are looking to create value in new ways.

Third, a successful expert must have integrity. The world wants to know that we can be trusted. Will we keep our Promise? Will we show up on time and be in the heat of the action? Most of all, do you really care? If love is our core drive, the motive for every way we create value, then our commitment will be authentic. That's literally priceless. Authentic commitment to create the Greatest Total Value possible is what the world desperately seeks. Integrity not only makes human sense, it makes market sense. If we can be trusted, we will be valued.

Fourth, we must also pair our expertise with virtuous wisdom. Knowledge has no inherent morality. Knowledge can be used to create biological weapons or a cure for cancer. There is no innate goodness in expert knowledge. The pursuit of virtuous goals requires our will to do so. What our world needs is experts willing to act in ways that save our future, plain and simple. To put expert knowledge to its highest purpose is to create the Greatest Total Value for humanity.

Fifth, an effective expert must be adept at social intelligence. This term was original coined by Dr. Daniel Goleman. Experts with high social intelligence listen not only to words but feelings. They don't just hear the content of others' concerns; they hear the intent of their emotions. An expert veterinarian, for example, does not just treat an animal's symptoms, she reads the emotional needs of the pet owner. People with high social intelligence are also able to collaborate, which means synthesizing other people's expert knowledge into new combinations. It means finding common ground, higher and higher up the mountain of value.

Finally, experts need to evangelize their vision and spread their knowledge. Expertise becomes more powerful when their knowledge is transmitted to others. Teaching, writing, communicating the essence of our wisdom is how all progress is accelerated. Keeping our Promise depends on us becoming an expert. An expert in "doing what we came for."

DON'T "FIT IN"

When we become an expert we no longer have to figure out where we fit into the world so we can make a living. As Loretta Lynn famously said, "Be first, best, or different." After all, fitting in will never make us outstanding. Rather, it is often where we *don't* fit that we can create our highest value and reap our greatest success. It is called unconventional job fit. Most of us can probably make our biggest difference by *being* different.

Let's say you went to a job center and tested out as a math-oriented, problem-solving introvert. You'd probably be told to become an accountant. You'd be encouraged to spend the rest of your life keeping track of other people's money. But what if you took those skills and talents and applied them in a new way? Today there is a whole new field of socially responsible investing. What if you made a specialty of tracking the *social* returns on financial investments? Unconventional application of conventional career skills is changing how business looks at itself.

Or consider this. Most people view filmmaking as just entertainment. But nothing has done more to change the way people view climate change than the Oscar-winning documentary, *An Inconvenient Truth*. In fact, social research is pretty clear that art and entertainment do more to change people's attitudes and behavior than laws or preaching. Socially conscious filmmaking is a way to take the gift of visual storytelling and use it to save the world.

It doesn't matter what your gifts and interests are. You can use them in a way that not only elevates you from the crowd, but also makes a difference in the world.

Don't compete, be unique. And turn up the volume. Greatness is always the result of being original. Don't *copy* greatness. Be great.

SIGNPOSTS OF A CAREER THAT MATTERS

Many people ask me, "How can I know what's possible for me? How can I know whether I am using my gifts and interests in ways that create my greatest value?" One way is to answer questions in the following 12 areas.

This will help you evaluate whether you are headed in the right direction:

1. Intrinsic Enjoyment

Would I do this work without pay? Is the inner payoff so direct and the process so engaging that I often have to be told to stop?

2. Energy Gain

Am I exhausted by my work or energized by it? Does my work generate the enthusiasm to do more and more of the same? Or am I a POW (Prisoner of Work)?

3. Soul Compatibility

Does my work reflect the longings of my soul? Is it something I feel called to do? Does it inherently satisfy the deepest core of me? Or would I secretly rather be doing something else?

4. True Choice

Would I choose to do this work if no one cared? If it didn't make anyone proud or create any social status, would it still be my choice? Would I choose to do it simply because I want to?

5. Success without Strain

Does success in my chosen area come relatively easily to me? Is the way I uniquely approach problems consistent with success in the work I am doing? Does the work just seem to make intuitive sense to me? Or do I have to put in long hours and make extraordinary effort just to achieve average results?

6. Desire for Mastery

Am I always naturally seeking to improve at what I do? Does the desire for mastery in this field come naturally to me? Am I a hungry learner or do I have to force myself to acquire new skills? Do I ask advice and seek mentors?

7. Growth

Is my work an avenue to new knowledge, new skills, and new experiences that make me feel as if I am personally growing? Does the work call me to become the person I desire to be?

8. Matters to Me

Do I personally think and feel this work is important? Do I think the world would miss out on something pretty special if I didn't do it?

9. Matters to Others

Does the work matter to others? Does it make a positive difference? Am I doing it *primarily* to make money or to create value in the world?

10. Best Opportunity

Does my work permit me to distinguish myself in such a way that I become a virtual category of one? Unique, indispensable, in demand? The "go to" person in my chosen skill area?

11. Compensation

If compensation were not an issue—that is, if I were paid the same whether I were president, salesperson, or janitor—is this the work I would choose to do? If so, is the pay I'm getting reasonable? Fair?

12. Collaboration versus Flying Solo

Do I like working collaboratively or flying solo? Does my work reflect this preference? Is my work aligned with my social nature?

IT REALLY IS ABOUT SAVING THE WORLD

The pinnacle of work value occurs when we see our work as a means to enrich and serve others. To do Good. This is true for every job. When singers and comedians are asked about their greatest satisfactions, many report that it comes from fan letters saying their song offered hope in a time of despair or their joke brought laughter in a time of sickness.

All of us are called to change the world. It starts when we decide to serve and lift others through the expression of our Design. Few of us will win a Nobel Prize or get our picture on a magazine cover. That doesn't matter. When we change *our* world, *the* world changes. And changing the world in a way we're Designed to is what we came to do.

Work in the twenty-first century offers the greatest opportunity for personal fulfillment in world history. Don't let your unsatisfying job turn into a career because you never took the time to decide what you most deeply desired. Become uniquely great at something you care about, then either start an enterprise or join one that is deeply committed to amplifying your value. In this day and age, anything less is a waste of your energy.

MAKE YOUR WORK GREAT

Lately a lot has been written about creating great, motivating, employee-centered workplaces. Lists of "employers of choice" abound the Internet. But reality slapped many of these well-meaning companies across the face in the recent "Great Recession." Layoffs, chain-sawed benefits, overwork and relentless stress caused many employees to become cynical about their "most admired" employer. Welcome to twenty-first century business.

Vicious business cycles, relentless competitive pressures and disruptive technologies are creating big gaps from what employees want from their organizations and what can be delivered. In the real world no one can promise you an excellent, personally supportive boss, friendly colleagues, adequate resources and meaningful work all of the time. So it's time to stare reality in the face and take responsibility to make our jobs great.

In a recent global workforce study reported in the Harvard Business Review, we increasingly want the same things from our work. Over 85 percent of us want work that contributes to a better society and a healthier environment. Second we want flexible working arrangements such as flextime and telecommuting. Yes, I know it sounds like confirmation that we want to save the world and still be home for dinner.

Well, our employers are increasingly giving us flexibility. It's becoming an accepted norm. As for meaning, that's our job. I went through the '80s helping companies write mission statements and declare their values. But a top-down approach to meaning doesn't work. Never did.

Most of the best social good and sustainability initiatives are innovations of employees rather than some overburdened CEO. While it's true that some companies have a toxic culture that strangles good before it can produce gain, there are millions of employers with positive intentions that can provide a platform for big ideas to save the world as long as it is economically sustainable. Remember Mike's redemptive sandals or Michael's film company, Patria's social work, Dave's leadership teaching or Parker's Bakery. The point is look carefully at your employer right now. Can you talk about creating the Greatest Total Value for all? If so, stand up and lead. Organizations with noble intentions and future-centered views can be found in virtually every town and city. If you are going to work for someone, work for someone you respect. And make them great.

Are the social and environmental issues that are important to you respected in your workplace?

Are you proud to work for your employer?

Is your company valued and respected by your employees?

Go to SavetheWorldBook.com and take the *Who Do You Work For?* survey or the *Who Works for You?* survey.

CHAPTER 28

THE TOTAL TRANSFORMATION
OF ENTERPRISE

Yes, the time has never been better to start or work for an enterprise that indeed "saves the world." This is because we are on the verge of whole new levels of technological breakthrough that will enable us to create everything we need directly from atoms and molecules instead of from iron ore, precious metals, and oil. We are on the verge of solving the problem of sustainable clean energy. We are on the verge of solving the riddles of disease. We are on the verge of creating sustainable abundance—based on the economics of ideas, rather than the economics of things.

But many of these advances will take 50 years or more to come into widespread use. If we are going to avoid planet burn-out, trade wars, structural unemployment, chronic under-employment, market disruptions, corporate extinction and a steady diet of boxed "mac and cheese," we need leadership of a different kind, NOW. Leadership that is committed to creating a future of sustainable abundance. This will require a huge leap in the evolution of capitalism.

It's not that capitalism is bad. It's just that on its own, it's not "good" either. Capitalism is morally neutral. It has no moral intent on its own. That's what humans are for. Capitalism without virtue rewards pollution, corruption, piracy, cartels, monopolies, exploiters, and unsafe working conditions more easily than innovation, quality, and good service. Raw, financially driven capitalism rewards anything that reduces cost and increases price. Anything. Even Adam Smith, capitalism's philosopher, knew that. Before he wrote *Wealth of Nations* he wrote *Moral Sentiments*, which makes the case that virtue is at the core of all enlightened self-interest. He never intended for butchers to cheat or bakers to poison their customers for a few shillings and then leave town. We live in an age that was unimagined by eighteenth century economic philosophers. The size and scope of power of global businesses tied to constant advances in technology have become the most potent force on our planet. Whether it's a force for good or is a force simply to concentrate more wealth and power without regard to the world we are creating is simply a leadership choice.

The problem we face is that global capitalism works so well it is destroying our resources at an ungodly rate. We should not be surprised by this. Capitalism's unending flaw is that short-term growth and profits easily mask the future suffering caused by greed and incompetence. This disconnection between immediate financial rewards and long-term value building is a huge fly in the ointment called our future. But the core problem is not capitalism itself. The problem is our refusal to use its power wisely. We must create a sustainable agenda for the future. We must take the efficiency of capitalism to a higher level of purpose. This is nothing less than the transformation of enterprise.

THE GREATEST ECONOMIC OPPORTUNITY IN HISTORY

Almost all social movements start with reformers shouting repentance. "Stop!" "Don't pollute!" "Don't waste!" "Don't buy all that stuff!" "Don't have all that fun!" They often get a lot of early converts. Angry folks. They shake their fists at the rest of us for our wasteful ways. However, after reformers get a core group of supporters, they mostly end up talking to themselves. They may publish magazines; they may have websites; they may be great at self-righteous chest-thumping. But they don't change the world.

Meaningful change only happens when the conversation shifts from "Don't do this" to "Let's do that." Instead of *don't pollute*, we shift to *heal the earth*.

Real change is all about opportunity, not reform.

The world craves products that are creatively conceived to offer solutions. Healthful and helpful products to replace the ones that are killing us. This is the great economic opportunity of the twenty-first century. Instead of "Don't buy that; it poisons" we say, "Here, buy this; it cures!"

CORPORATE SOCIAL OPPORTUNITY

The term Corporate Social Responsibility became popular a few years ago. It's the principle that business organizations have a responsibility to their workforce and the communities in which they operate to be good corporate citizens. CSR asks business leaders to reduce pollution, adopt fair labor practices, give to local charities, and use local suppliers. Most business leaders viewed Corporate Social Responsibility like a tax. It was something you have to do to maintain a positive reputation. So it was always about public relations getting their message out, encouraging employees to volunteer, and donating to usually local charities. Many businesses are still doing just that, CSR. Good, but not great.

Now the demand is for much more than that. Consumers want businesses to be responsible for how products are designed, manufactured, used, and disposed of. Highly talented employees are increasingly looking for employers who are committed to producing significant social and environmental benefits. For organizations that embrace this change, vast opportunity awaits. Opportunity to set themselves apart, to rethink how products are designed and used, and to take waste out of product development and manufacturing. And how to solve some of the most challenging problems of humanity. With this mindset, Corporate Social Responsibility is now becoming Corporate Social Opportunity (CSO).

CSO requires moral maturity at the highest level. It asks us to be more than law abiding, it asks us to be *good*. The highest level of ethics challenges us with the question, "How much good can we do?" When this is translated to a business enterprise, it stimulates the drive to do Good first, then Grow, and finally Gain. When a business culture thinks in terms of doing Good first, it opens up new ways of thinking that impact the purpose and quality of its products and services.

Imagine sitting in a strategy meeting where you were all gathered to answer the question, "How much good can we create for our customer and for each other?" I'm talking sustainable good. Smart good. Good that is so valued it creates a huge profit margin, even if that's not its primary intention.

At first you may think this kind of thinking is too idealistic. But it isn't. It is *strategic*. It's the level of thinking that truly creates sustainable abundance.

When Howard Schultz started Starbucks he knew he wanted it to stand for something. Something more than expensive, Italian-sounding coffee drinks. So he made a commitment that every employee that worked 20 hours would have full health insurance. An outrageous idea. Yet it's an idea that has generated a highly engaged employee culture in an industry notorious for indifference. Next he decided that he would promote fair-trade coffee meaning he would buy coffee from growers in developing nations at sustainable prices. Prices that insured growers a living wage. In the cutthroat cage fighting of global world commerce this makes no sense. But if you're after sustainable abundance, it makes perfect sense. Next time you visit a Starbucks pick up their pamphlet on all the humanitarian projects they have a hand in. All of these efforts have a huge brand payoff that helps drive Starbucks' positive mojo.

Corporate Social Opportunity is also blooming in the land of tulips. ING, the giant Dutch Bank, leases cars in Europe that have carbon offset payments built into the monthly lease payment. Thus every car they lease under the program is carbon neutral. Yes, CSO is ramping up. Nearly every cell phone and computer maker is trying to drastically reduce power consumption and make their products out of organic materials. Today cell phones have cute names like "chocolate." But tomorrow they may be edible! The point is CSO thinking is happening everywhere. In retail, manufacturing, transportation...everywhere.

Business becomes Corporate Social Opportunity if we simply look at it that way. Think about this: Virtually every product that we use is going to have to be reinvented in the next 50 years to be ecologically responsible and sustainable. Think about what an astonishing opportunity this presents. It's no less than the greatest economic opportunity in the history of the world.

Are you still interested in grumbling and shouting at others to stop, or are you ready to start?

BLANK SNOWBOARDS

I came across Rob, known as "Danger" to his friends, through a business associate, and I soon found that he is one guy who is all about seeing the opportunities of CSO. From the time Rob first got on a snowboard at the age of 10, he was hooked. And since then he has spent every spare moment on the mountain. It is his one true passion. He loves everything about it: the thrill of the ride, the friends, the gnarly beauty of nature and fresh powder. Even as he's gotten older, snowboarding has never lost its hold on him. After graduating from college, getting married, and having three kids, snowboarding remained on his mind. It's simply who he is. It's what he was made for. So Rob, along with some friends, created Blank Snowboards.

But Blank Snowboards isn't just another snowboard company; its entire business is founded on CSO. You see, Rob found that he can sell a board that's as good as or better than all of the big name boards but at a fraction of the cost by eliminating most of the waste. He sells most of his boards over his website (blanksnowboards.com) to cut out the middleman costs and reduce the carbon emissions created by shipping to stores that customers drive to. He does not pay pros to travel to promote his brand. His boards are literally blank. You are the rider. You are the brand. Pretty clever. So not only does he provide an amazing price to his customers, he reduces waste in the process.

Rob also wants to contribute proactively to healing the planet, so for every board he sells he makes a donation to a non-profit focused on planting trees and replenishing CO^2. You see, the core of his boards are wood. And the CO^2 generated by traveling to snowy mountains is significant. So for each board he sells, he makes a donation that replenishes the wood for your board and the carbon for your snow resort travel during the life of the board. He calls it "Buy a Board, Plant A Tree." After all, he says, if it stops snowing, the fun is over.

Rob has found that he can save the world and be home for dinner and have a great time doing it. He's doing it on his terms and he loves every minute. He sees the high competitive world we live in not as a burden but as an opportunity to do something healthy and innovative, and he sees his part in helping the environment not as a responsibility but as an opportunity to make a difference. That's Corporate Social Opportunity.

CHAPTER 29

A SHINING NEW IDEA

The leading edge of Corporate Social Opportunity is the transformation of enterprise into Socially Strategic Enterprise (SSE). Enterprise can be defined as organized human activity designed to create value. It used to be that we would broadly divide human enterprise into for-profit and not-for-profit. Non-profit enterprise would include charities and foundations as well as government services. Most everything else was business designed to make owners personally rich. As we've reached the vanishing point of sustainability Socially Strategic Enterprise has emerged. It incorporates the efficiencies, disciplines and rewards of for-profit business with the broader interests of directly solving humanitarian and environmental challenges.

Figure 29.1: Socially-Strategic Enterprise

Socially Strategic Enterprise is a far bigger idea than industrial or financial capitalism of the twentieth century. It literally transforms the ethical vision of Good, Grow, Gain into sustainable, profitable business. It challenges us to think about free enterprise not as the freedom to exploit, pollute, and poison, but rather as the freedom to create a better world. Free enterprise as a means for doing good. Imagine if we could rethink capitalism in this way.

We can. In fact, it's happening already.

I'm talking about much more than CSR. All that's good, but wholly insufficient to save the world. It's giving aspirin to a cancer victim. I'm even talking about much more than first stage CSO, which is moneymaking in a responsible, environmentally sustainable way. Socially Strategic Enterprise is based entirely on a new business model.

"Socially Strategic" means you earn your core Profit from 1) increasing People's well-being and/or 2) saving our Planet. Making money *by* saving the future. This demands a whole new way of thinking about how to produce a product or service and how it is used or consumed, and most of all what its beneficial impact will be. People, Planet, and Profit are the new triple bottom line of business. When we begin to measure the impacts of our choices on all three, the very way we create value changes.

Socially Strategic businesses go after huge challenges. They don't seek to limit ecological damage, they seek to reverse it. They seek to proactively heal our planet. You get the idea.

Socially strategic enterprises are not only good; they can be enormously successful. They can grow steadily and produce abundant profits. Often they are market leaders. They reward their employees, offer meaningful work and personal growth, benefit their communities, and improve the environment—all at the same time. The world is better off because of them.

Our future depends on this kind of company. If you're not working for one, you might want to be. Or you might want to think about starting one. Or turning your current job into a socially strategic position. The great social-entrepreneur, Muhammad Yunus has embraced this concept in a huge way. He calls it simply social business. He's helped found over 15 socially strategic, money-making enterprises bringing cell phone and Internet service to remote, rural areas. He's helped develop sustainable medical clinics, textile marketing co-ops and a yogurt production and sales business with the French company Donnone. That's Social Strategic Enterprise in action. Yunus has undoubtedly done more to lift people from grinding multi-generational poverty than any human being in history. Not bad for a college professor. And that's the point. Yunus wasn't a banker looking for new customers. He was an economist looking for a way to help millions out of poverty. His starting point changed everything.

Socially strategic thinking is just beginning to be noticed by the world's largest corporations. But at least they're talking about it. And some are doing great things. They are being inspired by small companies and non-profits that are changing the rules. Social Strategic Enterprise uses the energy of innovation and the urgency of competition to solve human problems such as poverty, illiteracy, environmental pollution, and pervasive health problems. It's all about doing well by doing good.

Socially Strategic Enterprise is the new wave. And it's crashing on the shores of commerce everywhere. Some of my clients including Johnson & Johnson, the health care company that sells us medicine, medical devices, band-aids, and baby powder is committing to creating a new sustainable business based on wellness because that's the great new frontier of creating value. General Electric is making wind-turbines and organic LED lights. Rainbird, the sprinkler company, is becoming a technological powerhouse in water conservation. But this isn't just for big companies. There are thousands of start-ups gaining ground with bio-fiber clothing, smog-eating cement coatings, algae based bio-fuels to name only a few.

An increasing number of clients and students ask me how they can conceive of Social Strategic Enterprise solutions to the challenges we face. I point them to a little model my colleague and I developed to accelerate our momentum to sustainable abundance.

What I help enterprises do is consider how they might add dramatically to the triple bottom line of People, Planet, and Profit in each one of these categories. In the workplace, how can we create more fully committed employees and suppliers by engaging them in value creation to save the world? In the marketplace, how can our organization create unique value by creating sustainable solutions through breaking down the barriers of cost, time, and skill that stand in the way of creating new customers? In our local and global communities, what problem can we

help solve that we are an expert in that will build our brand and excite
our people? What I find is that when we begin with the right questions
we will come up with new answers. And most times, those answers are
mind blowing.

Figure 29.2: Momentum to Sustainable Abundance
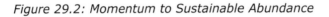

BIG PROMISE

For organizations to be authentically socially strategic, they must start
with a Big Promise. A Promise is more than good intentions. It's more
than a high tone mission statement. A Big Promise is a specific commitment to do something that matters to humanity. That Promise inspires
the core strategy of the enterprise, it is the driver of its culture, and it is
the substance of its brand. The whole enterprise is committed to their
Promise. Its direct advantage is the velocity of employee innovation and
the fierce loyalty of its customers.

BECOMING A SOCIALLY-STRATEGIC PERSON

Socially strategic thinking isn't just for companies. It's also for us, as
individuals. It promotes a virtuous cycle of unique value creation linked
to our social good, environmental health, and more fulfilling work. It

is hitting a tipping point. More of us want to work for and buy from companies who are wise enough to eliminate pollution, enhance the environment, and create new products that genuinely enrich our lives. As a society we are no longer preferring these qualities but insisting on them. We no longer have to feel helpless in the face of huge global and national problems. We can consciously invest our time, energy, ideas, and money in enterprises that are saving the world. Not all of us need to start or run significant businesses to participate in the new future. We can change the world today, right where we work.

Many of us are doing just that. We are figuring out how to create a future unlike the past. This future is based on all of us becoming indispensable as individuals rather than cogs in a faceless economic machine. It is based on the idea that each one of us has something uniquely valuable to offer the world. Each of us has a Promise to keep. Each of us really can change the world. Why do anything else?

CHANGE HOW YOU THINK ABOUT CHANGE

What is the unique value that you offer the world?

PART ELEVEN

JUST START

CHAPTER 30

YOUR BEST FUTURE

O ften it feels as if we should walk around with helmets on. Bad news seems to be exploding around us like cluster bombs. On our TVs, radios and computers. In our magazines and newspapers. Foreclosures, job losses, bank collapses, war, failing educational systems, broken health care systems, corruption, debt, crime, global warming...yikes!

But what does this have to do with our personal reality? Yours and mine? After all, we could say that the world is always going to hell. At least to some degree. Just ask someone who lived through the twentieth century. Two world wars, a depression with 25 percent unemployment, holocausts, the imminent threat of all-out nuclear war. For the first 50 years of the last century we lived without antibiotics and with legalized racism. And yet...the twentieth century was amazingly great. Nearly all of us got indoor plumbing, lived in houses with heat, got telephones and televisions, rode on jet planes, enjoyed great movies and music, got a high school and maybe even a college education, and expanded our lifespan by 35 years. And there was no nuclear war after all. And as I stated previously, Both + And thinking is the Swiss-army knife for creating sustainable abundance.

So was the twentieth century awful? Yes. Was it wonderful? Yes. And so is today. You see, reality is always a Both + And proposition. Our jobs are *both* satisfying *and* dissatisfying. So are our lifestyles, our homes and our 14-year-olds. Reality is messy. It's supposed to be. But the Grid likes to present reality as an Either-Or phenomenon. *Either* candidate "A" is the total answer, *or* he/she is the devil in disguise. *Either* we're in a full-scale financial collapse, *or* it's not even a recession.

Either our marriage is gloriously fulfilling every moment, *or* it's an un-bearable slog of emptiness.

But Either-Or thinking robs us of keeping a learning, flexible mind. One that is capable of thriving in a paradoxical world of disappointment and opportunity.

The truth is always more than we can presently see. It's always Both + And and so are the solutions we seek. Understanding the multi-dimensional nature of reality is essential to living our "good" life. Our choices are served up to our consciousness from our brains. And recent research has discovered that we rewire our brains minute by minute by our thoughts. Our thinking habits create mental highways that our thoughts zoom along like an endless chain of cars in a NASCAR race. And if we are not careful about *what* we think about and whether we nurture a Both + And solution orientation versus an Either-Or problem orientation, we can build a mental network of anxiety racetracks that drive our minds in endless laps of fear. We get in the habit of despair. The habit of anger. The habit of thinking like victims.

Or not.

It's simple; our brains give us the version of reality we choose. Every problem is an opportunity just as every opportunity is plagued with problems. The question is what we are going to do about it.

It's true we live in an economic, cultural, environmental, geo-political storm. It's also true that we live at a time where we have the personal freedom to choose our own path through it. It's no time to sit and hide. It's time to reflect on all the choices we've each made that have brought us to our particular place. It's time to carefully consider what our best choices are to take us closer to the life of our most noble desires. It's time to fill our minds with new, creative ideas. A time to learn new skills. Perhaps make new friends or re-kindle our best old friendships. It's a time to read inspiring books. It's a time to stand for something. It's a time to make our Promise. Yes life is *both* messy, *and* life is great. What an opportunity.

BUT HOW DO I START?
How do I start? What do I do? These are the common questions I am asked every day in my work, and they are good questions. Hard ones. After all, we only have so much time. So much energy. How can we be

sure we won't go off on a wild goose chase trying to save the world but instead make no difference and wreck our lives?

My answer to these questions has three parts. First, pay close attention to your current circumstances; be aware of where you are. Second, become clear on what really matters to you, your Promise. Third, just start.

WHERE ARE YOU STANDING?

Suppose you were living your life for a reason. Suppose that all your life experience up to this moment could be harnessed to make a difference in the world. Suppose that the job (or lack of one) you had, the place you lived, the family you lived with, the people you knew, and the things you most deeply cared about were all clues to revealing the difference you were meant to make today.

The point is not so much whether my proposal is true, rather, what if it *could* be true? Well, it could. And that possibility changes how we look at everything. Suddenly, everything in our life has a chance of being sacred. Sacred in the sense of being packed with meaning. Packed with opportunity for you to do Good, Grow, and Gain, in that order.

Sometimes your circumstances knock you to the ground and slap your face with opportunity. For instance, eighteen years ago my dad was dying of cancer and my younger brother, Tom, turned the light of his own compassion on high. He gave up his bachelor pad, moved home and spent six months helping Mom, getting Dad to therapy and providing the physical care he needed in his last moments.

Fourteen years later, Tom, still a bachelor, but now with an international trading business, moved home to take care of Mom who has been stricken with Alzheimer's. Tom rearranged his business so he could run it out of the house and has been serving my mother ever since. When my other brother, sister and I have suggested care-giving alternatives to Tom, he's refused. He says that this is exactly how he wants to live his life right now.

What's happened to my brother is remarkable. He has become one of the most loving, compassionate human beings I have ever personally known. He doesn't act like he's a hero. Instead he maintains, "This is why I am here. This is what I need to do right now and I am learning so much. It's a privilege to help Mom." No, I am not exaggerating. Yes,

Tom is a man's man with a messy room and big loud opinions. But he has learned what real love is in ways most of us never will.

So first look at your life as it stands right now. Examine your relationships, your lifestyle and your career. What brings you great satisfaction and what brings you pain? What are you afraid of? What are you trying to prove? (To help you get clear on where you stand, go to SavetheWorldBook.com and take the *Dream Life Assessment.* It's free and it will illuminate those places in your life where you are finding joy, satisfaction and meaning and those places where you long for more.)

Above all, where does your present life circumstance point your attention? How or for whom could you be making a difference right now? If you are indeed where you are right now for a reason, what might be the reason?

WHAT REALLY MATTERS TO YOU?

Let's now look at where you might invest your soul in saving the world. This is the drumbeat of your Promise. When I work with groups I categorize the challenges we face into six categories.

Figure 30.1: Challenges for Humanity

Human Rights	Education/Arts	Environment
Peace	Health	Wealth

This is simply a way of grouping the opportunities we have to create sustainable abundance for all humanity.

I find some people are more motivated when these opportunities are stated as challenges. For many people, problems fire us up more than opportunity so I restate the categories as:

Figure 30.2: Challenges for Humanity: Problems

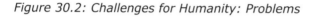

Human Rights	Education/Arts	Environment
Oppression	*Ignorance*	*Collapse*
Peace	Health	Wealth
Violence	*Disease*	*Poverty*

In each category there are many issues:

1. **Environment/Environmental Collapse**: climate change, dwindling energy resources, pollution, water shortages, resource depletion, conservation, park development and clean up, etc.
2. **Health/Disease**: wellness, disease prevention, education, research, children's health, access, affordability, cancer, aids, care giving, etc.
3. **Human Rights/Oppression**: equality, equal justice, dignity, women's and children's rights, tolerance, freedom of speech, worship, assembly, etc.
4. **Peace/Violence**: war, terrorism, nuclear non-proliferation, genocide, abuse, communication, negotiation, diplomacy, etc.
5. **Wealth/Poverty**: access to capital, food, housing, job creation, skill training, economic literacy, trade, homelessness, food banks, etc.
6. **Education/Ignorance**: literacy, graduation rates, arts education, science and math, women, computer/digital, early childhood, gifted and special needs, etc.

These six categories are not meant to be absolute so that every opportunity and problem will neatly fit in one. I use them simply to create a map so that people's internal moral compass will point them in a direction where they'd like to make their difference.

This is how:

Figure 30.3: Challenges for Humanity: Making a Difference

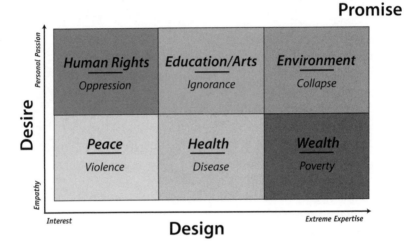

Again, what if you were perfectly designed to make the difference you most desired? This map of some of today's most formidable issues might point the way to action. The chart is not fixed. It's more like a Rubix cube. You can shift the boxes around so the one you put in the upper right is the one in which your persistent noble Desire and your expert Design meet. So for some our Promise might have to do with education, for others, health. For some it might be a unique mixture of several of the big issues. It's all individual. (e.g. Whitney wanted to lift girls from powerlessness through mentoring and education. Kate wanted to help children overcome their grief through mutual support.)

So we begin with a question. What problem are you persistently motivated to solve? What gets you jacked up emotionally? Asked a different way: what opportunity for humanity would you most want to expand? If you could wave a magic wand and solve one problem, relieve one type of suffering, or improve people or the planet in one way, what would that one way be?

Think about it like this. Our souls seem to be uniquely wired to resonate with specific ways to help humanity. For example, although most of us favor human rights and tolerance, Nelson Mandela *burned with a passion* for advancing these things. Many of us are motivated to fix the things that have hurt us the most or helped us the most. For instance, many business leaders warm up to mentoring inner city entrepreneurs because they emotionally resonate with the blessings of economic success. Look at how many people volunteer to raise money to find the cures for diseases that affect them or their loved ones.

Of course not all of us are driven by our pain. Some are deeply attracted to nature or animals in a positive way. I met a room full of them in a strategy workshop for SeaWorld San Diego. Their passion for the world's oceans and all creatures that swim in them was inspiring. They see themselves as using education and entertainment to spread their message of conservation of the marine environment. Their real mission is to make the whole world SeaWorld. That's quite a Promise.

What's important is to become conscious of whatever spins your needle. We all might care about issues in all six categories, but usually there are one or two that harmonize with the music inside us. That's what we most care about changing. That's where our Promise lies.

If we have a cause that grabs us with a persistent *Desire* to do something that matters, that's our ticket to action. We start by looking at our *Design* (our traits, talents, and track record) and investing the effort to become an expert in our particular niche. Remember, Bono got governments to offer debt relief to Africa because he became an expert on the economics of African poverty. He was mentored by Jeffrey Sachs, a renowned economist, among others. But he personally became effective by becoming an expert.

When we become more conscious of our Desire to make our difference and when we recognize *how* we make our strongest impact through our Design, our life circumstances become the canvas for painting our Promise. Often it's all laid out in front of us in high-def surround sound, just waiting for us to press the ON button.

SAVE THE WORLD RIGHT WHERE YOU ARE

Katherine is a legend in San Diego. She runs her executive relocation business as if it were a community trust. For eighteen years she's helped executives and their families who are moving to San Diego find the right

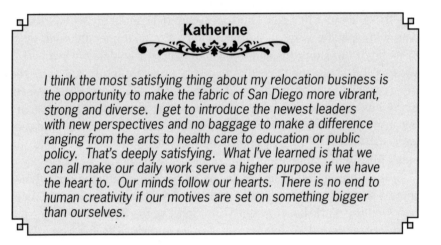

Katherine

I think the most satisfying thing about my relocation business is the opportunity to make the fabric of San Diego more vibrant, strong and diverse. I get to introduce the newest leaders with new perspectives and no baggage to make a difference ranging from the arts to health care to education or public policy. That's deeply satisfying. What I've learned is that we can all make our daily work serve a higher purpose if we have the heart to. Our minds follow our hearts. There is no end to human creativity if our motives are set on something bigger than ourselves.

neighborhoods, schools, churches and social clubs. But she has done so much more. She is an encyclopedia of local non-profits and their respective boards. She makes sure every willing executive becomes a board member of a non-profit where he or she will make the greatest impact. Over the years she has matched literally hundreds of leaders with worthy causes.

The non-profit angle is the primary reason Katherine runs the business she does. Her extreme talent and vivacious energy have netted her plenty of offers for easier, higher paying jobs, but she tells me that's not her calling. She believes that her work as a leadership recruiter for non-profits improves life for all of us. And she's right.

She also sits on six boards herself. Her husband is also cause-driven. He runs a bank that has a gigantic Wyland mural of whales painted on the side of its six-story building. That's called making a statement.

You see, most of the time our calling is in our circumstances. We just need to look for it through the lens of our Desire and Design.

START NOW

My experience is that most of us are waiting, most of the time. We're waiting to get out of school, waiting to meet the right person, waiting until we get out of debt, waiting to get promoted, waiting to find the right business partner, waiting for our children to move out... So we wait for the perfect time that never shows up.

It's time to quit waiting and start doing.

For 30 years I've sat in corporate strategy meetings. I've helped entrepreneurs develop business plans. I've seen the most elaborate market research, focus groups and competitive analyses, and guess what? Research confirms that only 1 in 10 businesses funded by the brightest venture capitalists succeeds in a big way. That's right. Although these very smart people use a rigorous process of planning, monitoring and mentoring, 7 out of their 10 new companies fail, two become self-sustaining but under-performing, and one, only one, is successful.

Interestingly, *5 out of 10* bootstrap entrepreneurs who *don't* seek venture capital or do sophisticated business planning succeed in creating self-sustaining businesses. They succeed by starting and then making adjustments on the fly. Consider this. Business leaders are trained to be professional decision makers, but research done at Ohio State University reveals that 50 percent of business decisions are wrong. Why? How could this be?

Perhaps it's because we simply don't know what we don't know. So what makes us most vulnerable is the stuff we *think* we know. As long as we are aware that we are flying without instruments, we're very careful pilots. We constantly scan the skies and watch the weather. We constantly make course corrections to keep us headed in the right direction. We use wisdom.

Those who wait until all the data is in never get off the ground.

There is no "right" way to make your difference. There are *billions* of right ways. If we are going to save the world, we must plunge in. The surest and simplest way to find out what the pitfalls are, what the laws and regulations are, is to jump in the deep end of the pool. If we wait until we have all the answers, we'll never get started.

But how can this work? It seems so chaotic. Happily, it is. And just like the mathematics of chaos theory, it's working. Chaos theory reveals that in seeming randomness a pattern of order emerges. Making our difference means plunging into the chaos and using the wisdom of good decisions to create order and momentum. When Abraham started raising money for his school in the Southern Sudan, he had no idea how he was going to pull it off. Neither did Kate with her foundation for grieving children, or John with his security business that's really a university of life. Muhammad Yunus had no idea his bank for the poor would survive let alone win him a Nobel Peace Prize. In fact, none of the people in this book had a fail-safe, fully funded plan to make their difference. They just started and then paid close attention to what was working and stopped doing everything that wasn't. They were bold and careful, visionary and practical, decisive and flexible. Above all they weren't concerned about being right. They just wanted to be effective. That's the spirit of standing for something right here, right now. Plunge in and then see what's working and what isn't working. Trial and error. Amplify what is working and eliminate what isn't. We must be passionate, persistent, and flexible, but most of all unafraid. Unafraid to do something right now.

Of course we need to be wise. We need to start by making decisions that are logical and practical as well as inspired. If we are going to fly, flying lessons are always a good idea first. We also need a reliable map with airports marked and a functioning radio so we can get guidance from the control towers. But we need to keep in mind that there's a good chance we won't end up where we thought we were headed.

So just start where you are. What are your circumstances calling you to do? What really matters to you? Figure it out, then take off. With your Promise as your compass, Design and Desire your wings, and your Drive as your fuel, you'll likely see things you've never imagined, land in amazing places and do things you never dreamed of. It's a lot better than riding the train I described in the opening pages—chugging down the tracks of a life put in place by others.

It's time to fly.

CHAPTER 31

BE WHO YOU ARE AND
DO WHAT YOU CAME TO DO

Each of us really is designed to play a crucial role in the world. And that role has nothing to do with snagging the right job title, the right wristwatch and the right retirement plan. I learned this for myself and have never looked back.

Up until I was 40, life was great. Not perfect, but great. I had it all figured out. I had success, I was doing what I loved doing, I was having fun along the way, I had a great family, and I was spiritually at peace. It's all good, right? And then it happened. I turned around one day and suddenly realized I was standing in the middle of a superhighway and the headlights were coming toward me. I was flattened. My guts splattered. My life blown to bits.

Then for nine years, the trucks kept coming. Every time I tried to crawl to safety, wham! Some force seemed to grab my ankles and drag me back on the highway of hell. Thump. Thump. I became intimately familiar with suffering.

My nature is to be resilient so I would constantly devise new strategies and directions to pull me off the highway. I'd be filled with optimism and then I'd turn around and hear the horns blast and see those damn headlights again.

One late summer evening I found myself in a cabin in the mountains. The sun was setting and I remember the sky being a rosy hue of purple. Purple, the color of love and compassion. I decided to spend a little quiet time and think about my father. He had died seven years earlier, a victim of cancer we thought was in remission but then came back and swallowed him whole.

I lay on my back on the floor, closed my eyes and tried to imagine my father's love for me. My father was a man of plain and powerful emotions. My first recollection of him was kneeling at my bedside teaching me to pray. He was a rancher and he taught me how to pray for rain. It seemed we always needed rain. After our prayer Dad would start kissing my face. His beard was scratchy but his love was like a heavy warm blanket that always made me feel safe. He was vigorous, strong, and outspoken. Even the day he died the intensity of his spirit never waned. That day I was at his bedside. In the moment of his passing he just went somewhere else.

So I lay there on the floor, imagining how it might feel to have him loving me right then and there, father to son. I was so black, so deeply hurting. I needed to feel that love. Suddenly, the indescribable happened. I felt as if I was *in* my father's being. I was in his heart, his mind. I could feel *his* feelings and think *his* thoughts. Then I saw him holding me as a tiny child. I could feel his pure, unrestrained love. Nothing held back. Tears were streaming down my face in silent joy. I had never expected to feel this, but it was just the beginning.

Soon I began to sense his actual presence. I can't explain it really. It seemed like a physical presence, not just in my mind, but out there in the room. He seemed to be hovering above me, mirroring my reclined position. His presence was unmistakable, just like when he walked into a room at home. He had that same powerful energy he'd always had.

I started to breathe a little more deeply. My mind was empty of thought but flooded with feeling. Then he spoke to me. Not out loud, but in *his* voice, with *his* thoughts. This was not something my suffering mind had created. He simply said, "Be who you are and do what you came for."

That's all. No fatherly wisdom. No "you can do it" encouragement. Just a plain and potent admonition. I know it sounds corny, like something you might hear on Oprah, so even as I was laying there I was wondering, "Is this really happening? Am I hallucinating?"

Dad lingered, and then it happened. He touched me. He touched my face. It was physical, yet not. It felt like the wispy brush of a feather. I opened my eyes to see if the wind was blowing something across my face. But no. I closed my eyes again, and he touched me again, or at least his spirit, his intention did. I felt it. Then he said, "This is real." He didn't so much say it as he intended it.

That experience happened a few years before I turned fifty, and it changed the way I view life. It changed what I view as important and what I am trying to accomplish. For most of my adult life I had tried to help people fulfill their real dreams, to live up to their highest potential, to fulfill their nature. But it was only after my father's visit that I really and truly got the fact that there is more to this journey than what we achieve. There *really* is an invisible essence to us that is more lasting and more important than our flesh and bones. And we are here to courageously un-cage that part of ourselves. To soar.

That is the point of every human existence.

Since that day my suffering has stopped. Except for the minor flesh wounds that are a part of everyday life. The quality of my journey has transcended anything I thought was possible. I am happy and incredibly grateful.

Today I have nine grandchildren and I am deeply concerned about the future they face. It seems to me that our mistaken belief that material existence is all there is has created a world that is unsustainable, physically, emotionally, mentally, and spiritually. At the same time I am encouraged that there is a rising tide moving in a counter-direction. Both trends are happening everywhere at once. It's a crazy, distressing, exciting time. Ultimately I am at peace because what I learned from my father that night was that what really matters is not what we do but what *we become through doing.*

I am convinced there is only one way to save the future. It is for each of us to come to the clear recognition of what's really important. It's far more than driving a hybrid or recycling our trash. Yes, these are good things, but what's important is no thing at all.

It is the *process* of discovering something to stand for and having the courage to stand for it.

This doesn't have to mean suffering and hardship. In fact, it means an end to suffering and hardship. We don't have to take a vow of poverty, only a vow of purpose. And when we do that, the real riches of life come rushing toward us like an overjoyed dog.

We *can* decide to have a better future. That's where we are today. Decision time. I know this because when I speak I actually see audiences liberate their thinking. The energy of the room changes and bam, we're off to the races.

How do we create that "we can change the world" feeling? It starts with changing *our own* world. Then *the* world changes. The way we change our world is entirely personal. But one thing is for sure: we don't have to wait for government corruption to end or health care to become available to all. We don't have to wait for world peace, sensible economic policy or the inspiration of a moral employer. Instead we *can* take control of what we actually can control. And we can do it thoughtfully and intentionally.

The magic of a free society is that it is free. It may not be completely *healthy* right now, but it is free. That means we can still choose to be self-governing in every way that matters. We can live where we want to. We can do what we most desire. We can love with grace and power. We can learn what we need to learn. In short, we can choose to keep our Promise.

In our town hall events, when audiences meet real people who have chosen to live inspiring lives, to run businesses that matter, or to attack social ills with big solutions, they begin to see the whole picture. And they go from slumping in their chairs to giving standing ovations. They aren't standing for me or even for the guests of honor. Rather, they are standing up for each other. For the hero that abides in all of us.

When you change *your* world, *the* world changes. And you're home in time to enjoy it with the ones you love. In the end, that's what matters most.

ENDNOTES

CHAPTER 1

P. 5   Jonathan Leake, "Last Warning: 10 Years to Save the World," *Times Online*, Jan. 28, 2007.

P. 8   As I was considering a term that captures the desires of people surveyed by the American Dream Project, I thought of the paradoxical goals of sustainability and abundance. It would seem all of us want a sustainable future with ample clean air, water, land and resources necessary for a decent life. At the same time we are delighted by the personal abundance brought about through harnessing electricity and modern technology. But this abundance cannot be sustained due to our current way of producing it. Obviously we are exploiting the earth's resources at a rate far more rapid than they can be naturally replenished. So the current abundance of the three billion of us who live on more than 3 dollars a day is on a collision course with scarcity for all in a dark future.

      As I researched this topic I came across the work of Belgium economist Bernard Lietaer who wrote of future scenarios in his book, *The Future of Money*. These five futures were: 1) More of the Same, which is the continuation of our current consumer driven system, 2) Corporate Millennium, in which global companies monopolize the world's resources by corrupting governments, 3) Careful Communities, super-rich elites wall themselves from the low wage poor, 4) Hell-on-Earth, in which disease epidemics and a total economic breakdown creates a new dark age, and 5) Sustainable Abundance, in which humanity's joint drive for a sustainable future stimulates a values revolution that harnesses economic incentives to benefit humanity. Although Professor Lietaer and I have a somewhat different view on what will produce sustainable abundance (he calls for alternate forms of money), we agree that our only best future must be an abundant one.

CHAPTER 2

P. 11   Michael R. Johnson and Nick Nordquist (Producers) and Will Marré (Writer), *Reclaiming Your American Dream* (American Dream Project and Will Marré, 2006). Industrial Strength Television and Thought Rocket Films. The American Dream, once more commonly know as "life, liberty and the pursuit of happiness," has been polluted by materialism and greed. *Reclaiming Your American Dream* takes a hard look at how these significant values and belief shifts have started a movement that will change business, government, products, services and our future. It helps individuals reignite the American Dream for themselves, their children, their workplace and their communities.

P. 13   Helen Keller, *The Story of My Life* (New York: Bantam Books, 1990).

P. 14   The Southern Sudan Education Project's mission is to empower Lost Boys and Girls to create peace and education in Southern Sudan and to connect people in Southern Sudan with friends in the United States. Their vision is that every child in Southern Sudan has access to quality education preparing them to enter the world competitively. For more information, please visit homepage.mac.com/globalhealing/SouthernSudanEd./Menu27.html.

P. 17   *The McKinsey Quarterly*, "The McKinsey Global Survey of Business Executives: Business and Society," January 2006. Can be found at: mckinseyquarterly.com/The_McKinsey_Global_Survey_of_Business_Executives__Business_and_Society_1741.

P. 17   Cone, Inc., "2007 Cone Cause Evolution and Environmental Survey," found at: coneinc.com/files/2007ConeSurveyReport.pdf.

CHAPTER 3

P. 20   U.S. Census Bureau, "Statistics about Business Size," U.S. Census Bureau, census.gov/epcd/www/smallbus.html (accessed Nov. 18, 2008).

CHAPTER 6

P. 55   Popular atheists, Richard Dawkins and Christopher Hitchens have written extensively about how the universe, despite its complexity, does not need a creator (*The God Delusion* by Richard Dawkins; *God is Not Great* by Christopher Hitchens). Hitchens has said that the universe does not owe us personal meaning. However, in a *Time Magazine* article ("God vs. Science," Nov. 2, 2006) that featured a debate with famed Christian Scientist, Francis Collins, he said that although he didn't believe in God with a long white beard, it was possible that there might be some sort of conscious, benevolent force. Perhaps the problem for evolutionary atheists is that many of them end up making evolution itself god complete with dogma, loyalty tests and a scientific priesthood.

P. 56   Science Encyclopedia, "Contemporary Genetics – Eugenics and the Issues of Selective Breeding (1900-1945)," Science Encyclopedia, Found at: science.jrank.org/pages/9488/Contemporary-Genetics-Eugenics-Ethical-Issues-Selective-Breeding-1900-1945.html (accessed Dec. 18, 2008).

P. 56   Daniel J. Kevles, "In the Name of Darwin" (1995), PBS can be found at: www.pbs.org/wgbh/evolution/darwin/nameof/index.html

P. 57   Bruce Rosenblum and Fred Kuttner, *Quantum Enigma: Physics Encounters Consciousness* (New York: Oxford University Press, 2006). This book discusses what the authors (professors at University of California Santa Cruz) call modern science's "skeleton in the closet." The problem they say is that quantum physics is not just a theory; it's a proven explanation of reality that powers our digital computers and cell phones. The problem is that it means the physical world is created by our perception of it. In fact what is most real is the non-physical reality of the quantum forces. The scientific problem with this is that it implies free will is a necessary part of consciousness. Taken further it calls into question the very basis of biology, because biological systems including our brains are just physical manifestations on a micro- invisible quantum reality, which is the basis of all existence. In other words, our brains and bodies are "created" by consciousness not the reverse. Maybe it's why placebos work. One thing is for sure. Nobody really knows what reality is.

P. 57   Allen S. Hamilton, M.D., *The Scalpel and the Soul* (New York: Penguin Publishing, 2008). For more information, visit allanhamilton.com.

P. 58   Maybe the biggest, most important truths are simply self-evident. Or, rather, soul-evident. How do I know I love my children, my wife, my mother…? Maybe I just know. How do I know that I exist, that I have an inner essence independent of my body? How do I know it's not just wishful thinking?

How? Deep in my soul, I know. "Soul knowledge" is neither a logical assertion nor an emotional belief; it's a profound and direct experience of being. It is a knowing beyond reason. Call it super-rational knowledge. Super-rational knowledge arises from our whole being, not just the limited tool of logic, not just the hot blood of emotion.

How do you get to super-rational knowledge? Simply turn off the noise of your mental arguments and listen for something deeper. If we quiet our minds and learn to pay *inner* attention, each of us can have super-rational experiences of truths beyond doubt. Soul-evident truths. The existence of our inner being, for example, needs no external proof. Only our *limited rational thinking* doubts our own inner existence. Our super-rational "soul" exists, without doubt, because we can experience it directly. More directly than any outer perception. In the quiet of sustained silence, it is simply there.

To listen in this quiet way we have to come to know a few powerful truths we may be deeply certain of. For instance:

- I exist.
- I have an enduring essence that is beyond space and time.
- Love is good and right. Fear and hatred lead to suffering.
- I am not alone in the universe.
- I am here for a reason.

These few vital "truths" may not be provable, but they need no proof. They are soul-evident. Direct and pure. They require only the courage to fully accept what we, at our purest core, already know. These precious gems become the bedrock of a fulfilling human life. The few things we know with inner certainty give us the courage to be open minded, flexible and non-dogmatic about all the many things we *don't* know.

CHAPTER 10

P. 89   In his seminar, *Unleash the Power Within*, Tony Robbins presents six human needs that drive our actions: certainty/comfort, variety, significance, connection/love, growth, and contribution.

CHAPTER 12

P. 97   Clark F. Power, Ann Higgins, and Lawrence Kohlberg, *Lawrence Kohlberg's Approach to Moral Education* (Columbia University Press, 1991).

CHAPTER 14

P. 117   Neal Gabler, *Walt Disney: The Triumph of the American Imagination* (Knopf, 2006).

CHAPTER 17

P. 130   Arthur F. Miller, Paul Brooks (Editor) and James Van Eerden, *Designed For Life* (Life Media, 2007).

P. 131   Christopher Petersen, PhD. and Martin Seligman, *Character Strengths and Virtues: A Handbook and Classification* (New York: Oxford University Press, 2004).

P. 133   Gary Erikson, *Raising the Bar: Integrity and Passion in Life and Business: The Story of Clif Bar & Co.* (San Francisco: Wiley Publishers, 2004).

CHAPTER 18

P. 140   Dan Sullivan is a thought leader in the area of discovering your "unique ability" and putting it to work in the service of others. He has a program called Strategic Coach designed to help entrepreneurs and business leaders succeed by doing just that. For more information see strategiccoach.com.

CHAPTER 19

P. 146   Girls For A Change, www.girlsforachange.org was founded in 2002 and focuses on social change projects to teach girls how to tackle community problems. Their goal is that the girls will leave their program with self-efficacy, authentic relationships with women volunteers, social change skills, and the ability and confidence to express and implement their ideas.

P. 148   Jim Loehr and Tony Schwartz, *The Power of Full Engagement* (New York: Free Press, 2003). Jim's programs at his Human Performance Institute have helped thousands of people expand their energy and focus their efforts to lead more productive lives.

CHAPTER 20

P. 153   Lisa Takeuchi Cullen, "How to Get Smarter, One Breath at a Time," *Time Magazine*, Jan. 16, 2006: 93.

P. 154   Jim Loehr and Tony Schwartz, *The Power of Full Engagement* (New York: Free Press, 2003).

P. 155   Dr. Bob Maurer, *One Small Step Can Change Your Life* (New York: Workman Publishing, 2004), 39-48. Bob Maurer is a very engaging teacher and speaker whose book is often called the real "Baby Steps" book made famous by Richard Dreyfuss's character in the film, *What About Bob?*.

P. 159   Mihaly Csikszentmihalyi, *Flow: The Psychology of Optimal Experience* (New York: Harper and Row, 1990).

CHAPTER 21

P. 163   Dr. Robert Kinsel Smith, *Discover Your Blind Spots: How to Stop Repeating Everyday Business Mistakes* (Texas: Clear Direction, Inc., 2004). Dr. Bob Smith has helped thousands of executives "see" their own blind spots by mapping their thinking biases. His analysis literally changed the way I make decisions. For more information visit cleardirection.com.

CHAPTER 22

P. 173   Triple bottom line is a term originally coined by John Elkington who founded a think-tank consultancy in 1987. The triple bottom line refers to accounting for the social, environmental and economic costs and benefits associated with organizational activity. The accurate accounting of the triple bottom line is a challenging task being undertaken by many private and public groups under the guidelines of the Global Reporting Initiative (GRI) which has established one of the world's most broadly used sustainability guidelines. The compelling idea of tracking social and environmental impacts as well as economic is that it gives societies and leaders a real measure to track progress toward sustainability.

P. 176   Matthew Kelly, *The Rhythm of Life: Living Every Day with Passion and Purpose* (New York: Beacon Publishing, 2004).

CHAPTER 23

P. 183   Shankar Vedantam, "Social Isolation Growing in U.S., Study Says," *Washington Post*, June 23, 2006, A03.

P. 184   *The Sourcebook for Teaching Science*, csun.edu/science/health/docs/tv&health.html (accessed Nov. 18, 2008).

P. 185   Christopher Petersen, *A Primer in Positive Psychology* (New York: Oxford University Press, 2006), 26.

P. 185   Barry Schwartz, *The Paradox of Choice: Why More is Less* (New York: Harper Collins, 2004), 6.

CHAPTER 24

P. 187   Many happiness surveys have confirmed that the happiest people on earth are married (See *Authentic Happiness* by Martin Seligman (authentichappiness.sas.upenn.edu).

P. 187   Rutgers University, The National Marriage Project, marriage.rutgers.edu.

P. 188   Schwartz, Barry, *The Paradox of Choice: Why More is Less* (New York: Harper Collins, 2004).

P. 190   John Ortberg, *Everybody's Normal Till You Get to Know Them* (Grand Rapids Zondervan Publishing House, 2003).

P. 190   John Gottman, PhD., The Gottman Institute, gottman.com/marriage/self_help.

P. 193   Willard, F. Harley, *His Needs, Her Needs* (Michigan: Fleming H. Revell, 2001).

P. 193   For more information on Dan Baker visit h2cleadership.com/resources/dan-baker.shtml.

CHAPTER 25

P. 197   Rick Foster and Greg Hicks, *How We Choose to be Happy: The 9
          Choices of Extremely Happy People—Their Secrets, Their Stories*
          (New York: The Berkley Publishing Group, 1999).
P. 201   Fight Global Warming, "Re-Thinking Energy in our Homes,"
          fightglobalwarming.com/page.cfm?tagID=262 (accessed Dec. 8,
          2008).

CHAPTER 27

P. 212   For more information on Nike's LIVESTRONG campaign, visit
          livestrong.com.
P. 216   Dr. Daniel Goleman, *Social Intelligence* (New York: Bantam
          Books, 2007).
P. 217   For more information on socially conscious filmmaking visit the
          International Social Action Film Festival at ISAFF.org.
P. 220   Sylvia Ann Hewlett, Laura Sherbin, and Karen Sumberg, "How
          Gen Y & Boomers Will Reshape Your Agenda," *Harvard Busi-
          ness Review*, July-Aug. 2009.

CHAPTER 28

P. 222   Adam Smith, *The Theory of Moral Sentiments* (New York: Co-
          simo Books, 2007, originally published in 1759).

CHAPTER 29

P. 228   For more information on Muhammad Yunus and Grameen Bank
          visit grameen.org.
P. 229   For more information on socially strategic thinking visit
          REALeadership.com.
P. 229   Michelle Sterling is a brilliant organizational development con-
          sultant. For more information visit buildingbsolutions.com.

CHAPTER 30

P. 241   For more information on SeaWorld, visit seaworld.com.
P. 242   For more information on Wyland visit wyland.com.
P. 243   *Journal of Business Venturing* 22, no. 5 (Sept. 2007).
P. 243   Jeff Grabmeier, "Why Decisions Fail," researchnews.osu.edu/
          archive/decfail.htm (accessed Nov. 18, 2008).

ACKNOWLEDGMENTS

I have been blessed my entire life with extraordinary people who encouraged me, taught me, supported me and above all understood the intent of my soul. Starting with my parents and continuing withy my children and grandchildren, I have been surrounded by a personal village of thoughtful authentic supporters who provide both insight and motivation for me to fulfill my design. To my wife, Debbie, who resurrected my motivation to turn up the volume on my love and my life. To my working colleague, Candie Perkins, who has tirelessly challenged my old thinking and helped me see the motivations of a new generation (and who also builds beautiful websites and miles of PowerPoint's). To Jeannie Foy who is effortlessly cheerful when she tells me what I write doesn't make much sense and then plunges in with her whole mind and heart to rescue the ideas that matter and bury the ones that don't. To Andy Wolfendon who is a brilliant writer/editor and whose big curious brain is always alert to reorganize, redraft and spark my words to be more than he received. To Michael Johnson who saw value in the message of this book and turned it into an award winning documentary and who's become a friend of endless patience and loyalty. To all the people whose stores inspired me in the book, and especially to Martyn Collins, Kate Atwood, Chris Osorio, John Kontopuls, Mark and Patria Lee, David Wyman, Mike Gass, and Katherine Kennedy who read and reviewed the manuscript. To all my colleagues at the American Dream Project who helped create hope for thousands that the future can be as good as we're willing to imagine it to be. To all the members of the American Dream Project whose insight and blog comments constantly amaze me. To my many clients whose examples and generosity have inspired me to be better. To Kathleen Hughes, my publisher, who has the vision to see what I'm trying to accomplish and provided a wide and open path to realize my own dreams. To all of you and to all who have touched my life I offer my sincere gratitude.

ABOUT THE AUTHOR

Will Marré (pronounce like hooray) is the co-founder and former president of the Covey Leadership Center where he translated the concepts of *The 7 Habits of Highly Effective People* into powerful leadership courses taught to millions worldwide. Will is a pioneer of socially strategic enterprise that transforms Corporate Social Responsibility into Corporate Social Opportunity. As CEO of the REALeadership Alliance Will works with corporations to create growth strategies by creating a unique value advantage driven by the triple bottom line strategy, harnessing the power of enterprise to improve the lives of *People* and the health of the *Planet* while generating a sustainable *Profit*.

Working with New York Stock Exchange companies to develop social-environmental commerce, Will co-founded the Seacology Foundation dedicated to saving the fragile environments and cultures of South Pacific Islanders.

In 2004 Will founded The American Dream Project to help leaders of the future create the next chapter in American and world history. Will recently received an Emmy Award® for writing the learning documentary *Reclaiming Your American Dream* that continues to air on PBS stations around the country.

Will is passionate about helping organizational leaders improve the quality of their personal lives and accelerate economic and social improvement throughout the world. As an expert in helping organizations develop cultures of fully engaged employees, he is the President of the Advisory Board of the Human Performance Institute of Johnson and Johnson. Will also serves as Consulting Director of the Corporate Responsibility Forum at the University of California San Diego and is the visiting Scholar of Social Enterprise at Clemson University where he teaches today's and tomorrow's leaders to embrace the triple bottom line strategy and increase their personal leadership impact.

Will is a frequent keynote speaker to business and non-profit groups evangelizing personal, social and corporate sustainability for the 21st century. For more information on Will, visit willmarre.com or visit his daily blog "Ten Years to Save the World" at thoughtrocket.com.